Simply
Logical

Simply
Logical

Intelligent Reasoning by Example

Peter Flach
Tilburg University, The Netherlands

JOHN WILEY & SONS
Chichester • New York • Brisbane • Toronto • Singapore

Figure 1.1 printed with permission from London Regional Transport
(LRT Registered User No. 94/1954)

Other Wiley Editorial Offices

John Wiley & Sons, Inc., 605 Third Avenue,
New York, NY 10158-0012, USA

Jacaranda Wiley Ltd, 33 Park Road, Milton,
Queensland 4064, Australia

John Wiley & Sons (Canada) Ltd, 22 Worcester Road,
Rexdale, Ontario M9W 1L1, Canada

John Wiley & Sons (SEA) Pte Ltd, 37 Jalan Pemimpin #05-04,
Block B, Union Industrial Building, Singapore 2057

Library of Congress Cataloging-in-Publication Data
Flach, Peter A.
    Simply logical : intelligent reasoning by example / P. Flach.
        p.   cm.
    Includes bibliographical references and index.
    ISBN 0 471 94152 2 — ISBN 0 471 94153 0
        1. Artificial intelligence.   2. Reasoning—Data processing.
    3. Logic, Symbolic and mathematical.   4. Prolog (Computer program
    language)   I. Title.
    Q335.F58   1994
    006.3—dc20   93-48745
                                                                CIP

British Library Cataloguing in Publication Data

A catalogue record for this book is available from the British Library

ISBN 0 471 94152 2;   0 471 94153 0 (disk);   0 471 94215 4 (book/disk set)

Produced from camera-ready copy supplied by the author using
Microsoft Word.
Printed and bound in Great Britain by Bookcraft Ltd, Midsomer Norton, Avon

Contents

Foreword

For many reasons it is a pleasure for me to recommend this book. I am especially pleased, in particular, because it relieves me of the temptation to write a revised edition of my own book, *Logic for Problem Solving*. Similarly to my own book, this book aims to introduce the reader to a number of topics — logic, Artificial Intelligence and computer programming — that are usually treated as distinct subjects elsewhere. Not only does this book succeed in its aim, but it goes further than my own book by showing how to implement the theory in runnable Prolog programs. Both the theory and the programs are presented incrementally in a style which is both pedagogically sound and, perhaps even more importantly, teaches the reader by example how new ideas and their implementations can be developed by means of successive refinement.

The latter parts of the book present a number of recent extensions of Logic Programming, most of which have been accessible previously only in conference proceedings and journal articles. As with the earlier parts of the book, this part shows how these extensions can be implemented effectively in Prolog. These extensions include abduction (the generation of explanations), default reasoning and Inductive Logic Programming. The Prolog implementations build upon the technique of metalogic programming, which is introduced earlier in the book, and which is one of the most powerful and characteristic techniques of Logic Programming.

The field of Logic Programming is fortunate in being well served by many excellent books covering virtually every aspect of the subject, including its theory, applications and programming. This book by Peter Flach is an important addition to these books, filling a gap both by including new material on abduction and Inductive Logic Programming and by relating Logic Programming theory and Prolog programming practice in a sound and convincing manner.

Bob Kowalski
Imperial College

Preface

This is a book about intelligent reasoning. *Reasoning* is the process of drawing conclusions; *intelligent* reasoning is the kind of reasoning performed by humans. This is not to say that this book is about the psychological aspects of human reasoning: rather, it discusses methods to implement intelligent reasoning by means of Prolog programs. The book is written from the shared viewpoints of Computational Logic, which aims at automating various kinds of reasoning, and Artificial Intelligence, which seeks to implement aspects of intelligent behaviour on a computer. The combination of these two viewpoints is a distinguishing feature of this book, which I think gives it a unique place among the many related books available.

Who should read this book

While writing this book, I had three kinds of readers in mind: Artificial Intelligence researchers or practitioners, Logic Programming researchers or practitioners, and students (advanced undergraduate or graduate level) in both fields.

The reader working in Artificial Intelligence will find a detailed treatment of how the power of logic can be used to solve some of her problems. It is a common prejudice among many practitioners of Artificial Intelligence that logic is a merely theoretical device, with limited significance when it comes to tackling practical problems. It is my hope that the many detailed programs in this book, which perform important tasks such as natural language interpretation, abductive and inductive reasoning, and reasoning by default, help to fight this unjust prejudice. On the other hand, those acquainted with Logic Programming will be interested in the practical side of many topics that get a mainly theoretical treatment in the literature. Indeed, many advanced programs presented and explained in this book are not, in a didactic form, available elsewhere.

The student unfamiliar with either field will profit from an integrated treatment of subjects that otherwise needs to be collected from different sources with widely varying degrees of sophistication. For instance, many treatments of the theory of Logic Programming employ an amount of mathematical machinery that has intimidated many a novice to the field. On the other hand, many practical treatments of programming for Artificial Intelligence display an almost embarrassing lack of theoretical foundations. This book aims at showing how much is gained by taking an intermediate position.

Style of presentation

As indicated by the title, this book presents intelligent reasoning techniques *by example*. This is meant to stress that every technique is accompanied by a Prolog program implementing it. These programs serve two didactic purposes. By running them, one can get a feeling what a particular technique is all about. But perhaps more importantly, the declarative reading of each program is an integral part of the explanation of the technique it implements. For the more elaborate programs, special attention is paid to their stepwise development, explaining key issues along the way. Thus, the book's focus is not just on the question 'How is this done in Prolog?', but rather on the question 'How should I solve this problem, were I to start from scratch?' In other words, the philosophy of this book is 'teaching by showing, learning by doing'.

This should not be taken to imply that the book is devoid of all theoretical underpinnings. On the contrary, a substantial part is devoted to the theoretical backgrounds of clausal logic and Logic Programming, which are put to use in subsequent presentations of advanced reasoning techniques. However, theoretical issues are not included for their own sake, but only insofar they are instrumental in understanding and implementing a particular technique. No attempt is made to give an encyclopedic coverage of the subjects covered. There exist specialised works in the literature which do exactly that for specific subjects, references to which are included.

Suggestions for teachers

This book can be used as a textbook for a graduate or advanced undergraduate course in Artificial Intelligence or Computational Logic. If one wishes to complement it with a second textbook, I would suggest either Genesereth and Nilsson's *Logical Foundations of Artificial Intelligence* (Morgan Kaufmann, 1987) or Kowalski's classic text *Logic for Problem Solving* (North-Holland, 1979) on the theoretical side; or, more practically, Ivan Bratko's *Prolog Programming for Artificial Intelligence* (Addison-Wesley, second edition, 1990) or Sterling and Shapiro's *The Art of Prolog* (MIT Press, 1986).

What can and cannot be found in this book

The book consists of three parts. Part I presents the necessary material on *Logic and Logic Programming*. In an introductory chapter, the main concepts in Logic Programming are introduced, such as program clauses, query answering, proof trees, and recursive data structures. This chapter is intended for the reader who is unfamiliar with Prolog programming, and is therefore written in a way intended to appeal to the student's intuition.

In Chapter 2, the topic of resolution theorem proving in clausal logic is addressed in a more rigorous fashion. Here, we deal with concepts such as Herbrand models and resolution refutations, as well as meta-theoretical notions like soundness and completeness. The presentation starts with propositional clausal logic, and proceeds via relational clausal logic (without functors) to full clausal logic, and finally arrives at definite clause logic.

Since the semantics of clausal logic is defined in its own terms, without reference to the kind of models employed in Predicate Logic, only a basic familiarity with the notion of a logic is required. Although I agree that a Herbrand model is, in some sense, a 'poor man's version' of a logical model, I believe that my presentation has didactic advantages over the standard treatment which defines Herbrand models in terms of Predicate Logic models. However, since this distinction is important, in a separate section I do address the relation between clausal logic and Predicate Logic.

In Chapter 3, the practical aspects of Prolog programming are discussed. The notion of an SLD-tree forms an important concept in this chapter, most notably in the treatment of cut. When explaining cut, I like to tell my students that it is much like the GO TO statement in imperative programming languages: it is there, it is needed at implementation level, but it should be replaced as much as possible by such higher-level constructs as `not` and if-then-else. Further practical issues include the treatment of arithmetic expressions in Prolog, second-order predicates like `setof`, and various programming techniques like accumulators and difference lists. Since meta-interpreters are very frequently used in the advanced programs in Part III, they are discussed here at some length as well. A final section in this chapter addresses some aspects of a general programming methodology.

Of course it is impossible to fully explain either the theory of Logic Programming or the practice of Prolog programming in a single chapter. I am certain that many lecturers will feel that something is missing which they consider important. However, my main intention has been to cover at least those subjects that are needed for understanding the programs presented in later chapters.

In Part II, I shift from the Logic Programming perspective to the Artificial Intelligence viewpoint. Here, the central notions are graphs and search. From the Prolog perspective, graphs occur in at least two ways: as the trees represented by terms (e.g. parse trees), and as the search spaces spanned by predicates (e.g. SLD-trees). These concepts are discussed in Chapter 4. Furthermore, several ways to represent inheritance hierarchies are investigated in section 4.3. Usually, this topic in Knowledge Representation gets a more or less historical treatment, introducing concepts like semantic networks, frames, and the like. I chose a complementary starting point, namely the question 'What are the possibilities for representing and reasoning about inheritance hierarchies in Prolog?' The justification for this is that I believe such a starting point to be closer to the student's initial position.

Intermezzi

Issues that are related to but somewhat aside from the current discussion are
highlighted in separate boxes, positioned at the top of the page.

In two subsequent chapters, the basic techniques for performing blind and informed
search are presented. In Chapter 5, the techniques for depth-first search, iterative deepening
and breadth-first search are discussed in the context of Logic Programming, and a breadth-
first Prolog meta-interpreter is developed as well as an (inefficient) interpreter for full
clausal logic. The concept of forward chaining is illustrated by a program which generates
Herbrand models of a set of clauses. Chapter 6 discusses best-first search and its optimality,
leading to the A* algorithm. The chapter is rounded off by a brief discussion of non-
exhaustive heuristic search strategies (beam search and hill-climbing).

If the material in Parts I and II is at all 'special', it is because some non-standard perspective
has been taken. Genuinely advanced and (mostly) new material is to be found in Part III,
again consisting of three chapters. In Chapter 7, I discuss the topics of natural language
parsing and interpretation. The close links between parsing context-free grammars and
definite clause resolution have been obvious from the early days of Prolog. I present a small
grammar accepting sentences like 'Socrates is human' and 'all humans are mortal', and
extend this grammar to a Definite Clause Grammar which builds the clauses representing
their meaning. This grammar is incorporated in a program for building and querying a small
knowledge base in natural language. A nice feature of this program is that it employs
sentence generation as well, by transforming the instantiated query back to a sentence
expressing the answer to the question in natural language.

Chapter 8 groups various topics under the heading *Reasoning with incomplete
information*. It discusses and implements default reasoning by means of negation as failure,
and by means of defeasible default rules. The semantics of incomplete information is
investigated through two completion methods, the Closed World Assumption and Predicate
Completion. Then, a detailed discussion of abductive reasoning follows, including how to
avoid inconsistencies when clauses contain negated literals, and an application to fault
diagnosis. In section 8.4, the various relations between these different ways of dealing with
incomplete information are discussed.

If Chapter 8 can be called an 'issues in …' chapter, then Chapter 9 is an '… in-depth'
chapter. It deals with the difficult subject of inductively inferring a logic program from
examples. Two programs which are able to induce predicates like append are developed.
Along the way, issues like generality between clauses and anti-unification are discussed and
implemented. This chapter covers some state-of-the-art material from the maturing field of
Inductive Logic Programming.

In a number of appendices, I give a brief overview of built-in predicates in Prolog, and
a small library of utility predicates used by many programs throughout the book.
Furthermore, two larger programs are listed for transforming a Predicate Logic formula to
clausal logic, and for performing Predicate Completion. In a third appendix, answers to

selected exercises are provided. The book is completed by an extensive index, providing many cross-references.

Exercises are integrated in the text, and aim at highlighting some aspect of the current discussion. Detailed answers to selected exercises are given in Appendix C. The student is encouraged to take advantage of the exercises to assess and improve her understanding. Also, she should not hesitate to play around with the various programs!

I would be grateful if people would inform me of their experiences with the book, either as a teacher, a student, or an interested reader. Please send suggestions, criticisms, bug reports and the like by electronic mail to `Peter.Flach@kub.nl`.

Acknowledgements

This book grew out of the lecture notes I wrote for an undergraduate course on Artificial Intelligence Techniques at the Management Information Science department of Tilburg University. I am grateful to my students, on whom I tried several incomplete drafts and lousy exercises, and some of whom wrote messy programs that I had to rewrite completely before they could be incorporated in the book. It is because of them that the teachers in this book invariably like their students.

I would like to thank the Faculty of Economics and the Institute for Language Technology and Artificial Intelligence at Tilburg University, for providing the environment which made this book possible. I also thank my colleagues there for letting me work on the book (and sometimes not). The Jožef Stefan Institute in Ljubljana was a very stimulating working place during a hot month in the Summer of '93.

Of the many people who contributed to this book, I can only name a few. Bob Kowalski's enthusiastic response to my bold request was more than I could hope for. Nada Lavrač and Luc De Raedt both worked their way through a draft manuscript and provided many useful suggestions. I have to apologise to Igor Mozetič, who provided the inspiration for the diagnosis example in section 8.3, but was unhappy with the outcome. The people at John Wiley were very helpful — I particularly like to thank Rosemary Altoft, Roslyn Meredith and Erica Howard for rescuing the London Underground map by obtaining copyright from London Regional Transport. The pictures in the Stuttgart Staatsgalerie were shot by Yvonne Kraan, Robert Meersman, and Jan van Schoot.

A final word of gratitude to the mysterious 'Maria', who is Peter's student in so many examples. In a certain sense, the opposite would have been more appropriate.

Tilburg, January 1994

I

Logic and Logic Programming

Logic Programming is the name of a programming paradigm which was developed in the 70s. Rather than viewing a computer program as a step-by-step description of an algorithm, the program is conceived as a logical theory, and a procedure call is viewed as a theorem of which the truth needs to be established. Thus, executing a program means searching for a proof. In traditional (imperative) programming languages, the program is a *procedural* specification of **how** a problem needs to be solved. In contrast, a logic program concentrates on a *declarative* specification of **what** the problem is. Readers familiar with imperative programming will find that Logic Programming requires quite a different way of thinking. Indeed, their knowledge of the imperative paradigm will be partly incompatible with the logic paradigm.

This is certainly true with regard to the concept of a program *variable*. In imperative languages, a variable is a name for a memory location which can store data of certain types. While the contents of the location may vary over time, the variable always points to the same location. In fact, the term 'variable' is a bit of a misnomer here, since it refers to a value that is well-defined at every moment. In contrast, a variable in a logic program is a variable in the mathematical sense, i.e. a placeholder that can take on any value. In this respect, Logic Programming is therefore much closer to mathematical intuition than imperative programming.

Imperative programming and Logic Programming also differ with respect to the *machine model* they assume. A machine model is an abstraction of the computer on which programs are executed. The imperative paradigm assumes a dynamic, state-based machine model, where the state of the computer is given by the contents of its memory. The effect of a program statement is a transition from one state to another. Logic Programming does not assume such a dynamic machine model. Computer plus program represent a certain amount of knowledge about the world, which is used to answer queries.

The first three chapters of the book are devoted to an introduction to Logic Programming. Chapter 1, *A brief introduction to clausal logic*, is an introductory chapter, introducing many concepts in Logic Programming by means of examples. These concepts get a more formal treatment in Chapter 2, *Clausal logic and resolution: theoretical backgrounds*. In Chapter 3, *Logic Programming and Prolog*, we take a closer look at Prolog as a logic programming language, explaining its main features and describing some common programming techniques.

1

A brief introduction to clausal logic

In this chapter, we will introduce clausal logic as a formalism for representing and reasoning with knowledge. The aim of this chapter is to acquaint the reader with the most important concepts, without going into too much detail. The theoretical aspects of clausal logic, and the practical aspects of Logic Programming, will be discussed in Chapters 2 and 3.

Our Universe of Discourse in this chapter will be the London Underground, of which a small part is shown in fig. 1.1. Note that this picture contains a wealth of information, about lines, stations, transit between lines, relative distance, etc. We will try to capture this information in logical statements. Basically, fig. 1.1 specifies which stations are directly connected by which lines. If we follow the lines from left to right (Northern downwards), we come up with the following 11 formulas:

```
connected(bond_street,oxford_circus,central).
connected(oxford_circus,tottenham_court_road,central).
connected(bond_street,green_park,jubilee).
connected(green_park,charing_cross,jubilee).
connected(green_park,piccadilly_circus,piccadilly).
connected(piccadilly_circus,leicester_square,piccadilly).
connected(green_park,oxford_circus,victoria).
connected(oxford_circus,piccadilly_circus,bakerloo).
connected(piccadilly_circus,charing_cross,bakerloo).
connected(tottenham_court_road,leicester_square,northern).
connected(leicester_square,charing_cross,northern).
```

Let's define two stations to be *nearby* if they are on the same line, with at most one station in between. This relation can also be represented by a set of logical formulas:

```
nearby(bond_street,oxford_circus).
nearby(oxford_circus,tottenham_court_road).
nearby(bond_street,tottenham_court_road).
nearby(bond_street,green_park).
nearby(green_park,charing_cross).
nearby(bond_street,charing_cross).
```

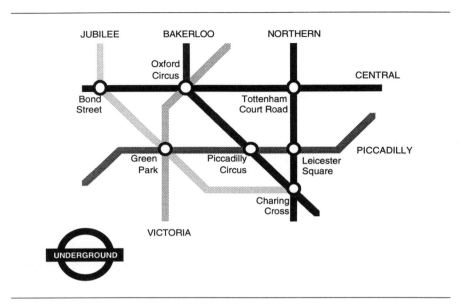

Figure 1.1. Part of the London Underground. Reproduced by permission of London Regional Transport (LRT Registered User No. 94/1954).

```
nearby(green_park,piccadilly_circus).
nearby(piccadilly_circus,leicester_square).
nearby(green_park,leicester_square).
nearby(green_park,oxford_circus).
nearby(oxford_circus,piccadilly_circus).
nearby(piccadilly_circus,charing_cross).
nearby(oxford_circus,charing_cross).
nearby(tottenham_court_road,leicester_square).
nearby(leicester_square,charing_cross).
nearby(tottenham_court_road,charing_cross).
```

These 16 formulas have been derived from the previous 11 formulas in a systematic way. If X and Y are directly connected via some line L, then X and Y are nearby. Alternatively, if there is some Z in between, such that X and Z are directly connected via L, and Z and Y are also directly connected via L, then X and Y are also nearby. We can formulate this in logic as follows:

```
nearby(X,Y):-connected(X,Y,L).
nearby(X,Y):-connected(X,Z,L),connected(Z,Y,L).
```

In these formulas, the symbol ':-' should be read as 'if', and the comma between connected(X,Z,L) and connected(Z,Y,L) should be read as 'and'. The uppercase letters stand for universally quantified variables, such that, for instance, the second formula means:

> **For any values** of *X*, *Y*, *Z* and *L*, *X* is nearby *Y* **if** *X* is directly connected to *Z* via L, **and** Z is directly connected to Y via L.

We now have two definitions of the nearby-relation, one which simply lists all pairs of stations that are nearby each other, and one in terms of direct connections. Logical formulas of the first type, such as

```
nearby(bond_street,oxford_circus)
```

will be called *facts*, and formulas of the second type, such as

```
nearby(X,Y):-connected(X,Z,L),connected(Z,Y,L)
```

will be called *rules*. Facts express unconditional truths, while rules denote conditional truths, i.e. conclusions which can only be drawn when the premises are known to be true. Obviously, we want these two definitions to be *equivalent*: for each possible query, both definitions should give exactly the same answer. We will make this more precise in the next section.

Exercise 1.1. Two stations are 'not too far' if they are on the same or a different line, with at most one station in between. Define rules for the predicate `not_too_far`.

1.1 Answering queries

A *query* like 'which station is nearby Tottenham Court Road?' will be written as

```
?-nearby(tottenham_court_road,W)
```

where the prefix '?-' indicates that this is a query rather than a fact. An *answer* to this query, e.g. 'Leicester Square', will be written {W→leicester_square}, indicating a *substitution* of values for variables, such that the statement in the query, i.e.

```
nearby(tottenham_court_road,leicester_square)
```

is true. Now, if the nearby-relation is defined by means of a list of facts, answers to queries are easily found: just look for a fact that *matches* the query, by which is meant that the fact and the query can be made identical by substituting values for variables in the query. Once we have found such a fact, we also have the substitution which constitutes the answer to the query.

If rules are involved, query-answering can take several of these steps. For answering the query `?-nearby(tottenham_court_road,W)`, we match it with the conclusion of the rule

```
nearby(X,Y):-connected(X,Y,L)
```

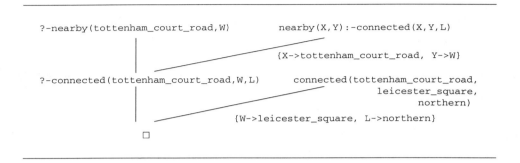

Figure 1.2. A proof tree for the query ?-nearby(tottenham_court_road,W).

yielding the substitution {X→tottenham_court_road, Y→W}. We then try to find an answer for the premises of the rule under this substitution, i.e. we try to answer the query

        ?-connected(tottenham_court_road,W,L).

That is, we can find a station nearby Tottenham Court Road, if we can find a station directly connected to it. This second query is answered by looking at the facts for direct connections, giving the answer {W→leicester_square, L→northern}. Finally, since the variable L does not occur in the initial query, we just ignore it in the final answer, which becomes {W→leicester_square} as above. In fig. 1.2, we give a graphical representation of this process. Since we are essentially *proving* that a statement follows logically from some other statements, this graphical representation is called a *proof tree*.

The steps in fig. 1.2 follow a very general reasoning pattern:

> to answer a query $?-Q_1, Q_2, \ldots, Q_n$, find a rule $A : -B_1, \ldots, B_m$ such that A matches with Q_1, and answer the query $?-B_1, \ldots, B_m, Q_2, \ldots, Q_n$.

This reasoning pattern is called *resolution*, and we will study it extensively in Chapters 2 and 3. Resolution adds a **procedural interpretation** to logical formulas, besides their declarative interpretation (they can be either true or false). Due to this procedural interpretation, logic can be used as a programming language. In an ideal logic programming system, the procedural interpretation would exactly match the declarative interpretation: everything that is calculated procedurally is declaratively true, and *vice versa*. In such an ideal system, the programmer would just bother about the declarative interpretation of the formulas she writes down, and leave the procedural interpretation to the computer. Unfortunately, in current logic programming systems the procedural interpretation does **not** exactly match the declarative interpretation: for example, some things that are declaratively true are not calculated at all, because the system enters an infinite loop. Therefore, the programmer should also be aware of the procedural interpretation given by the computer to her logical formulas.

The resolution proof process makes use of a technique that is known as *reduction to the absurd*: suppose that the formula to be proved is false, and show that this leads to a contradiction, thereby demonstrating that the formula to be proved is in fact true. Such a proof is also called a *proof by refutation*. For instance, if we want to know which stations are nearby Tottenham Court Road, we negate this statement, resulting in 'there are no stations nearby Tottenham Court Road'. In logic, this is achieved by writing the statement as a rule with an empty conclusion, i.e. a rule for which the truth of its premises would lead to falsity:

```
:-nearby(tottenham_court_road,W)
```

Thus, the symbols '?-' and ':-' are in fact equivalent. A contradiction is found if resolution leads to the empty rule, of which the premises are always true (since there are none), but the conclusion is always false. Conventionally, the empty rule is written as '□'.

At the beginning of this section, we posed the question: can we show that our two definitions of the nearby-relation are equivalent? As indicated before, the idea is that to be equivalent means to provide exactly the same answers to the same queries. To formalise this, we need some additional definitions. A *ground* fact is a fact without variables. Obviously, if G is a ground fact, the query ?-G never returns a substitution as answer: either it *succeeds* (G does follow from the initial assumptions), or it *fails* (G does not). The set of ground facts G for which the query ?-G succeeds is called the *success set*. Thus, the success set for our first definition of the nearby-relation consists simply of those 16 formulas, since they are ground facts already, and nothing else is derivable from them. The success set for the second definition of the nearby-relation is constructed by applying the two rules to the ground facts for connectedness. Thus we can say: two definitions of a relation are (procedurally) *equivalent* if they have the same success set (restricted to that relation).

Exercise 1.2. Construct the proof trees for the query
```
?-nearby(W,charing_cross).
```

1.2 Recursion

Until now, we have encountered two types of logical formulas: facts and rules. There is a special kind of rule which deserves special attention: the rule which defines a relation in terms of itself. This idea of 'self-reference', which is called *recursion*, is also present in most procedural programming languages. Recursion is a bit difficult to grasp, but once you've mastered it, you can use it to write very elegant programs, e.g.

```
IF N=0
THEN FAC:=1
ELSE FAC:=N*FAC(N-1).
```

is a recursive procedure for calculating the factorial of a given number, written in a Pascal-like procedural language. However, in such languages *iteration* (looping a pre-specified number of times) is usually preferred over recursion, because it uses memory more efficiently.

In Prolog, however, recursion is the **only** looping structure[1]. (This does not necessarily mean that Prolog is always less efficient than a procedural language, because there are ways to write recursive loops that are just as efficient as iterative loops, as we will see in section 3.6.) Perhaps the easiest way to think about recursion is the following: an arbitrarily large chain is described by describing how one link in the chain is connected to the next. For instance, let us define the relation of *reachability* in our underground example, where a station is reachable from another station if they are connected by one or more lines. We could define it by the following 20 ground facts:

```
reachable(bond_street,charing_cross).
reachable(bond_street,green_park).
reachable(bond_street,leicester_square).
reachable(bond_street,oxford_circus).
reachable(bond_street,piccadilly_circus).
reachable(bond_street,tottenham_court_road).
reachable(green_park,charing_cross).
reachable(green_park,leicester_square).
reachable(green_park,oxford_circus).
reachable(green_park,piccadilly_circus).
reachable(green_park,tottenham_court_road).
reachable(leicester_square,charing_cross).
reachable(oxford_circus,charing_cross).
reachable(oxford_circus,leicester_square).
reachable(oxford_circus,piccadilly_circus).
reachable(oxford_circus,tottenham_court_road).
reachable(piccadilly_circus,charing_cross).
reachable(piccadilly_circus,leicester_square).
reachable(tottenham_court_road,charing_cross).
reachable(tottenham_court_road,leicester_square).
```

Since any station is reachable from any other station by a route with at most two intermediate stations, we could instead use the following (non-recursive) definition:

```
reachable(X,Y):- connected(X,Y,L).
reachable(X,Y):- connected(X,Z,L1),connected(Z,Y,L2).
reachable(X,Y):- connected(X,Z1,L1),connected(Z1,Z2,L2),
                 connected(Z2,Y,L3).
```

Of course, if we were to define the reachability relation for the entire London underground, we would need a lot more, longer and longer rules. Recursion is a much more convenient and natural way to define such chains of arbitrary length:

```
reachable(X,Y):-connected(X,Y,L).
reachable(X,Y):-connected(X,Z,L),reachable(Z,Y).
```

The reading of the second rule is as follows: '*Y* is reachable from *X* if *Z* is directly connected to *X* via line *L*, and *Y* is reachable from *Z*'.

---

[1]If we take Prolog's procedural behaviour into account, there are alternatives to recursive loops such as the so-called *failure-driven loop* (see Exercise 7.5).

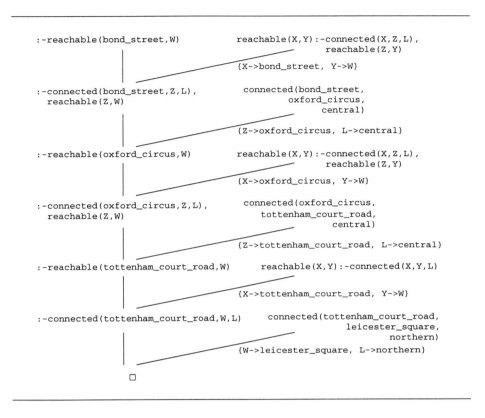

Figure 1.3. A proof tree for the query `?-reachable(bond_street,W)`.

We can now use this recursive definition to prove that Leicester Square is reachable from Bond Street (fig. 1.3). However, just as there are several routes from Bond Street to Leicester Square, there are several alternative proofs of the fact that Leicester Square is reachable from Bond Street. An alternative proof is given in fig. 1.4. The difference between these two proofs is that in the first proof we use the fact

```
connected(oxford_circus,tottenham_court_road,central)
```

while in the second proof we use

```
connected(oxford_circus,piccadilly_circus,bakerloo)
```

There is no reason to prefer one over the other, but since Prolog searches the given formulas top-down, it will find the first proof before the second. Thus, the order of the clauses determines the order in which answers are found. As we will see in Chapter 3, it sometimes even determines whether any answers are found at all.

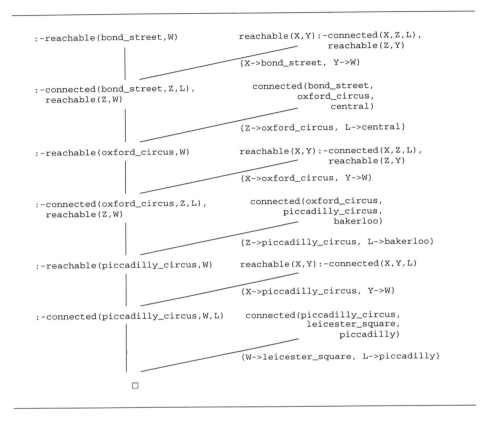

Figure 1.4. Alternative proof tree for the query `?-reachable(bond_street,W)`.

Exercise 1.3. Give a third proof tree for the answer {W→leicester_square}, and change the order of the facts for connectedness, such that this proof tree is constructed first.

In other words, Prolog's query-answering process is a *search process*, in which the answer depends on all the choices made earlier. A important point is that some of these choices may lead to a dead-end later. For example, if the recursive formula for the reachability relation had been tried before the non-recursive one, the bottom part of fig. 1.3 would have been as in fig. 1.5. This proof tree cannot be completed, because there are no answers to the query `?-reachable(charing_cross,W)`, as can easily be checked. Prolog has to recover from this failure by climbing up the tree, reconsidering previous choices. This search process, which is called *backtracking*, will be detailed in Chapter 5.

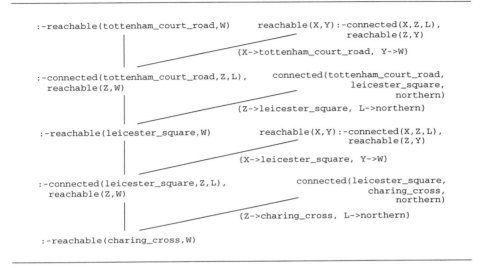

Figure 1.5. A failing proof tree.

1.3 Structured terms

Finally, we illustrate the way Prolog can handle more complex datastructures, such as a list of stations representing a route. Suppose we want to redefine the reachability relation, such that it also specifies the intermediate stations. We could adapt the non-recursive definition of `reachable` as follows:

```
reachable0(X,Y):-connected(X,Y,L).
reachable1(X,Y,Z):- connected(X,Z,L1),
                    connected(Z,Y,L2).
reachable2(X,Y,Z1,Z2):- connected(X,Z1,L1),
                        connected(Z1,Z2,L2),
                        connected(Z2,Y,L3).
```

The suffix of reachable indicates the number of intermediate stations; it is added to stress that relations with different number of arguments are really different relations, even if their names are the same. The problem now is that we have to know the number of intermediate stations in advance, before we can ask the right query. This is, of course, unacceptable.

We can solve this problem by means of *functors*. A functor looks just like a mathematical function, but the important difference is that *functor expressions are never evaluated to determine a value*. Instead, they provide a way to name a complex object

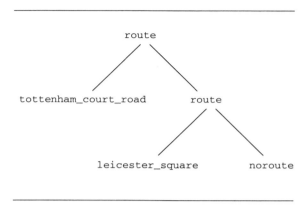

Figure 1.6. A complex object as a tree.

composed of simpler objects. For instance, a route with Oxford Circus and Tottenham Court Road as intermediate stations could be represented by

```
route(oxford_circus,tottenham_court_road)
```

Note that this is not a ground fact, but rather an argument for a logical formula. The reachability relation can now be defined as follows:

```
reachable(X,Y,noroute):-connected(X,Y,L).
reachable(X,Y,route(Z)):- connected(X,Z,L1),
                            connected(Z,Y,L2).
reachable(X,Y,route(Z1,Z2)):- connected(X,Z1,L1),
                                connected(Z1,Z2,L2),
                                connected(Z2,Y,L3).
```

The query `?-reachable(oxford_circus,charing_cross,R)` now has three possible answers:

```
{R→route(piccadilly_circus)}
{R→route(tottenham_court_road,leicester_square)}
{R→route(piccadilly_circus,leicester_square)}
```

As argued in the previous section, we prefer the recursive definition of the reachability relation, in which case we use functors in a somewhat different way.

```
reachable(X,Y,noroute):-connected(X,Y,L).
reachable(X,Y,route(Z,R)):- connected(X,Z,L),
                             reachable(Z,Y,R).
```

At first sight, there does not seem to be a big difference between this and the use of functors in the non-recursive program. However, the query

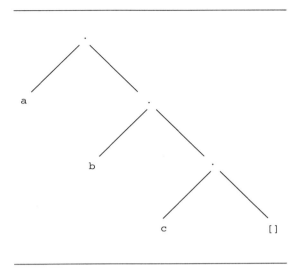

Figure 1.7. The list [a,b,c] as a tree.

```
?-reachable(oxford_circus,charing_cross,R)
```

now has the following answers:

```
{R→route(tottenham_court_road,
         route(leicester_square,noroute))}
{R→route(piccadilly_circus,noroute)}
{R→route(piccadilly_circus,
         route(leicester_square,noroute))}
```

The functor route is now also recursive in nature: its first argument is a station, but *its second argument is again a route*. For instance, the object

```
route(tottenham_court_road,route(leicester_square,noroute))
```

can be pictured as in fig. 1.6. Such a figure is called a *tree* (we will have a lot more to say about trees in chapter 4). In order to find out the route represented by this complex object, we read the leaves of this tree from left to right, until we reach the 'terminator' noroute. This would result in a linear notation like

```
[tottenham_court_road,leicester_square].
```

For user-defined functors, such a linear notation is not available. However, Prolog provides a built-in 'datatype' called *lists*, for which both the tree-like notation and the linear notation may be used. The functor for lists is . (dot), which takes two arguments: the first element of the list (which may be any object), and the rest of the list (which must be a list). The list terminator is the special symbol [], denoting the empty list. For instance, the term

```
.(a,.(b,.(c,[])))
```

denotes the list consisting of a followed by b followed by c (fig. 1.7). Alternatively, we may use the linear notation, which uses square brackets:

```
[a,b,c]
```

To increase readability of the tree-like notation, instead of

```
.(First,Rest)
```

one can also write

```
[First|Rest]
```

Note that Rest is a list: e.g., [a,b,c] is the same list as [a|[b,c]]. a is called the *head* of the list, and [b,c] is called its *tail*. Finally, to a certain extent the two notations can be mixed: at the head of the list, you can write any number of elements in linear notation. For instance,

```
[First,Second,Third|Rest]
```

denotes a list with three or more elements.

Exercise 1.4. A list is either the empty list [], or a non-empty list [First|Rest] where Rest is a list. Define a relation list(L), which checks whether L is a list. Adapt it such that it succeeds only for lists of (*i*) even length and (*ii*) odd length.

The recursive nature of such datastructures makes it possible to ignore the size of the objects, which is extremely useful in many situations. For instance, the definition of a route between two underground stations does not depend on the length of the route; all that matters is whether there is an intermediate station or not. For both cases, there is a clause. Expressing the route as a list, we can state the final definition of the reachability relation:

```
reachable(X,Y,[]):-connected(X,Y,L).
reachable(X,Y,[Z|R]):-connected(X,Z,L),reachable(Z,Y,R).
```

The query ?-reachable(oxford_circus,charing_cross,R) now results in the following answers:

```
{R→[tottenham_court_road,leicester_square]}
{R→[piccadilly_circus]}
{R→[piccadilly_circus, leicester_square]}
```

Note that Prolog writes out lists of fixed length in the linear notation.

Should we for some reason want to know from which station Charing Cross can be reached via a route with four intermediate stations, we should ask the query

```
?-reachable(X,charing_cross,[A,B,C,D])
```

which results in two answers:

```
{ X→bond_street, A→green_park, B→oxford_circus,
  C→tottenham_court_road, D→leicester_square }
{ X→bond_street, A→green_park, B→oxford_circus,
  C→piccadilly_circus, D→leicester_square }.
```

Exercise 1.5. Construct a query asking for a route from Bond Street to Piccadilly Circus with at least two intermediate stations.

1.4　What else is there to know about clausal logic?

The main goal of this chapter has been to introduce the most important concepts in clausal logic, and how it can be used as a reasoning formalism. Needless to say, a subject like this needs a much more extensive and precise discussion than has been attempted here, and many important questions remain. To name a few:

- what are the limits of expressiveness of clausal logic, i.e. what can and what cannot be expressed?
- what are the limits of reasoning with clausal logic, i.e. what can and what cannot be (efficiently) computed?
- how are these two limits related: is it for instance possible to enhance reasoning by limiting expressiveness?

In order to start answering such questions, we need to be more precise in defining what clausal logic is, what expressions in clausal logic mean, and how we can reason with them. That means that we will have to introduce some theory in the next chapter. This theory will not only be useful for a better understanding of Logic Programming, but it will also be the foundation for most of the topics in Part III (*Advanced reasoning techniques*).

Another aim of Part I of this book is to teach the skill of programming in Prolog. For this, theory alone, however important, will not suffice. Like any programming language, Prolog has a number of built-in procedures and datastructures that you should know about. Furthermore, there are of course numerous programming techniques and tricks of the trade, with which the Prolog programmer should be familiar. These subjects will be discussed in Chapter 3. Together, Chapters 2 and 3 will provide a solid foundation for the rest of the book.

2
Clausal logic and resolution: theoretical backgrounds

In this chapter we develop a more formal view of Logic Programming by means of a rigorous treatment of clausal logic and resolution theorem proving. Any such treatment has three parts: syntax, semantics, and proof theory. *Syntax* defines the logical language we are using, i.e. the alphabet, different kinds of 'words', and the allowed 'sentences'. *Semantics* defines, in some formal way, the meaning of words and sentences in the language. As with most logics, semantics for clausal logic is *truth-functional*, i.e. the meaning of a sentence is defined by specifying the conditions under which it is assigned certain *truth values* (in our case: **true** or **false**). Finally, *proof theory* specifies how we can obtain new sentences (theorems) from assumed ones (axioms) by means of pure symbol manipulation (inference rules).

Of these three, proof theory is most closely related to Logic Programming, because answering queries is in fact no different from proving theorems. In addition to proof theory, we need semantics for deciding whether the things we prove actually make sense. For instance, we need to be sure that the truth of the theorems is assured by the truth of the axioms. If our inference rules guarantee this, they are said to be *sound*. But this will not be enough, because sound inference rules can be actually very weak, and unable to prove anything of interest. We also need to be sure that the inference rules are powerful enough to eventually prove any possible theorem: they should be *complete*.

Concepts like soundness and completeness are called *meta-theoretical*, since they are not expressed **in** the logic under discussion, but rather belong to a theory **about** that logic ('meta' means above). Their significance is not merely theoretical, but extends to logic programming languages like Prolog. For example, if a logic programming language is unsound, it will give wrong answers to some queries; if it is incomplete, it will give no answer to some other queries. Ideally, a logic programming language should be sound and complete; in practice, this will not be the case. For instance, in the next chapter we will see that Prolog is both unsound and incomplete. This has been a deliberate design choice: a sound and complete Prolog would be much less efficient. Nevertheless, any Prolog programmer should know exactly the circumstances under which Prolog is unsound or incomplete, and avoid these circumstances in her programs.

The structure of this chapter is as follows. We start with a very simple (propositional) logical language, and enrich this language in two steps to full clausal logic. For each of these three languages, we discuss syntax, semantics, proof theory, and meta-theory. We then discuss definite clause logic, which is the subset of clausal logic used in Prolog. Finally, we relate clausal logic to Predicate Logic, and show that they are essentially equal in expressive power.

2.1 Propositional clausal logic

Informally, a *proposition* is any statement which is either true or false, such as '2 + 2 = 4' or 'the moon is made of green cheese'. These are the building blocks of propositional logic, the weakest form of logic.

Syntax. Propositions are abstractly denoted by *atoms*, which are single words starting with a lowercase character. For instance, `married` is an atom denoting the proposition 'he/she is married'; similarly, `man` denotes the proposition 'he is a man'. Using the special symbols ': -' (**if**), ';' (**or**) and ',' (**and**), we can combine atoms to form *clauses*. For instance,

```
married;bachelor:-man,adult
```

is a clause, with intended meaning: 'somebody is married **or** a bachelor **if** he is a man **and** an adult'[2]. The part to the left of the if-symbol ': -' is called the *head* of the clause, and the right part is called the *body* of the clause. The head of a clause is always a disjunction (**or**) of atoms, and the body of a clause is always a conjunction (**and**).

Exercise 2.1. Translate the following statements into clauses, using the atoms `person`, `sad` and `happy`:
- (*a*)   persons are happy or sad;
- (*b*)   no person is both happy and sad;
- (*c*)   sad persons are not happy;
- (*d*)   non-happy persons are sad.

A *program* is a set of clauses, each of them terminated by a period. The clauses are to be read conjunctively; for example, the program

```
woman;man:-human.
human:-woman.
human:-man.
```

has the intended meaning '(**if** someone is human **then** she/he is a woman **or** a man) **and** (**if** someone is a woman **then** she is human) **and** (**if** someone is a man **then** he is human)', or, in other words, 'someone is human **if and only if** she/he is a woman **or** a man'.

---

[2]It is often more convenient to read a clause in the opposite direction: '**if** somebody is a man **and** an adult **then** he is married **or** a bachelor'.

Semantics. The *Herbrand base* of a program P is the set of atoms occurring in P. For the above program, the Herbrand base is {woman, man, human}. A *Herbrand interpretation* (or interpretation for short) for P is a mapping from the Herbrand base of P into the set of truth values {**true**, **false**}. For example, the mapping {woman→**true**, man→**false**, human→**true**} is a Herbrand interpretation for the above program. A Herbrand interpretation can be viewed as describing a possible state of affairs in the Universe of Discourse (in this case: 'she is a woman, she is not a man, she is human'). Since there are only two possible truth values in the semantics we are considering, we could abbreviate such mappings by listing only the atoms that are assigned the truth value **true**; by definition, the remaining ones are assigned the truth value **false**. Under this convention, which we will adopt in this book, a Herbrand interpretation is simply a subset of the Herbrand base. Thus, the previous Herbrand interpretation would be represented as {woman, human}.

Since a Herbrand interpretation assigns truth values to every atom in a clause, it also assigns a truth value to the clause as a whole. The rules for determining the truth value of a clause from the truth values of its atoms are not so complicated, if you keep in mind that the body of a clause is a conjunction of atoms, and the head is a disjunction. Consequently, the body of a clause is **true** if every atom in it is **true**, and the head of a clause is **true** if at least one atom in it is **true**. In turn, the truth value of the clause is determined by the truth values of head and body. There are four possibilities:

(*i*)   the body is **true**, and the head is **true**;

(*ii*)   the body is **true**, and the head is **false**;

(*iii*) the body is **false**, and the head is **true**;

(*iv*) the body is **false**, and the head is **false**.

The intended meaning of the clause is '**if** body **then** head', which is obviously **true** in the first case, and **false** in the second case.

What about the remaining two cases? They cover statements like '**if** the moon is made of green cheese **then** $2 + 2 = 4$', in which there is no connection at all between body and head. One would like to say that such statements are neither **true** nor **false**. However, our semantics is not sophisticated enough to deal with this: it simply insists that clauses should be assigned a truth value in every possible interpretation. Therefore, we consider the clause to be **true** whenever its body is **false**. It is not difficult to see that under these truth conditions a clause is equivalent with the statement 'head **or not** body'. For example, the clause married;bachelor:-man,adult can also be read as 'someone is married **or** a bachelor **or not** a man **or not** an adult'. Thus, a clause is a disjunction of atoms, which are negated if they occur in the body of the clause. Therefore, the atoms in the body of the clause are often called *negative literals*, while those in the head of the clause are called *positive literals*.

To summarise: a clause is assigned the truth value **true** in an interpretation, if and only if at least one of the following conditions is true: (*a*) at least one atom in the body of the clause is **false** in the interpretation (cases (*iii*) and (*iv*)), or (*b*) at least one atom in the head of the clause is **true** in the interpretation (cases (*i*) and (*iii*)). If a clause is **true** in an interpretation, we say that the interpretation is a *model* for the clause. An interpretation is a model for a program if it is a model for each clause in the program. For example, the above program has the following models: ∅ (the empty model, assigning **false** to every atom), {woman, human}, {man, human}, and {woman, man, human}. Since there are eight possible interpretations for a Herbrand base with three atoms, this means that the program contains enough information to rule out half of these.

Adding more clauses to the program means restricting its set of models. For instance, if we add the clause woman (a clause with an empty body) to the program, we rule out the first and third model, which leaves us with the models {woman, human}, and {woman, man, human}. Note that in both of these models, human is **true**. We say that human is a logical consequence of the set of clauses. In general, a clause C is a *logical consequence* of a program P if every model of the program is also a model of the clause; we write $P \models C$.

Exercise 2.2. Given the program
```
married;bachelor:-man,adult.
man.
:-bachelor.
```
determine which of the following clauses are logical consequences of this program:
(a) married:-adult;
(b) married:-bachelor;
(c) bachelor:-man;
(d) bachelor:-bachelor.

Of the two remaining models, obviously {woman, human} is the intended one; but the program does not yet contain enough information to distinguish it from the non-intended model {woman, man, human}. We can add yet another clause, to make sure that the atom man is mapped to **false**. For instance, we could add

```
:-man
```

(it is not a man) or

```
:-man,woman
```

(nobody is both a man and a woman). However, explicitly stating everything that is false in the intended model is not always feasible. Consider, for example, an airline database consulted by travel agencies: we simply want to say that if a particular flight (i.e., a combination of plane, origin, destination, date and time) is not listed in the database, then it does not exist, instead of listing all the dates that a particular plane does **not** fly from Amsterdam to London.

So, instead of adding clauses until a single model remains, we want to add a rule to our semantics which tells us which of the several models is the intended one. The airline example shows us that, in general, we only want to accept something as **true** if we are really forced to, i.e. if it is **true** in every possible model. This means that we should take the intersection of every model of a program in order to construct the intended model. In the example, this is {woman, human}. Note that this model is *minimal* in the sense that no subset of it is also a model. Therefore, this semantics is called a *minimal model semantics*.

Unfortunately, this approach is only applicable to a restricted class of programs. Consider the following program:

```
woman;man:-human.
human.
```

This program has three models: {woman, human}, {man, human}, and {woman, man, human}. The intersection of these models is {human}, but this interpretation is not a model of the first clause! The program has in fact not one, but **two** minimal models, which is caused by the fact that the first clause has a disjunctive head. Such a clause is called *indefinite*, because it does not permit definite conclusions to be drawn.

On the other hand, if we would only allow *definite* clauses, i.e. clauses with a single positive literal, minimal models are guaranteed to be unique. We will deal with definite clauses in section 2.4, because Prolog is based on definite clause logic. In principle, this means that clauses like woman;man:-human are not expressible in Prolog. However, such a clause can be transformed into a 'pseudo-definite' clause by moving one of the literals in the head to the body, extended with an extra negation. This gives the following two possibilities:

```
woman:-human,not(man).
man:-human,not(woman).
```

In Prolog, we have to choose between these two clauses, which means that we have only an approximation of the original indefinite clause. Negation in Prolog is an important subject with many aspects. In Chapter 3, we will show how Prolog handles negation in the body of clauses. In Chapter 8, we will discuss particular applications of this kind of negation.

Proof theory. Recall that a clause C is a logical consequence of a program P ($P \models C$) if every model of P is a model of C. Checking this condition is, in general, unfeasible. Therefore, we need a more efficient way of computing logical consequences, by means of inference rules. If C can be derived from P by means of a number of applications of such inference rules, we say that C can be *proved* from P. Such inference rules are purely syntactic, and do not refer to any underlying semantics.

The proof theory for clausal logic consists of a single inference rule called *resolution*. Resolution is a very powerful inference rule. Consider the following program:

```
married;bachelor:-man,adult.
has_wife:-man,married.
```

This simple program has no less than 26 models, each of which needs to be considered if we want to check whether a clause is a logical consequence of it.

Exercise 2.3. Write down the six Herbrand interpretations that are not models of the program.

The following clause is a logical consequence of this program:

```
has_wife;bachelor:-man,adult
```

By means of resolution, it can be produced in a single step. This step represents the following line of reasoning: 'if someone is a man and an adult, then he is a bachelor or

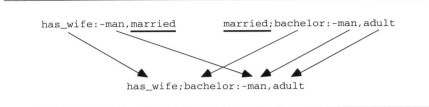

Figure 2.1. A resolution step.

married; but if he is married, he has a wife; therefore, if someone is a man and an adult, then he is a bachelor or he has a wife'. In this argument, the two clauses in the program are related to each other by means of the atom married, which occurs in the head of the first clause (a positive literal) and in the body of the second (a negative literal). The derived clause, which is called the *resolvent*, consists of all the literals of the two input clauses, except married (the literal *resolved upon*). The negative literal man, which occurs in both input clauses, appears only once in the derived clause. This process is depicted in fig. 2.1.

Resolution is most easily understood when applied to definite clauses. Consider the following program:

```
square:-rectangle,equal_sides.
rectangle:-parallelogram,right_angles.
```

Applying resolution yields the clause

```
square:-parallelogram,right_angles,equal_sides
```

That is, the atom rectangle in the body of the first clause is replaced by the body of the second clause (which has rectangle as its head). This process is also referred to as *unfolding* the second clause into the first one (fig. 2.2).

A resolvent resulting from one resolution step can be used as input for the next. A *proof* or *derivation* of a clause *C* from a program *P* is a sequence of clauses such that each

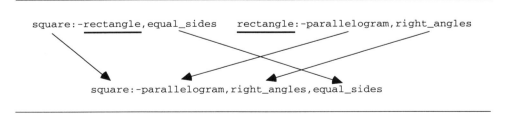

Figure 2.2. Resolution with definite clauses.

clause is either in the program, or the resolvent of two previous clauses, and the last clause is *C*. If there is a proof of *C* from *P*, we write $P \vdash C$.

Exercise 2.4. Give a derivation of friendly from the following program:
```
happy;friendly:-teacher.
friendly:-teacher,happy.
teacher;wise.
teacher:-wise.
```

Meta-theory. It is easy to show that propositional resolution is **sound**: you have to establish that every model for the two input clauses is a model for the resolvent. In our earlier example, every model of married;bachelor:-man,adult and has_wife:-man,married must be a model of has_wife;bachelor:-man,adult. Now, the literal resolved upon (in this case married) is either assigned the truth value **true** or **false**. In the first case, every model of has_wife:-man,married is also a model of has_wife:-man; in the second case, every model of married;bachelor:-man,adult is also a model of bachelor:-man,adult. In both cases, these models are models of a subclause of the resolvent, which means that they are also models of the resolvent itself.

In general, proving **completeness** is more complicated than proving soundness. Still worse, proving completeness of resolution is impossible, because resolution is not complete at all! For instance, consider the clause a:-a. This clause is a so-called *tautology*: it is true under any interpretation. Therefore, any model of an arbitrary program *P* is a model for it, and thus $P \models$ a:-a for any program *P*. If resolution were complete, it would be possible to derive the clause a:-a from some program *P* in which the literal a doesn't even occur! It is clear that resolution is unable to do this.

However, this is not necessarily bad, because although tautologies follow from any set of clauses, they are not very interesting. Resolution makes it possible to guide the inference process, by implementing the question 'is *C* a logical consequence of *P*?' rather than 'what are the logical consequences of *P*?'. We will see that, although resolution is unable to generate every logical consequence of a set of clauses, it is complete in the sense that resolution can always determine whether a specific clause is a logical consequence of a set of clauses.

The idea is analogous to a proof technique in mathematics called 'reduction to the absurd'. Suppose for the moment that *C* consists of a single positive literal a; we want to know whether $P \models$ a, i.e. whether every model of *P* is also a model of a. It is easily checked that an interpretation is a model of a if, and only if, it is **not** a model of :-a. Therefore, every model of *P* is a model of a if, and only if, there is no interpretation which is a model of both :-a and *P*. In other words, a is a logical consequence of *P* if, and only if, :-a and *P* are mutually *inconsistent* (don't have a common model). So, checking whether $P \models$ a is equivalent to checking whether $P \cup \{:\text{-a}\}$ is inconsistent.

Resolution provides a way to check this condition. Note that, since an inconsistent set of clauses doesn't have a model, it trivially satisfies the condition that any model of it is a model of any other clause; therefore, an inconsistent set of clauses has every possible clause as its logical consequence. In particular, the absurd or *empty* clause, denoted by □[3], is a logical consequence of an inconsistent set of clauses. Conversely, if □ is a logical consequence of a set of clauses, we know it must be inconsistent. Now, resolution is complete in the sense that *if P set of clauses is inconsistent, it is always possible to derive* □ *by resolution*. Since resolution is sound, we already know that if we can derive □ then the input clauses must be inconsistent. So we conclude: a is a logical consequence of *P* if, and only if, the empty clause can be deduced by resolution from *P* augmented with :-a. This process is called *proof by refutation*, and resolution is called *refutation complete*.

This proof method can be generalised to the case where *B* is not a single atom. For instance, let us check by resolution that a:-a is a tautology, i.e. a logical consequence of any set of clauses. Logically speaking, this clause is equivalent to 'a **or not** a', the negation of which is '**not** a **and** a', which is represented by two separate clauses :-a and a. Since we can derive the empty clause from these two clauses in a single resolution step without using any other clauses, we have in fact proved that a:-a is a logical consequence of an empty set of clauses, hence a tautology.

Exercise 2.5. Prove by refutation that `friendly:-has_friends` is a logical consequence of the following clauses:

                happy:-has_friends.
                friendly:-happy.

Finally, we mention that although resolution can always be used to prove inconsistency of a set of clauses it is not always fit to prove the opposite, i.e. consistency of a set of clauses. For instance, a is not a logical consequence of a:-a; yet, if we try to prove the inconsistency of :-a and a:-a (which should fail) we can go on applying resolution forever! The reason, of course, is that there is a loop in the system: applying resolution to :-a and a:-a again yields :-a. In this simple case it is easy to check for loops: just maintain a list of previously derived clauses, and do not proceed with clauses that have been derived previously.

However, as we will see, this is not possible in the general case of full clausal logic, which is *semi-decidable* with respect to the question 'is *B* a logical consequence of *A*': there is an algorithm which derives, in finite time, a proof if one exists, but there is no algorithm which, for any *A* and *B*, halts and returns 'no' if no proof exists. The reason for this is that interpretations for full clausal logic are in general infinite. As a consequence, some Prolog programs may loop forever (just like some Pascal programs). One might suggest that it should be possible to check, just by examining the source code, whether a program is going to loop or not, but, as Alan Turing showed, this is, in general, impossible (the Halting Problem). That is, you can write programs for checking termination of programs, but for any such termination checking program you can write a program on which it will not terminate itself!

---

[3] □ is called the empty clause because it has empty body and head, and therefore it is not satisfiable by any interpretation.

2.2   Relational clausal logic

Propositional clausal logic is rather coarse-grained, because it takes propositions (i.e. anything that can be assigned a truth value) as its basic building blocks. For example, it is not possible to formulate the following argument in propositional logic:

Peter likes all his students
Maria is one of Peter's students
Therefore, Peter likes Maria

In order to formalise this type of reasoning, we need to talk about individuals like Peter and Maria, sets of individuals like Peter's students, and relations between individuals, such as 'likes'. This refinement of propositional clausal logic leads us into relational clausal logic.

Syntax.   Individual names are called *constants*; we follow the Prolog convention of writing them as single words starting with a lowercase character (or as arbitrary strings enclosed in single quotes, like `'this is a constant'`). Arbitrary individuals are denoted by *variables*, which are single words starting with an uppercase character. Jointly, constants and variables are denoted as *terms*. A *ground* term is a term without variables[4].

Relations between individuals are abstractly denoted by *predicates* (which follow the same notational conventions as constants). An *atom* is a predicate followed by a number of terms, enclosed in brackets and separated by commas, e.g. `likes(peter,maria)`. The terms between brackets are called the *arguments* of the predicate, and the number of arguments is the predicate's *arity*. The arity of a predicate is assumed to be fixed, and predicates with the same name but different arity are assumed to be different. A *ground* atom is an atom without variables.

All the remaining definitions pertaining to the syntax of propositional clausal logic, in particular those of literal, clause and program, stay the same. So, the following clauses are meant to represent the above statements:

```
likes(peter,S):-student_of(S,peter).
student_of(maria,peter).
likes(peter,maria).
```

The intended meaning of these clauses are, respectively, '**if** *S* is a student of Peter **then** Peter likes *S*', 'Maria is a student of Peter', and 'Peter likes Maria'. Clearly, we want our logic to be such that the third clause follows logically from the first two, and we want to be able to prove this by resolution. Therefore, we must extend the semantics and proof theory in order to deal with variables.

Semantics.   The *Herbrand universe* of a program *P* is the set of ground terms (i.e. constants) occurring in it. For the above program, the Herbrand universe is {`peter`, `maria`}. The Herbrand universe is the set of all individuals we are talking about in our clauses. The *Herbrand base* of *P* is the set of **ground** atoms that can be constructed using the predicates in *P* and the ground terms in the Herbrand universe. This set represents all the things we can say about the individuals in the Herbrand universe.

---

[4]In relational clausal logic, ground terms are necessarily constants. However, this is not the case in full clausal logic, as we will see in section 2.3.

Logical   variables

Variables in clausal logic are very similar to variables in mathematical formulas:
they are placeholders that can be substituted by arbitrary ground terms from the
Herbrand universe. It is very important to notice that *logical variables are global
within a clause* (i.e. if the variable occurs at several positions within a clause, it
should be substituted everywhere by the same term), *but not within a program.* This
can be clearly seen from the semantics of relational clausal logic, where grounding
substitutions are applied to clauses rather than programs. As a consequence,
variables in two different clauses are distinct by definition,
even if they have the same name. It will sometimes be useful to rename the
variables in clauses, such that no two clauses share a variable; this is called
standardising the clauses *apart.*

The Herbrand base of the above program is

```
{ likes(peter,peter),likes(peter,maria),
  likes(maria,peter),likes(maria,maria),
  student_of(peter,peter),student_of(peter,maria),
  student_of(maria,peter),student_of(maria,maria) }
```

As before, a *Herbrand interpretation* is the subset of the Herbrand base whose elements are
assigned the truth value **true**. For instance,

```
{likes(peter,maria),student_of(maria,peter)}
```

is an interpretation of the above program.

Clearly, we want this interpretation to be a model of the program, but now we have to
deal with the variables in the program. A *substitution* is a mapping from variables to terms.
For example, {S→maria} and {S→X} are substitutions. A substitution can be *applied* to a
clause, which means that all occurrences of a variable occurring on the lefthand side in a
substitution are replaced by the term on the righthand side. For instance, if C is the clause

```
likes(peter,S):-student_of(S,peter)
```

then the above substitutions yield the clauses

```
likes(peter,maria):-student_of(maria,peter)
```

```
likes(peter,X):-student_of(X,peter)
```

Notice that the first clause is ground; it is said to be a *ground instance* of C, and the
substitution {S→maria} is called a *grounding substitution.* All the atoms in a ground
clause occur in the Herbrand base, so reasoning with ground clauses is just like reasoning
with propositional clauses. An interpretation is a model for a non-ground clause if it is a
model for every ground instance of the clause. Thus, in order to show that

$$M = \{\texttt{likes(peter,maria),student\_of(maria,peter)}\}$$

is a model of the clause *C* above, we have to construct the set of the ground instances of *C* over the Herbrand universe {peter, maria}, which is

```
{ likes(peter,maria):-student_of(maria,peter),
  likes(peter,peter):-student_of(peter,peter) }
```

and show that *M* is a model of every element of this set.

Exercise 2.6. How many models does *C* have over the Herbrand universe {peter, maria}?

Proof theory. Because reasoning with ground clauses is just like reasoning with propositional clauses, a naive proof method in relational clausal logic would apply grounding substitutions to every clause in the program before applying resolution. Such a method is naive, because a program has many different grounding substitutions, most of which do not lead to a resolution proof. For instance, if the Herbrand universe contains four constants, then a clause with two distinct variables has 16 different grounding substitutions, and a program consisting of three such clauses has 4096 different grounding substitutions.

Instead of applying arbitrary grounding substitutions before trying to apply resolution, we will derive the required substitutions from the clauses themselves. Recall that in order to apply propositional resolution, the literal resolved upon should occur in both input clauses (positive in one clause and negative in the other). In relational clausal logic, atoms can contain variables. Therefore, we do not require that exactly the same atom occurs in both clauses; rather, we require that there is a pair of atoms *which can be made equal by substituting terms for variables*. For instance, let *P* be the following program:

```
likes(peter,S):-student_of(S,peter).
student_of(maria,T):-follows(maria,C),teaches(T,C).
```

The second clause is intended to mean: 'Maria is a student of any teacher who teaches a course she follows'. From these two clauses we should be able to prove that 'Peter likes Maria **if** Maria follows a course taught by Peter'. This means that we want to resolve the two clauses on the student_of literals.

The two atoms student_of(S,peter) and student_of(maria,T) can be made equal by replacing S by maria and T by peter, by means of the substitution {S→maria, T→peter}. This process is called *unification*, and the substitution is called a *unifier*. Applying this substitution yields the following two clauses:

```
likes(peter,maria):-student_of(maria,peter).
student_of(maria,peter):-follows(maria,C),
                                teaches(peter,C).
```

(Note that the second clause is not ground.) We can now construct the resolvent in the usual way, by dropping the literal resolved upon and combining the remaining literals, which yields the required clause

```
likes(peter,maria):-follows(maria,C),teaches(peter,C)
```

Exercise 2.7. Write a clause expressing that Peter teaches all the first-year courses, and apply resolution to this clause and the above resolvent.

Consider the following two-clause program P':

```
likes(peter,S):-student_of(S,peter).
student_of(X,T):-follows(X,C),teaches(T,C).
```

which differs from the previous program P in that the constant `maria` in the second clause has been replaced by a variable. Since this generalises the applicability of this clause from Maria to any of Peter's students, it follows that any model for P' over a Herbrand universe including `maria` is also a model for P, and therefore $P' \models P$. In particular, this means that all the logical consequences of P' are also logical consequences of P. For instance, we can again derive the clause

```
likes(peter,maria):-follows(maria,C),teaches(peter,C)
```

from P' by means of the unifier {S→maria, X→maria, T→peter}.

Unifiers are not necessarily grounding substitutions: the substitution {X→S, T→peter} also unifies the two `student_of` literals, and the two clauses then resolve to

```
likes(peter,S):-follows(S,C),teaches(peter,C)
```

The first unifier replaces more variables by terms than strictly necessary, while the second contains only those substitutions that are needed to unify the two atoms in the input clauses. As a result, the first resolvent is a special case of the second resolvent, that can be obtained by means of the additional substitution {S→maria}. Therefore, the second resolvent is said to be *more general* than the first[5]. Likewise, the second unifier is called a more general unifier than the first.

As it were, more general resolvents summarise a lot of less general ones. It therefore makes sense to derive only those resolvents that are as general as possible, when applying resolution to clauses with variables. This means that we are only interested in a *most general unifier* (mgu) of two literals. Such an mgu, if it exists, is always unique, apart from an arbitrary renaming of variables (e.g. we could decide to keep the variable X, and replace S by X). If a unifier does not exist, we say that the two atoms are not unifiable. For instance, the atoms `student_of(maria,peter)` and `student_of(S,maria)` are not unifiable.

As we have seen before, the actual proof method in clausal logic is proof by refutation. If we succeed in deriving the empty clause, then we have demonstrated that the set of clauses is inconsistent *under the substitutions that are needed for unification of literals*. For instance, consider the program

```
likes(peter,S):-student_of(S,peter).
student_of(S,T):-follows(S,C),teaches(T,C).
teaches(peter,ai_techniques).
follows(maria,ai_techniques).
```

---

[5]We will have more to say about the generality of clauses in Chapter 9.

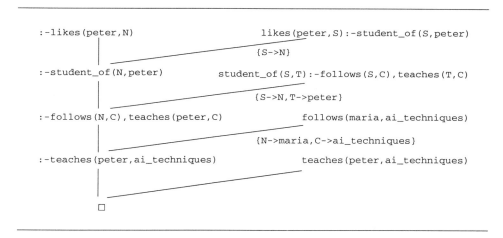

Figure 2.3. A refutation proof which finds someone whom Peter likes.

If we want to find out if there is anyone whom Peter likes, we add to the program the negation of this statement, i.e. 'Peter likes nobody' or `:-likes(peter,N)`; this clause is called a *query* or a *goal*. We then try to refute this query by finding an inconsistency by means of resolution. A refutation proof is given in fig. 2.3. In this figure, which is called a *proof tree*, two clauses on a row are input clauses for a resolution step, and they are connected by lines to their resolvent, which is then again an input clause for a resolution step, together with another program clause. The mgu's are also shown. Since the empty clause is derived, the query is indeed refuted, but only under the substitution {N→maria}, which constitutes the *answer* to the query.

In general, a query can have several answers. For instance, suppose that Peter does not only like his students, but also the people his students like (and the people those people like, and …):

```
likes(peter,S):-student_of(S,peter).
likes(peter,Y):-likes(peter,X),likes(X,Y).
likes(maria,paul).
student_of(S,T):-follows(S,C),teaches(T,C).
teaches(peter,ai_techniques).
follows(maria,ai_techniques).
```

The query `:-likes(peter,N)` will now have two answers.

Exercise 2.8. Draw the proof tree for the answer {N→paul}.

Meta-theory.   As with propositional resolution, relational resolution is sound (i.e. it always produces logical consequences of the input clauses), refutation complete (i.e. it always detects an inconsistency in a set of clauses), but not complete (i.e. it does not always generate every logical consequence of the input clauses). An important characteristic of relational clausal logic is that the Herbrand universe (the set of individuals we can reason about) is always finite. Consequently, models are finite as well, and there are a finite number of different models for any program. This means that, in principle, we could answer the question 'is *C* a logical consequence of *P*?' by enumerating all the models of *P*, and checking whether they are also models of *C*. The finiteness of the Herbrand universe will ensure that this procedure always terminates. This demonstrates that relational clausal logic is decidable, and therefore it is (in principle) possible to prevent resolution from looping if no more answers can be found. As we will see in the next section, this does not hold for full clausal logic.

2.3 Full clausal logic

Relational logic extends propositional logic by means of the logical variable, which enables us to talk about arbitrary un-named individuals. However, consider the following statement:

Everybody loves somebody.

The only way to express this statement in relational clausal logic, is by explicitly listing every pair of persons such that the first loves the second, e.g.

```
loves(peter,peter).
loves(anna,paul).
loves(paul,anna).
```

First of all, this is not a precise translation of the above statement into logic, because it is too explicit (e.g. the fact that Peter loves himself does not follow from the original statement). Secondly, this translation works only for *finite* domains, while the original statement also allows infinite domains. Many interesting domains are infinite, such as the set of natural numbers. Full clausal logic allows us to reason about infinite domains by introducing more complex terms besides constants and variables. The above statement translates into full clausal logic as

```
loves(X,person_loved_by(X))
```

The fact loves(peter,person_loved_by(peter)) is a logical consequence of this clause. Since we know that everybody loves somebody, there must exist someone whom Peter loves. We have given this person the *abstract name*

```
person_loved_by(peter)
```

without explicitly stating whom it is that Peter loves. As we will see, this way of composing complex names from simple names also gives us the possibility to reflect the structure of the domain in our logical formulas.

Exercise 2.9. Translate to clausal logic:
(*a*)   every mouse has a tail;
(*b*)   somebody loves everybody;
(*c*)   every two numbers have a maximum.

Syntax.   A *term* is either simple or complex. Constants and variables are *simple terms*. A *complex term* is a functor (which follows the same notational conventions as constants and predicates) followed by a number of terms, enclosed in brackets and separated by commas, e.g. `eldest_child_of(anna,paul)`. The terms between brackets are called the *arguments* of the functor, and the number of arguments is the functor's *arity*. Again, a *ground* term is a term without variables. All the other definitions (atom, clause, literal, program) are the same as for relational clausal logic.

Semantics.   Although there is no **syntactic** difference in full clausal logic between terms and atoms, their **meaning** and use is totally different, a fact which should be adequately reflected in the semantics. A term always denotes an individual from the domain, while an atom denotes a proposition about individuals, which can get a truth value. Consequently, we must change the definition of the Herbrand universe in order to accomodate for complex terms: given a program *P*, the *Herbrand universe* is the set of ground terms that can be constructed from the constants and functors in *P* (if *P* contains no constants, choose an arbitrary one). For instance, let *P* be the program

```
plus(0,X,X).
plus(s(X),Y,s(Z)):-plus(X,Y,Z).
```

then the Herbrand universe of *P* is {0, s(0), s(s(0)), s(s(s(0))), ...}. Thus, as soon as a program contains a functor, the Herbrand universe (the set of individuals we can reason about) is an infinite set.

Exercise 2.10. Determine the Herbrand universe of the following program:
```
                    length([],0).
                    length([X|Y],s(L)):-length(Y,L).
```
(Hint: recall that `[]` is a constant, and that `[X|Y]` is an alternative notation for the complex term `.(X,Y)` with binary functor '`.`'!)

The *Herbrand base* of *P* remains the set of ground atoms that can be constructed using the predicates in *P* and the ground terms in the Herbrand universe. For the above program, the Herbrand base is

```
{plus(0,0,0),plus(s(0),0,0),...,
 plus(0,s(0),0),plus(s(0),s(0),0),...,
 ...,
 plus(s(0),s(s(0)),s(s(s(0)))),...}
```

Unification vs. evaluation

Functors should not be confused with mathematical functions. Although both can be viewed as mappings from objects to objects, *an expression containing a functor is not evaluated* to determine the value of the mapping, as in mathematics. Rather, the outcome of the mapping is a name, which is determined by *unification*. For instance, given the complex term `person_loved_by(X)`, if we want to know the name of the object to which Peter is mapped, we unify X with `peter` to get `person_loved_by(peter)`; this ground term is not evaluated any further.

This approach has the disadvantage that we introduce different names for individuals that might turn out to be identical, e.g. `person_loved_by(peter)` might be the same as `peter`. Consequently, reasoning about equality (of different names for the same object) is a problem in clausal logic. Several possible solutions exist, but they fall outside the scope of this book.

As before, a *Herbrand interpretation* is a subset of the Herbrand base, whose elements are assigned the truth value **true**. For instance,

```
{plus(0,0,0),plus(s(0),0,s(0)),plus(0,s(0),s(0))}
```

is an interpretation of the above program.

Is this interpretation also a model of the program? As in the propositional case, we define an interpretation to be a model of a program if it is a model of every ground instance of every clause in the program. But since the Herbrand universe is infinite, there are an infinite number of grounding substitutions, hence we must generate the ground clauses in a systematic way, e.g.

```
plus(0,0,0)
plus(s(0),0,s(0)):-plus(0,0,0)
plus(s(s(0)),0,s(s(0))):-plus(s(0),0,s(0))
plus(s(s(s(0))),0,s(s(s(0)))):-plus(s(s(0)),0,s(s(0)))
...
plus(0,s(0),s(0))
plus(s(0),s(0),s(s(0))):-plus(0,s(0),s(0))
plus(s(s(0)),s(0),s(s(s(0)))):-plus(s(0),s(0),s(s(0)))
...
plus(0,s(s(0)),s(s(0)))
plus(s(0),s(s(0)),s(s(s(0)))):-plus(0,s(s(0)),s(s(0)))
plus(s(s(0)),s(s(0)),s(s(s(s(0))))):-
                          plus(s(0),s(s(0)),s(s(s(0))))
...
```

Now we can reason as follows: according to the first ground clause, `plus(0,0,0)` must be in any model; but then the second ground clause requires that `plus(s(0),0,s(0))` must be in any model, the third ground clause requires `plus(s(s(0)),0,s(s(0)))` to be in any model, and so on. Likewise, the second group of ground clauses demands that

```
plus(0,s(0),s(0))
plus(s(0),s(0),s(s(0)))
plus(s(s(0)),s(0),s(s(s(0))))
...
```

are in the model; the third group of ground clauses requires that

```
plus(0,s(s(0)),s(s(0)))
plus(s(0),s(s(0)),s(s(s(0))))
plus(s(s(0)),s(s(0)),s(s(s(s(0)))))
...
```

are in the model, and so forth.

In other words, *every model of this program is necessarily infinite*. Moreover, as you should have guessed by now, it contains every ground atom such that the number of s's in the third argument equals the number of s's in the first argument **plus** the number of s's in the second argument. The way we generated this infinite model is particularly interesting, because it is essentially what was called the naive proof method in the relational case: generate all possible ground instances of program clauses by applying every possible grounding substitution, and then apply (propositional) resolution as long as you can. While, in the case of relational clausal logic, there inevitably comes a point where applying resolution will not give any new results (i.e. you reach a *fixpoint*), in the case of full clausal logic with infinite Herbrand universe you can go on applying resolution forever. On the other hand, as we saw above, we get a clear idea of what the infinite model[6] we're constructing looks like, which means that it is still a fixpoint in some sense. There are mathematical techniques to deal with such infinitary fixpoints, but we will not dive into this subject here.

Although the introduction of only a single functor already results in an infinite Herbrand universe, models are not necessarily infinite. Consider the following program:

```
reachable(oxford,charing_cross,piccadilly).
reachable(X,Y,route(Z,R)):-
    connected(X,Z,L),
    reachable(Z,Y,R).
connected(bond_street,oxford,central).
```

with intended meaning 'Charing Cross is reachable from Oxford Circus via Piccadilly Circus', '**if** X is connected to Z by line L **and** Y is reachable from Z via R **then** Y is reachable from X via a route consisting of Z and R' and 'Bond Street is connected to Oxford Circus by the Central line'. The minimal model of this program is the finite set

```
{connected(bond_street,oxford,central),
reachable(oxford,charing_cross,piccadilly),
reachable(bond_street,charing_cross,route(oxford,piccadilly))}
```

A Prolog program for constructing models of a given set of clauses (or submodels if the models are infinite) can be found in section 5.4.

---

[6]For definite clauses this method of bottom-up model construction always yields the unique minimal model of the program.

Proof theory.   Resolution for full clausal logic is very similar to resolution for relational clausal logic: we only have to modify the unification algorithm in order to deal with complex terms. For instance, consider the atoms

```
plus(s(0),X,s(X))
```

and

```
plus(s(Y),s(0),s(s(Y)))
```

Their mgu is {Y→0, X→s(0)}, yielding the atom

```
plus(s(0),s(0),s(s(0)))
```

In order to find this mgu, we first of all have to make sure that the two atoms do not have any variables in common; if needed some of the variables should be renamed. Then, after making sure that both atoms contain the same predicate (with the same arity), we scan the atoms from left to right, searching for the first **subterms** at which the two atoms differ. In our example, these are 0 and Y. If one of these subterms is not a variable, then the two atoms are not unifiable; otherwise, substitute the other term for all occurrences of the variable in both atoms, and remember this partial substitution (in the above example: {Y→0}), because it is going to be part of the unifier we are constructing. Then, proceed with the next subterms at which the two atoms differ. Unification is finished when no such subterms can be found (the two atoms are made equal).

Although the two atoms initially have no variables in common, this may change during the unification process. Therefore, it is important that, before a variable is replaced by a term, we check whether the variable already occurs in that term; this is called the *occur check*. If the variable does not occur in the term by which it is to be replaced, everything is in order and we can proceed; if it does, the unification should fail, because it would lead to circular substitutions and infinite terms. To illustrate this, consider again the clause

```
loves(X,person_loved_by(X))
```

We want to know whether this implies that someone loves herself; thus, we add the query `:-loves(Y,Y)` to this clause and try to apply resolution. To this end, we must unify the two atoms. The first subterms at which they differ are the first arguments, so we apply the partial substitution Y→X to the two atoms, resulting in

```
loves(X,person_loved_by(X))
```

and

```
loves(X,X)
```

The next subterms at which these atoms differ are their second arguments, one of which is a variable. Suppose that we ignore the fact that this variable, X, already occurs in the other term; we construct the substitution X→person_loved_by(X). Now, we have reached the end of the two atoms, so unification has succeeded, we have derived the empty clause, and the answer to the query is

```
X→person_loved_by(person_loved_by(person_loved_by(...)))
```

which is an infinite term.

Now we have two problems. The first is that we did not define any semantics for infinite terms, because there are no infinite terms in the Herbrand base. But even worse, the fact that there exists someone who loves herself is not a logical consequence of the above clause! That is, this clause has models in which nobody loves herself. So, *unification without occur check would make resolution unsound.*

Exercise 2.11. If possible, unify the following pairs of terms:
(*a*)   `plus(X,Y,s(Y))` and `plus(s(V),W,s(s(V)))`;
(*b*)   `length([X|Y],s(0))` and `length([V],V)`;
(*c*)   `larger(s(s(X)),X)` and `larger(V,s(V))`.

The disadvantage of the occur check is that it can be computationally very costly. Suppose that you need to unify X with a list of thousand elements, then the complete list has to be searched in order to check whether X occurs somewhere in it. Moreover, cases in which the occur check is needed often look somewhat exotic. Since the developers of Prolog were also taking the efficiency of the Prolog interpreter into consideration, they decided to omit the occur check from Prolog's unification algorithm. On the whole, this makes Prolog unsound; but this unsoundness only occurs in very specific cases, and it is the duty of the programmer to avoid such cases. In case you really need sound unification, most available Prolog implementations provide it as a library routine, but you must build your own Prolog interpreter in order to incorporate it. In Chapter 3, we will see that this is in fact amazingly simple: it can even be done in Prolog!

Meta-theory. Most meta-theoretical results concerning full clausal logic have already been mentioned. Full clausal resolution is sound (as long as unification is performed with the occur check), refutation complete but not complete. Moreover, due to the possibility of infinite interpretations full clausal logic is only semi-decidable: that is, if *A* is a logical consequence of *B*, then there is an algorithm that will check this in finite time; however, if *A* is not a logical consequence of *B*, then there is no algorithm which is guaranteed to check this in finite time for arbitrary *A* and *B*. Consequently, there is no general way to prevent Prolog from looping if no (further) answers to a query can be found.

2.4 Definite clause logic

In the foregoing three sections, we introduced and discussed three variants of clausal logic, in order of increasing expressiveness. In this section, we will show how an additional restriction on each of these variants will significantly improve the efficiency of a computational reasoning system for clausal logic. This is the restriction to definite clauses, on which Prolog is based. On the other hand, this restriction also means that definite clause logic is less expressive than full clausal logic, the main difference being that clausal logic can handle negative information. If we allow negated literals in the body of a definite clause then we obtain a so-called general clause, which is probably the closest we can get to full clausal logic without having to sacrifice efficiency.

Consider the following program:

```
married(X);bachelor(X):-man(X),adult(X).
man(peter).
adult(peter).
:-married(maria).
:-bachelor(maria).
man(paul).
:-bachelor(paul).
```

There are many clauses that are logical consequences of this program. In particular, the following three clauses can be derived by resolution:

```
married(peter);bachelor(peter)
:-man(maria),adult(maria)
married(paul):-adult(paul)
```

Exercise 2.12. Draw the proof tree for each of these derivations.

In each of these derivations, the first clause in the program is used in a different way. In the first one, only literals in the body are resolved away; one could say that the clause is used from right to left. In the second derivation the clause is used from left to right, and in the third one literals from both the head and the body are resolved away. The way in which a clause is used in a resolution proof cannot be fixed in advance, because it depends on the thing we want to prove (the query in refutation proofs).

On the other hand, this indeterminacy substantially increases the time it takes to find a refutation. Let us decide for the moment to use clauses only in one direction, say from right to left. That is, we can only resolve the negative literals away in a clause, as in the first derivation above, but not the positive literals. But now we have a problem: how are we going to decide whether Peter is married or a bachelor? We are stuck with a clause with two positive literals, representing a disjunctive or *indefinite* conclusion.

This problem can in turn be solved by requiring that clauses have exactly one positive literal, which leads us into *definite clause logic*. Consequently, a definite clause

$$A:-B_1,\ldots,B_n$$

will always be used in the following way: A is proved by proving each of $B_1,\ldots,B_n$. This is called the *procedural interpretation* of definite clauses, and its simplicity makes the search for a refutation much more efficient than in the indefinite case. Moreover, it allows for an implementation which limits the amount of memory needed, as will be explained in more detail in Chapter 5.

But how do we express in definite clause logic that adult men are bachelors or married? Even if we read the corresponding indefinite clause from right to left only, it basically has two different procedural interpretations:

(*i*)   to prove that someone is married, prove that he is a man and an adult, and prove that he is not a bachelor;

(*ii*)   to prove that someone is a bachelor, prove that he is a man and an adult, and prove that he is not married.

We should first choose one of these procedural interpretations, and then convert it into a 'pseudo-definite' clause. In case (*i*), this would be

```
married(X):-man(X),adult(X),not bachelor(X)
```

and case (*ii*) becomes

```
bachelor(X):-man(X),adult(X),not married(X)
```

These clauses do not conform to the syntax of definite clause logic, because of the negation symbol `not`. We will call them *general clauses*.

If we want to extend definite clause logic to cover general clauses, we should extend resolution in order to deal with negated literals in the body of a clause. In addition, we should extend the semantics. This topic will be addressed in section 8.2. Without going into too much detail here, we will demonstrate that preferring a certain procedural interpretation corresponds to preferring a certain minimal model. Reconsider the original indefinite clause

```
married(X);bachelor(X):-man(X),adult(X)
```

Supposing that `john` is the only individual in the Herbrand universe, and that `man(john)` and `adult(john)` are both true, then the models of this clause are

```
{man(john),adult(john),married(john)}
{man(john),adult(john),bachelor(john)}
{man(john),adult(john),married(john),bachelor(john)}
```

Note that the first **two** models are minimal, as is characteristic for indefinite clauses. If we want to make the clause definite, we should single out one of these two minimal models as the *intended* model. If we choose the first model, in which John is married but not a bachelor, we are actually preferring the general clause

```
married(X):-man(X),adult(X),not bachelor(X)
```

Likewise, the second model corresponds to the general clause

```
bachelor(X):-man(X),adult(X),not married(X)
```

Exercise 2.13. Write a clause for the statement 'somebody is innocent unless proven guilty', and give its intended model (supposing that `john` is the only individual in the Herbrand universe).

An alternative approach to general clauses is to treat `not` as a special Prolog predicate, as will be discussed in the next chapter. This has the advantage that we need not extend the proof theory and semantics to incorporate general clauses. However, a disadvantage is that in this way `not` can only be understood procedurally.

2.5   The relation between clausal logic and Predicate Logic

Clausal logic is a formalism especially suited for automated reasoning. However, the form of logic usually presented in courses on Symbolic Logic is (first-order) Predicate Logic. Predicate logic is more expressive in the sense that statements expressed in Predicate Logic often result in shorter formulas than would result if they were expressed in clausal logic. This is due to the larger vocabulary and less restrictive syntax of Predicate Logic, which includes quantifiers ('for all' ($\forall$) and 'there exists' ($\exists$)), and various logical connectives (conjunction ($\land$), disjunction ($\lor$), negation ($\lnot$), implication ($\rightarrow$), and equivalence ($\leftrightarrow$)) which may occur anywhere within a formula.

Being syntactically quite different, clausal logic and Predicate Logic are semantically equivalent in the following sense: every set of clauses is, after minor modifications, a formula in Predicate Logic, and conversely, every formula in Predicate Logic can be rewritten to an 'almost' equivalent set of clauses. Why then bother about Predicate Logic at all in this book? The main reason is that in Chapter 8, we will discuss an alternative semantics of logic programs, defined in terms of Predicate Logic. In this section, we will illustrate the semantic equivalence of clausal logic and Predicate Logic. We will assume a basic knowledge of the syntax and semantics of Predicate Logic.

We start with the propositional case. Any clause like

```
married;bachelor:-man,adult
```

can be rewritten by reversing head and body and replacing the ': -' sign by an implication '$\rightarrow$', replacing ', ' by a conjunction '$\land$', and replacing '; ' by a disjunction '$\lor$', which yields

```
man ∧ adult → married ∨ bachelor
```

By using the logical laws $A \rightarrow B \equiv \lnot A \lor B$ and $\lnot (C \land D) \equiv \lnot C \lor \lnot D$, this can be rewritten into the logically equivalent formula

```
¬man ∨ ¬adult ∨ married ∨ bachelor
```

which, by the way, clearly demonstrates the origin of the terms *negative* literal and *positive* literal!

A set of clauses can be rewritten by rewriting each clause separately, and combining the results into a single conjunction, e.g.

```
married;bachelor:-man,adult.
has_wife:-man,married.
```

becomes

```
(¬man ∨ ¬adult ∨ married ∨ bachelor) ∧
(¬man ∨ ¬married ∨ has_wife)
```

Formulas like these, i.e. conjunctions of disjunctions of atoms and negated atoms, are said to be in *conjunctive normal form* (CNF).

The term 'normal form' here indicates that *every formula of Predicate Logic can be rewritten into a unique equivalent formula in conjunctive normal form*, and therefore to a unique equivalent set of clauses. For instance, the formula

```
(married ∨ ¬child) → (adult ∧ (man ∨ woman))
```

The order of logics

A logic with propositions (statements that can be either true or false) as basic building blocks is called a propositional logic; a logic built on predicates is called a Predicate Logic. Since propositions can be viewed as nullary predicates (i.e. predicates without arguments), any propositional logic is also a Predicate Logic.

A logic may or may not have variables for its basic building blocks. If it does not include such variables, both the logic and its building blocks are called *first-order*; this is the normal case. Thus, in first-order Predicate Logic, there are no predicate variables, but only first-order predicates.

Otherwise, an nth order logic has variables (and thus quantifiers) for its $(n-1)$th order building blocks. For instance, the statement

$$\forall X \forall Y: \texttt{equal(X,Y)} \leftrightarrow (\forall P: P(X) \leftrightarrow P(Y))$$

defining two individuals to be equal if they have the same properties, is a statement from second-order Predicate Logic, because P is a variable ranging over first-order predicates.

Another example of a statement from second-order Predicate Logic is

$$\forall P: \texttt{transitive(P)} \leftrightarrow (\forall X \forall Y \forall Z: P(X,Y) \land P(Y,Z) \rightarrow P(X,Z))$$

This statement defines the transitivity of binary relations. Since `transitive` has a second-order variable as argument, it is called a *second-order predicate*.

---

can be rewritten into CNF as (replace $A \rightarrow B$ by $\neg A \lor B$, push negations inside by means of De Morgan's laws: $\neg(C \land D) \equiv \neg C \lor \neg D$ and $\neg(C \lor D) \equiv \neg C \land \neg D$, and distribute $\land$ over $\lor$ by means of $(A \land B) \lor C \equiv (A \lor C) \land (B \lor C)$):

```
(¬married ∨ adult) ∧ (¬married ∨ man ∨ woman) ∧
(child ∨ adult) ∧ (child ∨ man ∨ woman)
```

and hence into clausal form as

```
adult:-married.
man;woman:-married.
child;adult.
child;man;woman.
```

Using a normal form has the advantage that the language contains no redundancy: formulas are only equivalent if they are **identical** (up to the order of the subformulas). A slight disadvantage is that normal forms are often longer and less understandable (the same objection can be made against resolution proofs).

For rewriting clauses from full clausal logic to Predicate Logic, we use the same rewrite rules as for propositional clauses. Additionally, we have to add universal quantifiers for every variable in the clause. For example, the clause

```
reachable(X,Y,route(Z,R)):-
    connected(X,Z,L),
    reachable(Z,Y,R).
```

becomes

$$\forall X \forall Y \forall Z \forall R \forall L: \texttt{¬connected(X,Z,L)} \lor \texttt{¬reachable(Z,Y,R)} \lor$$
$$\texttt{reachable(X,Y,route(Z,R))}$$

The reverse process of rewriting a formula of Predicate Logic into an equivalent set of clauses is somewhat complicated if existential quantifiers are involved (the exact procedure is given as a Prolog program in Appendix B.1). An existential quantifier allows us to reason about individuals without naming them. For example, the statement 'everybody loves somebody' is represented by the Predicate Logic formula

$$\forall X \exists Y: \texttt{loves(X,Y)}$$

Recall that we translated this same statement into clausal logic as

```
loves(X,person_loved_by(X))
```

These two formulas are not logically equivalent! That is, the Predicate Logic formula has models like {`loves(paul,anna)`} which are **not** models of the clause. The reason for this is, that in clausal logic we are forced to introduce abstract names, while in Predicate Logic we are not (we use existential quantification instead). On the other hand, every model of the Predicate Logic formula, if not a model of the clause, can always be converted to a model of the clause, like {`loves(paul,person_loved_by(paul))`}. Thus, we have that the formula has a model if and only if the clause has a model (but not necessarily the same model).

So, existential quantifiers are replaced by functors. The arguments of the functor are given by the universal quantifiers in whose scope the existential quantifier occurs. In the above example, ∃Y occurs within the scope of ∀X, so we replace Y everywhere in the formula by `person_loved_by(X)`, where `person_loved_by` should be a **new** functor, not occurring anywhere else in the clause (or in any other clause). This new functor is called a *Skolem functor*, and the whole process is called *Skolemisation*. Note that, if the existential quantifier does not occur inside the scope of a universal quantifier, the Skolem functor does not get any arguments, i.e. it becomes a *Skolem constant*. For example, the formula

$$\exists X \forall Y: \texttt{loves(X,Y)}$$

('somebody loves everybody') is translated to the clause

```
loves(someone_who_loves_everybody,X)
```

Finally, we illustrate the whole process of converting from Predicate Logic to clausal logic by means of an example. Consider the sentence 'Everyone has a mother, but not every woman has a child'. In Predicate Logic, this can be represented as

$$\forall Y \exists X: \texttt{mother\_of(X,Y)} \ \land \ \neg \forall Z \exists W: \texttt{woman(Z)} \rightarrow \texttt{mother\_of(Z,W)}$$

First, we push the negation inside by means of the equivalences $\neg \forall X: F \equiv \exists X: \neg F$ and $\neg \exists Y: G \equiv \forall Y: \neg G$, and the previously given propositional equivalences, giving

∀Y∃X: mother_of(X,Y) ∧ ∃Z∀W: woman(Z) ∧ ¬mother_of(Z,W)

The existential quantifiers are Skolemised: X is replaced by `mother(Y)`, because it is in the scope of the universal quantifier ∀Y. Z, however, is not in the scope of a universal quantifier; therefore it is replaced by a Skolem constant `childless_woman`. The universal quantifiers can now be dropped:

    mother_of(mother(Y),Y) ∧ woman(childless_woman) ∧
    ¬mother_of(childless_woman,W)

This formula is already in CNF, so we obtain the following set of clauses:

    mother_of(mother(Y),Y).
    woman(childless_woman).
    :-mother_of(childless_woman,W).

Exercise 2.14. Translate to clausal logic:
(a) ∀X∃Y: mouse(X)→tail_of(Y,X);
(b) ∀X∃Y: loves(X,Y)∧(∀Z: loves(Y,Z));
(c) ∀X∀Y∃Z: number(X)∧number(Y)→maximum(X,Y,Z).

Further reading

Many (but not all) aspects of Artificial Intelligence are amenable to logical analysis. An early advocate of this approach is Kowalski (1979). Overviews of different types of logics used in Artificial Intelligence can be found in (Turner, 1984; Genesereth & Nilsson, 1987; Ramsay, 1988). Bläsius and Bürckert (1989) discuss more technical aspects of automated theorem proving.

The main source for theoretical results in Logic Programming is (Lloyd, 1987). Hogger (1990) gives a more accessible introduction to this theory. (Mendelson, 1987) is an excellent introduction to Predicate Logic.

K.H. BLÄSIUS & H.J. BÜRCKERT (eds) (1989), *Deduction Systems in Artificial Intelligence*, Ellis Horwood.

M.R. GENESERETH & N.J. NILSSON (1987), *Logical Foundations of Artificial Intelligence*, Morgan Kaufmann.

C.J. HOGGER (1990), *Essentials of Logic Programming*, Oxford University Press.

R.A. KOWALSKI (1979), *Logic for Problem Solving*, North-Holland.

J.W. LLOYD (1987), *Foundations of Logic Programming*, Springer-Verlag, second edition.

E. MENDELSON (1987), *Introduction to Mathematical Logic*, Wadsworth & Brooks/Cole, third edition.

R. TURNER (1984), *Logics for Artificial Intelligence*, Ellis Horwood.

A. RAMSAY (1988), *Formal Methods in Artificial Intelligence*, Cambridge University Press.

3
Logic Programming and Prolog

In the previous chapters we have seen how logic can be used to represent knowledge about a particular domain, and to derive new knowledge by means of logical inference. A distinct feature of logical reasoning is the separation between model theory and proof theory: a set of logical formulas determines the set of its models, but also the set of formulas that can be derived by applying inference rules. Another way to say the same thing is: logical formulas have both a *declarative* meaning and a *procedural* meaning. For instance, declaratively the order of the atoms in the body of a clause is irrelevant, but procedurally it may determine the order in which different answers to a query are found.

Because of this procedural meaning of logical formulas, logic can be used as a programming language. If we want to solve a problem in a particular domain, we write down the required knowledge and apply the inference rules built into the logic programming language. Declaratively, this knowledge specifies **what** the problem is, rather than **how** it should be solved. The distinction between declarative and procedural aspects of problem solving is succinctly expressed by Kowalski's equation

algorithm = logic + control

Here, *logic* refers to declarative knowledge, and *control* refers to procedural knowledge. The equation expresses that both components are needed to solve a problem algorithmically.

In a purely declarative programming language, the programmer would have no means to express procedural knowledge, because logically equivalent programs would behave identical. However, Prolog is not a purely declarative language, and therefore the procedural meaning of Prolog programs cannot be ignored. For instance, the order of the literals in the body of a clause usually influences the efficiency of the program to a large degree. Similarly, the order of clauses in a program often determines whether a program will give an answer at all. Therefore, in this chapter we will take a closer look at Prolog's inference engine and its built-in features (some of which are non-declarative). Also, we will discuss some common programming techniques.

3.1 SLD-resolution

Prolog's proof procedure is based on resolution refutation in definite clause logic. Resolution refutation has been explained in the previous chapter. In order to turn it into an executable proof procedure, we have to specify how a literal to resolve upon is selected, and how the second input clause is found. Jointly, this is called a *resolution strategy*. Consider the following program:

```
student_of(X,T):-follows(X,C),teaches(T,C).
follows(paul,computer_science).
follows(paul,expert_systems).
follows(maria,ai_techniques).
teaches(adrian,expert_systems).
teaches(peter,ai_techniques).
teaches(peter,computer_science).
```

The query `?-student_of(S,peter)` has two possible answers: {S→paul} and {S→maria}. In order to find these answers, we first resolve the query with the first clause, yielding

```
:-follows(S,C),teaches(peter,C)
```

Now we have to decide whether we will search for a clause which resolves on `follows(S,C)`, or for a clause which resolves on `teaches(peter,C)`. This decision is governed by a *selection rule*. Prolog's selection rule is left to right, thus Prolog will search for a clause with a positive literal unifying with `follows(S,C)`. There are three of these, so now we must decide which one to try first. Prolog searches the clauses in the program top-down, so Prolog finds the answer {S→paul} first. Note that the second choice leads to a dead end: the resolvent is

```
:-teaches(peter,expert_systems)
```

which doesn't resolve with any clause in the program.

This process is called *SLD-resolution*: **S** for selection rule, **L** for *linear* resolution (which refers to the shape of the proof trees obtained), and **D** for *definite* clauses. Graphically, SLD-resolution can be depicted as in fig. 3.1. This *SLD-tree* should not be confused with a proof tree: first, only the resolvents are shown (no input clauses or unifiers), and second, it contains every possible resolution step. Thus, every leaf of an SLD-tree which contains the empty clause □ corresponds to a refutation and hence to a proof tree; such a leaf is also called a *success branch*. An underlined leaf which does not contain □ represents a *failure branch*.

Exercise 3.1. Draw the proof trees for the two success branches in fig. 3.1.

As remarked already, Prolog searches the clauses in the program top-down, which is the same as traversing the SLD-tree from left to right. This not only determines the order in which answers (i.e. success branches) are found: it also determines whether any answers are

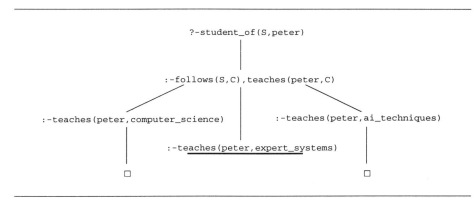

Figure 3.1. An SLD-tree.

found at all, because an SLD-tree may contain infinite branches, if some predicates in the program are recursive. As an example, consider the following program:

```
brother_of(X,Y):-brother_of(Y,X).
brother_of(paul,peter).
```

An SLD-tree for the query ?-brother_of(peter,B) is depicted in fig. 3.2. If we descend this tree taking the left branch at every node, we will never reach a leaf. On the other hand, if we take the right branch at every node, we almost immediately reach a success

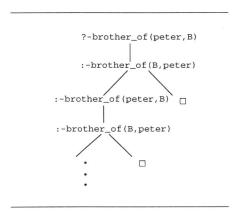

Figure 3.2. An SLD-tree with infinite branches.

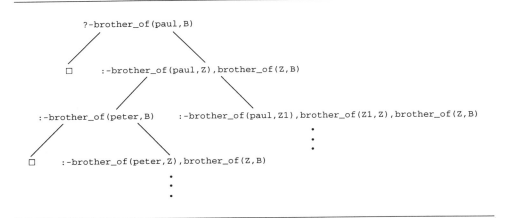

Figure 3.3. An SLD-tree with infinite branches and expanding resolvents.

branch. Taking right branches instead of left branches in an SLD-tree corresponds to searching the clauses from bottom to top. The same effect would be obtained by reversing the order of the clauses in the program, and the SLD-tree clearly shows that this is enough to prevent Prolog from looping on this query. This is a rule of thumb that applies to most cases: *put non-recursive clauses before recursive ones.*

However, note that, even after this modification, the program still has some problems. For one thing, the query `?-brother_of(peter,B)` will be answered an infinite number of times, because there are infinitely many refutations of it. But, even worse, consider a query that does **not** have an answer, like `?-brother(peter,maria)`. No matter the order in which the SLD-tree is descended, Prolog will never discover that the query has in fact no answer, *simply because the SLD-tree is infinite.* So, one should be careful with programs like the above, which define a predicate to be *symmetric*.

Another property of predicates which can cause similar problems is *transitivity*. Consider the following program:

```
brother_of(paul,peter).
brother_of(peter,adrian).
brother_of(X,Y):-brother_of(X,Z),brother_of(Z,Y).
```

The third clause ensures that `brother_of(paul,adrian)` is a logical consequence of the program. The SLD-tree for the query `?-brother_of(paul,B)` is depicted in fig. 3.3. Not only is this SLD-tree infinite, but the resolvents get longer and longer on deeper levels in the tree.

We have encountered two problems with SLD-resolution: (*i*) we might never reach a success branch in the SLD-tree, because we get 'trapped' into an infinite subtree, and (*ii*) any infinite SLD-tree causes the inference engine to loop if no (more) answers are to be found. The first problem means that Prolog is *incomplete*: some logical consequences of a program may never be found. Note carefully that this incompleteness is **not** caused by the inference rule of resolution, which is refutation complete. Indeed, for any program and any query, all the possible answers will be represented by success branches in the SLD-tree. The incompleteness of SLD-resolution is caused by the way the SLD-tree is searched.

There exists a solution to this problem: if we descend the tree layer by layer rather than branch-by-branch, we will find any leaf before we descend to the next level. However, this also means that we must keep track of **all** the resolvents on a level, instead of just a single one. Therefore, this *breadth-first* search strategy needs much more memory than the *depth-first* strategy used by Prolog. In fact, Prolog's incompleteness was a deliberate design choice, sacrificing completeness in order to obtain an efficient use of memory[7]. As we saw above, this problem can often be avoided by ordering the clauses in the program in a specific way (which means that we have to take the procedural meaning of the program into account).

As for the second problem, we already saw that this is due to the semi-decidability of full clausal logic, which means that there is no general solution to it.

Exercise 3.2. Draw the SLD-tree for the following program:
```
list([]).
list([H|T]):-list(T).
```
and the query ?-list(L).

3.2 Pruning the search by means of cut

As shown in the previous section, Prolog constantly searches the clauses in a program in order to reach a success branch in the SLD-tree for a query. If a failure branch is reached (i.e., a non-empty resolvent which cannot be reduced any further), Prolog has to 'unchoose' the last-chosen program clause, and try another one. This amounts to going up one level in the SLD-tree, and trying the next branch to the right. This process of reconsidering previous choices is called *backtracking*. Note that backtracking requires that all previous resolvents are remembered for which not all alternatives have been tried yet, together with a pointer to the most recent program clause that has been tried at that point. Because of Prolog's depth-first search strategy, we can easily record all previous resolvents in a *goal stack*: backtracking is then implemented by popping the upper resolvent from the stack, and searching for the next program clause to resolve with.

As an illustration, consider again the SLD-tree in fig. 3.1. The resolvent in the middle branch

```
:-teaches(peter,expert_systems)
```

cannot be reduced any further, and thus represents a failure branch. At that point, the stack contains (top-down) the previous resolvents

---

[7]The efficiency and completeness of search strategies will be discussed in Chapters 5 and 6.

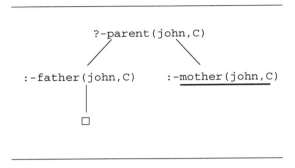

Figure 3.4. SLD-tree for the query
?-parent(john,C).

```
:-follows(S,C),teaches(peter,C)
?-student_of(S,peter)
```

The top one is popped from the stack; it has been most recently resolved with follows(paul,expert_systems), so we continue searching the program from that clause, finding follows(maria,ai_techniques) as the next alternative.

A node in the SLD-tree which is not a leaf is called a *choice point*, because the subtree rooted at that node may contain several success branches, each of which may be reached by a different choice for a program clause to resolve with. Now, suppose a subtree contains only one success branch, yielding an answer to our query. If we want to know whether there are any alternative answers, we can force Prolog to backtrack. However, since the rest of the subtree does not contain any success branches, we might as well skip it altogether, thus speeding up backtracking. But how do we tell Prolog that a subtree contains only one success branch? For this, Prolog provides a control device which is called *cut* (written !), because it cuts away (or prunes) part of the SLD-tree.

To illustrate the effect of cut, consider the following program.

```
parent(X,Y):-father(X,Y).
parent(X,Y):-mother(X,Y).
father(john,paul).
mother(mary,paul).
```

The SLD-tree for the query ?-parent(john,C) is given in fig. 3.4. The answer given by Prolog is {C→paul}. By asking whether there are any other answers, we force Prolog to backtrack to the most recent choice point for which there are any alternatives left, which is the root of the SLD-tree (i.e. the original query). Prolog tries the second clause for parent, but discovers that this leads to a failure branch.

Of course, **we** know that this backtracking step did not make sense: if John is a father of anyone, he can't be a mother. We can express this by adding a cut to the first parent clause:

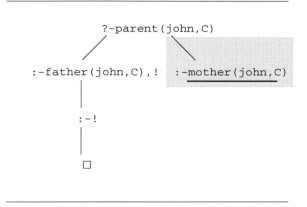

Figure 3.5. The effect of cut.

```
parent(X,Y):-father(X,Y),!.
parent(X,Y):-mother(X,Y).
```

The cut says: *once you've reached me, stick to all the variable substitutions you've found after you entered my clause*. That is: don't try to find any alternative solutions to the literals left of the cut, and also: don't try any alternative clauses for the one in which the cut is found. Given this modified program, the SLD-tree for the same query is shown in fig. 3.5. Since ! is true by definition, the resolvent : - ! reduces to the empty clause. The shaded part represents the part of the SLD-tree which is pruned as a result of the cut. That is: every alternative at choice points below and including ?-parent(john,C), which are on the stack when the cut is reached, are pruned. Note carefully that a cut does not prune **every** choice point. First of all, pruning does not occur above the choice point containing the head of the clause in which the cut is found. Secondly, choice points created by literals to the right of the cut, which are below the cut in the SLD-tree but are not yet on the stack when the cut is reached, are not pruned either (fig. 3.6).

A cut is harmless if it does not cut away subtrees containing success branches. If a cut prunes success branches, then some logical consequences of the program are not returned as answers, resulting in a procedural meaning different from the declarative meaning. Cuts of the first kind are called *green* cuts, while cuts of the second kind are called *red* cuts. A green cut merely stresses that the conjunction of literals to its left is *deterministic*: it does not give alternative solutions. In addition, it signifies that if those literals give a solution, the clauses below it will not result in any alternatives.

This seems to be true for the above program: John is the father of only one child, and no-one is both a father and a mother. However, note that we only analysed the situation with regard to a particular query. We can show that the cut is in fact red by asking the query ?-parent(P,paul) (fig. 3.7). The answer {P→mary} is pruned by the cut. That is, the

```
p(X,Y):-q(X,Y).
p(X,Y):-r(X,Y).

q(X,Y):-s(X),!,t(X).
```

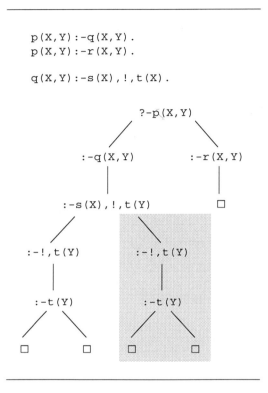

Figure 3.6. Cut prunes away alternative solutions for s, but not for t. Also, choice points above :-q(X,Y) are not pruned.

literal `father(X,Y)` left to the cut is only deterministic if X is *instantiated* (is substituted by a non-variable value).

Note that success branches are also pruned for the first query if John has several children:

```
parent(X,Y):-father(X,Y),!.
parent(X,Y):-mother(X,Y).
father(john,paul).
father(john,peter).
mother(mary,paul).
mother(mary,peter).
```

The SLD-tree for the query ?-parent(john,C) is given in fig. 3.8. Indeed, the second answer {C→peter} is pruned by the cut. This clearly shows that the effect of a cut is not

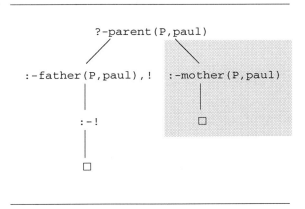

Figure 3.7. A success branch is pruned.

only determined by the clause in which it occurs but also by other clauses. Therefore, the effect of a cut is often hard to understand.

Programs with cuts are not only difficult to understand; this last example also shows that their procedural interpretation (the set of answers they produce to a query) may be different from their declarative interpretation (the set of its logical consequences). Logically, cut has no meaning: it always evaluates to **true**, and therefore it can always be added or removed from the body of a clause without affecting its declarative interpretation. Procedurally, cut may have many effects, as the preceding examples show. This

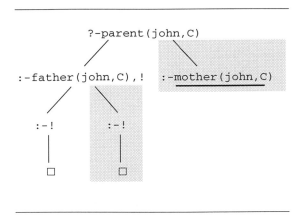

Figure 3.8. Another success branch is pruned.

incompatibility between declarative and procedural interpretation makes it a very problematic concept. Much research in Logic Programming aims at replacing it by higher-level constructs which have cleaner declarative meanings and which are easier to understand. The most important of these will be considered in the next two sections.

Exercise 3.3. Draw the SLD-tree for the query `?-likes(A,B)`, given the following program:

```
likes(peter,Y):-friendly(Y).
likes(T,S):-student_of(S,T).
student_of(maria,peter).
student_of(paul,peter).
friendly(maria).
```

Add a cut in order to prune away one of the answers {A→peter, B→maria}, and indicate the result in the SLD-tree. Can this be done without pruning away the third answer?

3.3 Negation as failure

The following program computes the maximum of two integers:

```
max(M,N,M):-M >= N.
max(M,N,N):-M =< N.
```

`>=` and `=<` are built-in predicates with meaning 'greater than or equal' and 'less than or equal', respectively[8]. Declaratively, the program captures the intended meaning, but procedurally there are two different ways to solve queries of the form `?-max(N,N,M)`. The reason for this is that the bodies of the two clauses are not exclusive: they both succeed if the first two values of the `max` predicate are equal. We could of course remove one of the equality symbols, but suppose that we use a cut instead:

```
max(M,N,M):-M >= N,!.
max(M,N,N).
```

With a red cut, this program can only be understood procedurally. The question is: does the procedural meaning correspond to the intended meaning? Perhaps surprisingly, the answer is no! For instance, the query

```
?-max(5,3,3).
```

succeeds: the cut is never reached, because the literal in the query does not unify with the head of the first clause. The second program is in fact a very bad program: the declarative and procedural meanings differ, and **neither** of them captures the intended meaning.

---

[8]Written this way to distinguish them from the arrows => and <=.

Exercise 3.4. Show that this cut is red, by drawing an SLD-tree in which a success branch is pruned.

The procedural meaning of the program would be correct if its use is restricted to queries with uninstantiated third argument. It illustrates a very common use of cut: to ensure that the bodies of the clauses are mutually exclusive. In general, if we have a program of the form

```
p:-q,!,r.
p:-s.
```

its meaning is something like

```
p:-q,r.
p:-not_q,s.
```

How should `not_q` be defined, in order to make the second program work? If `q` succeeds, `not_q` should fail. This is expressed by the following clause:

```
not_q:-q,fail
```

where `fail` is a built-in predicate, which is always **false**. If `q` fails, `not_q` should succeed. This can be realised by the program

```
not_q:-q,!,fail.
not_q.
```

The cut in the first clause is needed to prevent backtracking to the second clause when `q` succeeds.

This approach is not very practical, because it only works for a single proposition symbol, without variables. We would like to treat the literal to be negated as a parameter, as in

```
not(Goal):- /* execute Goal, */ !,fail.
not(Goal).
```

The problem now is to execute a goal which is passed to the predicate `not` as a term. Prolog provides two facilities for this. One is the built-in predicate `call`, which takes a goal as argument and succeeds if and only if execution of that goal succeeds. The second facility[9] is merely a shorthand for this: instead of writing `call(Goal)`, one may simply write `Goal`, as in

```
not(Goal):-Goal,!,fail.
not(Goal).
```

This is a slight abuse of the syntax rules, because a variable (a term) occurs in a position where only atoms are allowed. As long as the variable is instantiated to a goal before it is reached, this will, however, cause no problem (if it is not correctly instantiated, Prolog will generate an error-message). Predicates like `not` and `call` are called *meta-predicates*, that

---

[9]This is not allowed by every Prolog interpreter.

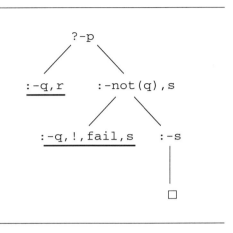

Figure 3.9. SLD-tree with `not`.

take formulas from the same logical language in which they are written as arguments. As we will see in later chapters, meta-predicates play an important role in this book.

We illustrate the operation of `not` by means of the following propositional program:

```
p:-q,r.
p:-not(q),s.
s.
```

and the query `?-p`. The SLD-tree is shown in fig. 3.9. The first clause for `p` leads to a failure branch, because `q` cannot be proved. The second clause for `p` is tried, and `not(q)` is

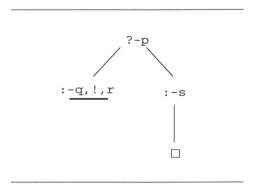

Figure 3.10. Equivalent SLD-tree with cut.

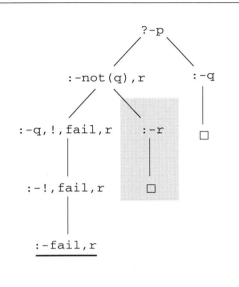

Figure 3.11. `:-not(q)` fails because `:-q` succeeds.

evaluated by trying to prove q. Again, this fails, which means that the second clause for not is tried, which succeeds. Thus, not(q) *is proved by failing to prove* q! Therefore, this kind of negation is called *negation as failure*.

Fig. 3.9 shows, that Prolog tries to prove q twice. Consequently, the program with not is slightly less efficient than the version with cut:

```
p:-q,!,r.
p:-s.
s.
```

which leads to the SLD-tree shown in fig. 3.10. Here, q is tried only once. However, in general we prefer the use of not, because it leads to programs of which the declarative meaning corresponds more closely to the procedural meaning.

In the following program, `:-not(q)` fails because `:-q` succeeds:

```
p:-not(q),r.
p:-q.
q.
r.
```

The SLD-tree for the query ?-p is shown in fig. 3.11. Since q succeeds, fail ensures that not(q) fails. The cut is needed to ensure that everything following the not is pruned, even if it contains a success branch.

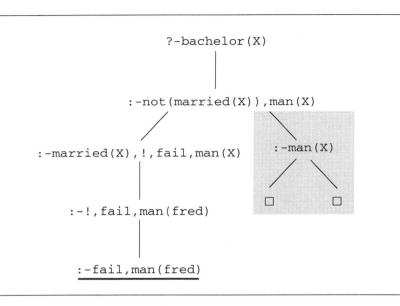

Figure 3.12. There are no bachelors?!

The implementation of `not` illustrated above can lead to problems if variables are involved. Take a look at the following program:

```
bachelor(X):-not(married(X)),man(X).
man(fred).
man(peter).
married(fred).
```

Exercise 3.5. Draw the SLD-trees for the queries ?-bachelor(fred) and ?-bachelor(peter).

Consider the query

```
?-bachelor(X)
```

for which the SLD-tree is depicted in fig. 3.12. According to negation as failure, Prolog tries to prove `not(married(X))` by trying `married(X)` first. Since this succeeds for X=fred, the cut is reached and the success branch to the right (representing the correct answer {X→peter}) is pruned. Thus, :-not(married(X)) fails because :-married(X) succeeds for one value of X. That is, not(married(X)) is interpreted

---

Negation as failure vs. logical negation

Negation as failure is not the same as logical negation: if we cannot prove q, we know that q is not a logical consequence of the program, but this does not mean that its negation :-q is a logical consequence of the program. Adopting negation as failure is similar to saying 'I cannot prove that God exists, therefore I conclude God does not exist'. It is a kind of reasoning that is applicable in some contexts, but inadequate in others. Logical negation can only be expressed by indefinite clauses, as in the following program:

```
p:-q,r.
p;q:-s.
s.
```

Semantically speaking, if we don't have enough information to conclude that a formula *F* is true or false, the truth value of its logical negation will also be undecided, but not(*F*) will be true. This property of negation as failure can be very useful when dealing with exceptions to rules: if we don't know that something is an exception to a rule, we assume that it's not, so we only have to list the exceptions and not the normal cases. This approach will be extensively discussed in Chapter 8 on reasoning with incomplete information.

---

as 'it is false that somebody is married', or equivalently, 'nobody is married'. But this means that the clause

```
bachelor(X):-not(married(X)),man(X)
```

is interpreted as '*X* is a bachelor if nobody is married and *X* is a man', which is of course not as intended.

Thus, if G is instantiated to a goal containing variables at the time not(G) is called, the result may be not in accordance with negation as failure. *It is the programmer's responsibility to avoid this.* A simple remedy that will often work is to ensure the grounding of G by literals preceding not(G) in the body of the clause, i.e.

```
bachelor(X):-man(X),not(married(X))
```

Exercise 3.6. Show that the modified program produces the right answer, by drawing the SLD-tree for the query ?-bachelor(X).

Thus, we see that changing the order of the literals in the body of a clause does not only affect the order in which answers to a query are found, but it may also change the set of answers! Of course, this is very much against the spirit of declarative programming, because the declarative interpretation of a clause does not depend on the order of the literals. Therefore, some Prolog interpreters provide a mechanism which defers the evaluation of `not(G)` until G is ground. However, with standard Prolog it is the programmer's duty to ensure that `not` is never called with a non-ground argument.

Let's summarise the points made about negation in Prolog. It is often used to ensure that only one of several possible clauses is applicable. The same effect can be achieved by means of cut, but in general we prefer the use of `not`, although it is somewhat less efficient[10]. `not` is supplied by Prolog as a meta-predicate (i.e. a predicate which takes formulas from the same logical language in which it is written as arguments). It is only a partially correct implementation of negation as failure, since it does not operate correctly when its argument is a goal containing variables.

3.4 Other uses of cut

Consider the following propositional program:

```
p:-q,r,s,!,t.
p:-q,r,u.
q.
r.
u.
```

Exercise 3.7. Show that the query ?-p succeeds, but that q and r are tried twice.

This inefficiency can be avoided by putting s, ! at the beginning of the body of the first clause. However, in full clausal logic the goals preceding s might supply necessary variable bindings, which requires them to be called first. A possible solution would be the introduction of an extra proposition symbol:

```
p:-q,r,if_s_then_t_else_u.
if_s_then_t_else_u:-s,!,t.
if_s_then_t_else_u:-u.
```

Exercise 3.8. Show that q and r are now tried only once.

Just as we did with `not`, we can rewrite this new proposition symbol to a generally applicable meta-predicate:

```
if_then_else(S,T,U):-S,!,T.
if_then_else(S,T,U):-U.
```

---

[10]Since efficiency is an implementation issue, it is suggested that `not` is replaced by `!` only in the final stage of program development.

Note that we can nest applications of `if_then_else`, for instance

```
if_then_else_else(P,Q,R,S,T):-
    if_then_else(P,Q,if_then_else(R,S,T)).
```

Unfolding the definition of `if_then_else` yields

```
if_then_else_else(P,Q,R,S,T):-P,!,Q.
if_then_else_else(P,Q,R,S,T):-R,!,S.
if_then_else_else(P,Q,R,S,T):-T.
```

which clearly shows the meaning of the predicate: 'if *P* then *Q* else if *R* then *S* else *T* '. This resembles the CASE-statement of procedural languages, only the above notation is much more clumsy. Most Prolog interpreters provide the notation `P->Q;R` for if-then-else; the nested variant then becomes `P->Q;(R->S;T)`. The parentheses are not strictly necessary, but in general the outermost if-then-else literal should be enclosed in parentheses. A useful lay-out is shown by the following program:

```
diagnosis(Patient,Condition):-
    temperature(Patient,T),
    ( T=<37         ->   blood_pressure(Patient,Condition)
    ; T>37,T<38     ->   Condition=ok
    ; otherwise     ->   diagnose_fever(Patient,Condition)
    ).
```

`otherwise` is always assigned the truthvalue **true**, so the last rule applies if all the others fail.

not and if-then-else show that many uses of cut can be replaced by higher-level constructs, which are easier to understand. However, this is not true for every use of cut. For instance, consider the following program:

```
play(Board,Player):-
    lost(Board,Player).
play(Board,Player):-
    find_move(Board,Player,Move),
    make_move(Board,Move,NewBoard),
    next_player(Player,Next),
    play(NewBoard,Next).
```

This program plays a game by recursively looking for best moves. Suppose one game has been finished; that is, the query `?-play(Start,First)` (with appropriate instantiations of the variables) has succeeded. As usual, we can ask Prolog whether there are any alternative solutions. Prolog will start backtracking, looking for alternatives for the most recent move, then for the move before that one, and so on. That is, *Prolog has maintained all previous board situations, and every move made can be undone.* Although this seems a desirable feature, in reality it is totally unpractical because of the memory requirements: after a few moves you would get a stack overflow. In such cases, we tell Prolog not to reconsider any previous moves, by placing a cut just before the recursive call. This way, we pop the remaining choice points from the stack before entering the next recursion. In fact, this technique results in a use of memory similar to that of iterative loops in procedural languages.

Note that this only works if the recursive call is the last call in the body. In general, it is advisable to write your recursive predicates like `play` above: the non-recursive clause before the recursive one, and the recursive call at the end of the body. A recursive predicate written this way is said to be *tail recursive*. If in addition the literals before the recursive call are deterministic (yield only one solution), some Prolog interpreters may recognise this and change recursion into iteration. This process is called *tail recursion optimisation*. As illustrated above, you can force this optimisation by placing a cut before the recursive call.

3.5 Arithmetic expressions

In Logic Programming, recursion is the only looping control structure. Consequently, recursive datatypes such as lists can be expressed very naturally. Natural numbers also have a recursive nature: '0 is a natural number, and if *X* is a natural number, then the successor of *X* is also a natural number'. In Prolog, this is expressed as

```
nat(0).
nat(s(X)):-nat(X).
```

Addition of natural numbers is defined in terms of successors:

```
add(0,X,X).
add(s(X),Y,s(Z)):-add(X,Y,Z).
```

The following query asks for the sum of two and three:

```
?-add(s(s(0)),s(s(s(0))),Z).
Z = s(s(s(s(s(0)))))
```

We can also find an *X* such that the sum of *X* and *Y* is *Z* (i.e., subtract *Y* from *Z*):

```
?-add(X,s(s(s(0))),s(s(s(s(s(0)))))).
X = s(s(0))
```

We can even find all *X* and *Y* which add up to a given sum. Thus, this program is fully declarative. Similarly, multiplication is repeated addition:

```
mul(0,X,0).
mul(s(X),Y,Z):-mul(X,Y,Z1),add(Y,Z1,Z).
```

There are two problems with this approach to representing and manipulating natural numbers. First, naming natural numbers by means of the constant symbol 0 and the functor s is very clumsy, especially for large numbers. Of course, it would be possible to write a translator from decimal notation to successor notation, and back. However, the second problem is more fundamental: multiplication as repeated addition is extremely inefficient compared to the algorithm for multiplicating numbers in decimal notation. Therefore, Prolog has built-in arithmetic facilities, which we will discuss now.

Consider the arithmetic expression `5+7-3`. Prolog will view this expression as the term `+(5,-(7,3))`, with the functors + and – written as infix operators. We want to

---

Operators

In Prolog, functors and predicates are collectively called *operators*. An operator is
declared by the query `?-op(Priority,Type,Name)`, where `Priority` is a number
between 0 and 1200 (lower priority binds stronger), and `Type` is `fx` or `fy` for
prefix, `xfx`, `xfy` or `yfx` for infix, and `xf` or `yf` for postfix. The x and y determine
associativity: for instance, `xfx` means not associative (you cannot write `X op Y`
`op Z`, but must either write `(X op Y) op Z` or `X op (Y op Z)`), `xfy` means
right-associative (`X op Y op Z` means `op(X,op(Y,Z))`), and `yfx` means left-
associative (`X op Y op Z` means `op(op(X,Y),Z)`). Every special symbol of
Prolog, such as `:-` and `,` (conjunction in the body of a clause), is a predefined
operator. The interpretation of operators can be visualised by means of the
predicate `display`, which writes a term without operators. For instance,
the query `?-display((p:-q,r,s))` writes `:-(p,','(q,','(r,s)))`.
The extra parentheses are needed because `:-` binds very weakly.

---

evaluate this expression, i.e. we want a single numerical value which represents somehow
the same number as the expression. A program for doing this would look something like

```
is(V,E1+E2):-
    is(V1,E1),is(V2,E2),
    fast_add(V1,V2,V).
is(V,E1-E2):-
    is(V1,E1,),is(V2,E2),
    fast_sub(V1,V2,V).
is(E,E):-
    number(E).
```

Here, `fast_add` and `fast_sub` represent the fast, built-in procedures for addition and
subtraction, which are not directly available to the user. These procedures are **not** reversible:
its first two arguments must be instantiated. Therefore, the predicate `is` will include a test
for groundness of its second argument (the arithmetic expression), and will quit with an
error-message if this test fails.

The `is` predicate is a built-in feature of Prolog, and is declared as an infix operator. Its
behaviour is illustrated by the following queries:

```
?-X is 5+7-3
  X = 9

?-9 is 5+7-3
  Yes

?-9 is X+7-3
  Error in arithmetic expression

?-X is 5*3+7/2
  X = 18.5
```

The last example shows, that arithmetic expressions obey the usual precedence rules (which can be overruled using parentheses). Also, note that the `is` predicate can handle real numbers.

Prolog also provides a built-in predicate =, but this predicate behaves quite differently from `is`, since it performs *unification* rather than arithmetic evaluation (see also section 2.3). The following queries illustrate the operation of =:

```
?-X = 5+7-3
   X = 5+7-3

?-9 = 5+7-3
   No

?-9 = X+7-3
   No

?-X = Y+7-3
   X = _947+7-3
   Y = _947

?-X = f(X)
   X = f(f(f(f(f(f(f(f(f(f(f(f(f(f(f(f(f(f(f(f(f(f(f(f(f(f(f
   (f(f(f(f
   (f(f(f(f(f(f(f(f(f(f(f(f(f(f(f(f(f(f(f(f(f(f(f(f(f(f(f(f(
   f(f(f(f(
   Error: term being written is too deep
```

The first query just unifies X with the term 5+7-3 (i.e. +(5,-(7,3))), which of course succeeds. In the second and third query, we try to unify a constant with a complex term, which fails. The fourth query succeeds, leaving Y unbound (_947 is an internal variable name, generated by Prolog).

The fifth query illustrates that Prolog indeed omits the occur check (section 2.3) in unification: the query should have failed, but instead it succeeds, resulting in the circular binding {X→f(X)}. The problem only becomes apparent when Prolog tries to write the resulting term, which is infinite. Just to stress that Prolog quite happily constructs circular bindings, take a look at the following strange program:

```
strange:-X=f(X).
```

The query `?-strange` succeeds, and since there is no answer substitution, it is not apparent that there is a circular binding involved.

Exercise 3.9. Write a predicate `zero(A,B,C,X)` which, given the coefficients a, b and c, calculates both values of x for which $ax^2+bx+c=0$.

Finally, we mention that Prolog provides a number of other useful arithmetic predicates, including the inequality tests < and >, and their reflexive counterparts =< and >=. For these tests, both arguments should be instantiated to numbers.

3.6 Accumulators

The condition that the righthand-side of `is` should not contain variables sometimes determines the ordering of literals in the body of the clause. For instance, in the program below, which computes the length of a list, the `is` literal should be placed after the recursive `length` call, which instantiates M. This means that the resolvent first collects as many `is` literals as there are elements in the list, before doing the actual calculation. Each of these literals contains some 'local' variables that require some space in memory. The total memory requirements are thus proportional to the depth of the recursion.

```
length([],0).
length([H|T],N):-length(T,M),N is M+1.
```

Exercise 3.10. Draw the proof tree for the query ?-length([a,b,c],N).

Programs with tail recursion need less memory because they do all the work on one recursive level before proceeding to the next. There is a common trick to transform even the `length` predicate above into a tail recursive program, using an auxiliary argument called an *accumulator*.

```
length_acc(L,N):-length_acc(L,0,N).

length_acc([],N,N).
length_acc([H|T],N0,N):-N1 is N0+1,length_acc(T,N1,N).
```

`length_acc(L,N0,N)` is true if N is the number of elements in L plus N0. Initialising N0 to 0 results in N returning the length of L. Note that the actual counting is done by the second argument: only when the list is empty is the third argument unified with the second argument. The main point is that, since the accumulator is given an initial value of 0, it is always instantiated, such that the `is` literal can be placed before the recursive call.

Exercise 3.11. Draw the proof tree for the query ?-length_acc([a,b,c],N).

Accumulators can be used in very many programs. Suppose we want to reverse the order of elements in a list. We could do this by recursively reversing the tail of the list, and putting the head at the end of the result:

```
naive_reverse([],[]).
naive_reverse([H|T],R):-
    naive_reverse(T,R1),
    append(R1,[H],R).

append([],Y,Y).
append([H|T],Y,[H|Z]):-
    append(T,Y,Z).
```

This predicate is called 'naive' because a lot of unnecessary work is done by the `append` calls in the recursive clause.

Exercise 3.12. Draw the proof tree for the query `?-naive_reverse([a,b,c],R)`.

By using an accumulator, we can get rid of the `append` predicate, as follows:

```
reverse(X,Y):-
    reverse(X,[],Y).

reverse([],Y,Y).
reverse([H|T],Y0,Y):-
    reverse(T,[H|Y0],Y).
```

`reverse(X,Y0,Y)` is true if Y consists of the reversal of X followed by Y0. Initialising Y0 to `[]` results in Y returning the reversal of X.

The use of an accumulator in this more efficient program for reversing a list is closely related to another programming trick for increasing the efficiency of list handling. The idea is not to represent a list by a single term, but instead by a pair of terms L1-L2, such that the list actually represented is the **difference** between L1 and L2. The term L1-L2 is appropriately called a *difference list*; L1 is called the *plus list*, and L2 is called the *minus list*. For instance, the difference list `[a,b,c,d]-[d]` represents the simple list `[a,b,c]`, as does the difference list `[a,b,c,1234,5678]-[1234,5678]`, and even the difference list `[a,b,c|X]-X`. The last difference list can be seen as summarising every possible difference list representing the same simple list, by introducing a variable for the part which is not contained in the simple list.

As was remarked above, `reverse(X,Y0,Y)` is true if Y consists of the reversal of X followed by Y0. Another way to say the same thing is that the reversal of X is the difference between Y and Y0. That is, the reversal of X is represented by the difference list Y-Y0! We can make this explicit by a small syntactic change to `reverse`, resulting in the following program:

```
reverse_dl(X,Y):-
    reverse_dl(X,Y-[]).

reverse_dl([],Y-Y).
reverse_dl([H|T],Y-Y0):-
    reverse_dl(T,Y-[H|Y0]).
```

For instance, the third clause in this program says: if the reversal of T is represented by the difference list Y-[H|Y0], then adding H to the head of T is the same as removing H from the minus list in the difference list.

If the minus list is a variable, it can be used as a pointer to the end of the represented list. It is this property which makes difference lists so useful. For instance, if we unify `[a,b,c|X]-X` with Y-[d,e], we get Y=[a,b,c,d,e] — we have managed to append two lists together in a single unification step! In this example, the second term is not a difference list, nor is the result. If we want to append two difference lists

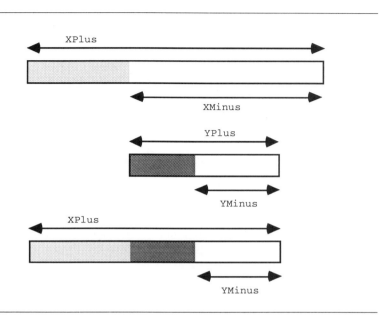

Figure 3.13. Appending two difference lists: the 'length' of XMinus is adjusted by unification with YPlus, the result is given by XPlus-YMinus.

```
[a,b,c|XMinus]-XMinus
```

and

```
[d,e|YMinus]-YMinus
```

we must unify XMinus with [d,e|YMinus] (the plus list of the second difference list), such that the first difference list becomes

```
[a,b,c,d,e|YMinus]-[d,e|YMinus]
```

Combining the plus list of this difference list with YMinus, we get exactly what we want.

In general, given two difference lists XPlus-XMinus and YPlus-YMinus, we unify XMinus with YPlus, and the result is given by XPlus-YMinus (fig. 3.13):

```
append_dl(XPlus-XMinus,YPlus-YMinus,XPlus-YMinus):-
                                        XMinus=YPlus.
```

or even shorter

```
append_dl(XPlus-YPlus,YPlus-YMinus,XPlus-YMinus).
```

Appending a simple list to another simple list of *n* elements requires *n* resolution steps; appending two difference lists requires no resolution at all, just one unification. Using difference lists is almost always a good idea if you have to do a lot of list processing.

Exercise 3.13. In the `naive_reverse` predicate, represent the reversed list by a difference list, use `append_dl` instead of `append`, and show that this results in the predicate `reverse_dl` by unfolding the definition of `append_dl`.

3.7 Second-order predicates

Suppose we need a program to determine, given two lists of persons of equal length, whether a person in the first list is the parent of the corresponding person in the second list. The following program will do the job:

```
parents([],[]).
parents([P|Ps],[C|Cs]):-
    parent(P,C),
    parents(Ps,Cs).
```

We can generalise this program by including the relation which must hold between corresponding elements of the two lists as a parameter:

```
rel(R,[],[]).
rel(R,[X|Xs],[Y|Ys]):-
    R(X,Y),
    rel(R,Xs,Ys).
```

A term like `R(X,Y)` is allowed at the position of an atom in the body of a clause, as long as it is correctly instantiated at the time it is called.

Some Prolog interpreters don't allow this, in which case you must explicitly construct the literal by means of the built-in predicate '`=..`' (sometimes called *univ*). It is a fully declarative predicate, which can both be used to construct a term from a list of arguments preceded by a functor, or to decompose a term into its constituents:

```
?-Term =.. [parent,X,peter]
  Term = parent(X,peter)

?-parent(maria,Y) =.. List
  List = [parent,maria,Y]
```

'`=..`' is declared as an infix operator in Prolog.

Exercise 3.14. Rewrite the program for `rel`, using `=..`

The predicate `rel` is called a *second-order* predicate, because it takes a (first-order) predicate as an argument[11]. We can now define the `parents` predicate as

```
parents(Ps,Cs):-rel(parent,Ps,Cs).
```

Suppose now you have the following facts in your program, and you want to collect all the children of a particular parent in a list:

```
parent(john,peter).
parent(john,paul).
parent(john,mary).
parent(mick,davy).
parent(mick,dee).
parent(mick,dozy).
```

Of course, it is easy to generate all the children upon backtracking; the problem is to collect them in a global list. To this end, Prolog provides the second-order predicates `findall`, `bagof`, and `setof`. For instance, we could use the following program and query:

```
children(Parent,Children):-
    findall(C,parent(Parent,C),Children).

?-children(john,Children).
  Children = [peter,paul,mary]
```

In general, the query

```
?-findall(X,Goal,ListofX)
```

generates all the possible solutions of the query `?-Goal`, recording the substitutions for `X` for each of these solutions in the list `ListofX` (`Goal` must be instantiated to a term representing a Prolog goal).

The `bagof` predicate acts similarly. However, its behaviour is different when the goal contains free variables. Consider the query

```
?-bagof(C,parent(P,C),L)
```

---

[11]Recall the discussion about the order of a logic in section 2.5.

in which the variable P is unbound. This query has two possible interpretations: 'find a parent and a list of his children', and 'find the list of children *that have a parent*'. In the first case, we get a possible value for P and a list of P's children, which means that there are two solutions:

```
?-bagof(C,parent(P,C),L).
  C = _951
  P = john
  L = [peter,paul,mary];

  C = _951
  P = mick
  L = [davy,dee,dozy]
```

In the second case, the goal to prove is 'there exists a P such that parent(P,C) is true', which means that the variable P is existentially quantified. This is signalled by prefixing the goal with P^:

```
?-bagof(C,P^parent(P,C),L).
  C = _957
  P = _958
  L = [peter,paul,mary,davy,dee,dozy]
```

The query ?-findall(C,parent(P,C),L) (without existential quantification) can only generate this second solution.

Finally, Prolog provides the predicate setof, which acts just like bagof, except that the resulting list is sorted and does not contain duplicates. Thus, setof is slightly less efficient than bagof, and the latter is preferred in cases where the list of solutions is known not to contain duplicates.

Exercise 3.15. Write a program which sorts and removes duplicates from a list, using setof.

3.8 Meta-programs

Prolog represents a clause Head:-Body in the same way as a term :-(Head,Body). Thus, it is easy to write programs that manipulate clauses. In the first case, ':-' is treated as a predicate, and in the second case it is treated as a functor. The combination of these two interpretations occurs frequently in Prolog programs, and can be applied to any predicate p. Such programs are called *meta-programs*; the interpretation of p as a predicate occurs on the *object-level*, and the interpretation as a functor occurs on the *meta-level*. (Note that the difference between meta-predicates and higher-order predicates is that meta-predicates take object-level *clauses* as arguments, while the latter take lower-order *predicates* as arguments.)

For instance, suppose we have the following biological knowledge, expressed as propositional if-then rules:

```
% if A and B then C means if(then(and(A,B),C))
:-op(900,fx,if).
:-op(800,xfx,then).
:-op(700,yfx,and).

% object-level rules
if has_feathers and lays_eggs then is_bird.
if has_gills and lays_eggs then is_fish.
if tweety then has_feathers.
if tweety then lays_eggs.
```

Suppose we want to prove that Tweety is a bird. That is, we want to show that the rule

```
if tweety then is_bird
```

follows logically from the given rules This can be done by a meta-program, which manipulates the rules on the object-level:

```
% meta-program
derive(if Assumptions then Goal):-
    if Body then Goal,
    derive(if Assumptions then Body).
derive(if Assumptions then Goal1 and Goal2):-
    derive(if Assumptions then Goal1),
    derive(if Assumptions then Goal2).
derive(if Assumptions then Goal):-
    assumed(Goal,Assumptions).

assumed(A,A).
assumed(A,A and As).
assumed(A,B and As):-
    assumed(A,As).
```

The three clauses for the `derive` predicate represent the three possible cases:
(*i*)   a goal matches the head of a rule, in which case we should proceed with the body;
(*ii*)   a goal is a conjunction (for instance, because it was produced in the previous step), of which each conjunct is derived separately;
(*iii*) a goal is among the assumptions.
As explained above, `if` is a predicate on the object-level, and a functor on the meta-level.

Exercise 3.16. Draw the SLD-tree for the query
```
?-derive(if tweety then is_bird).
```

Since propositional definite clauses are similar to the above if-then rules, one could view this program as a propositional Prolog simulator. In fact, it is possible to push the resemblance closer, by adopting the Prolog-representation of clauses at the object-level. One minor complication is that the clause constructor ':-' is not directly available as an object-level predicate. Instead, Prolog provides the built-in predicate `clause`: a query `?-clause(H,B)` succeeds if `H:-B` unifies with a clause in the internal Prolog database (if `H` unifies with a fact, `B` is unified with `true`). A further modification with respect to the above program is that Prolog queries do not have the form `if Assumptions then Goal`; instead, the `Assumptions` are added to the object-level program, from which a proof of `Goal` is attempted.

Following these observations, the predicate `derive` is changed as follows:

```
prove(Goal):-
    clause(Goal,Body),
    prove(Body).
prove((Goal1,Goal2)):-
    prove(Goal1),
    prove(Goal2).
prove(true).
```

This program nicely reflects the process of constructing a resolution proof:
- (*i*)   if the resolvent contains a single atom, find a clause with that atom in the head and proceed with its body;
- (*ii*) if the resolvent contains various atoms, start with the first and proceed with the rest;
- (*iii*) if the resolvent is empty, we're done.

Some Prolog interpreters have problems if `clause` is called with the first argument instantiated to `true` or a conjunction, because `true` and '`,`' (comma) are built-in predicates. To avoid these problems, we should add the conditions `not A=true` and `not A=(X,Y)` to the first clause. A less declarative solution is to reorder the clauses and use cuts:

```
prove(true):-!.
prove((A,B)):-!,
    prove(A),
    prove(B).
prove(A):-
    /* not A=true, not A=(X,Y) */
    clause(A,B),
    prove(B).
```

We will adopt this less declarative version for pragmatic reasons: it is the one usually found in the literature. As this program illustrates, whenever you use cuts it is normally a good idea to add a declarative description of their effect between comment brackets.

A meta-program interpreting programs in the same language in which it is written is called a *meta-interpreter*. In order to 'lift' this propositional meta-interpreter to clauses containing variables, it is necessary to incorporate unification into the third clause. Suppose we are equipped with predicates `unify` and `apply`, such that `unify(T1,T2,MGU,T)` is **true** if `T` is the result of unifying `T1` and `T2` with most general unifier `MGU`, and `apply(T,Sub,TS)` is **true** if `TS` is the term obtained from `T` by applying substitution `Sub`. The meta-interpreter would then look like this:

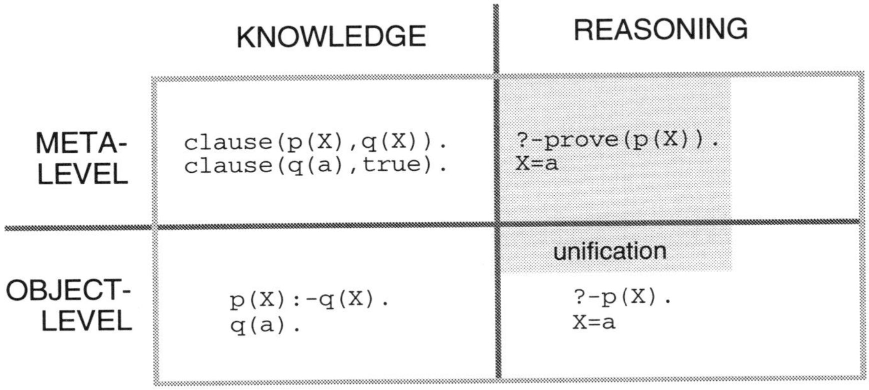

Figure 3.14. The `prove` meta-interpreter embodies a declarative implementation of the resolution proof procedure, making use of built-in unification.

```
prove_var(true):-!.
prove_var((A,B)):-!,
     prove(A),
     prove(B).
prove_var(A):-
     clause(Head,Body),
     unify(A,Head,MGU,Result),
     apply(Body,MGU,NewBody),
     prove_var(NewBody).
```

Prolog's own unification predicate = does not return the most general unifier explicitly, but rather unifies the two original terms implicitly. Therefore, if we want to use the built-in unification algorithm in our meta-interpreter, we do not need the `apply` predicate, and we can write the third clause as

```
prove_var(A):-
     clause(Head,Body),
     A=Head,
     prove_var(Body)
```

If we now change the explicit unification in the body of this clause to an implicit unification in the head, we actually obtain the propositional meta-interpreter again! That is, while this program is read **declaratively** as a meta-interpreter for propositional programs, it nevertheless operates **procedurally** as an interpreter of first-order clauses (fig. 3.14).

Exercise 3.17. Draw the SLD-tree for the query ?-prove(is_bird(X)), given the following clauses:

```
is_bird(X):-has_feathers(X),lays_eggs(X).
is_fish(X):-has_gills(X),lays_eggs(X).
has_feathers(tweety).
lays_eggs(tweety).
```

Note that this meta-interpreter is able to handle only 'pure' Prolog programs, without system predicates like cut or is, since there are no explicit clauses for such predicates.

A variety of meta-interpreters will be encountered in this book. Each of them is a variation of the above 'canonical' meta-interpreter in one of the following senses:

(*i*)   application of a different search strategy;

(*ii*)   application of a different proof procedure;

(*iii*) enlargement of the set of clauses that can be handled;

(*iv*)   extraction of additional information from the proof process.

The first variation will be illustrated in section 5.3, where the meta-interpreter adopts a breadth-first search strategy. In the same section, this meta-interpreter is changed to an interpreter for full clausal logic (*iii*). Different proof procedures are extensively used in Chapters 8 and 9. Here, we will give two example variations. In the first example, we change the meta-interpreter in order to handle general clauses by means of negation as failure (*iii*). All we have to do is to add the following clause:

```
prove(not A):-
    not prove(A)
```

This clause gives a declarative description of negation as failure.

The second variation extracts additional information from the SLD proof procedure by means of a proof tree (*iv*). To this end, we need to make a slight change to the meta-interpreter given above. The reason for this is that the second clause of the original meta-interpreter breaks up the current resolvent if it is a conjunction, whereas in a proof tree we want the complete resolvent to appear.

```
% meta-interpreter with complete resolvent
prove_r(true):-!.
prove_r((A,B)):-!,
    clause(A,C),
    conj_append(C,B,D),
    prove_r(D).
prove_r(A):-
    clause(A,B),
    prove_r(B).

%%% conj_append/3: see Appendix A.2
```

We now extend prove_r/1 with a second argument, which returns the proof tree as a list of pairs p(Resolvent,Clause):

```
% display a proof tree
prove_p(A):-
    prove_p(A,P),
    write_proof(P).

% prove_p(A,P) <- P is proof tree of A
prove_p(true,[]):-!.
prove_p((A,B),[p((A,B),(A:-C))|Proof]):-!,
    clause(A,C),
    conj_append(C,B,D),
    prove_p(D,Proof).
prove_p(A,[p(A,(A:-B))|Proof]):-
    clause(A,B),
    prove_p(B,Proof).

write_proof([]):-
    tab(15),write('[]'),nl.
write_proof([p(A,B)|Proof]):-
    write((:-A)),nl,
    tab(5),write('|'),tab(10),write(B),nl,
    tab(5),write('|'),tab(20),write('/'),nl,
    write_proof(Proof).
```

For instance, given the following clauses:

```
student_of(S,T):-teaches(T,C),follows(S,C).
teaches(peter,cs).
teaches(peter,ai).
follows(maria,cs).
follows(paul,ai).
```

and the query ?-prove_p(student_of(S,T)), the program writes the following proof trees:

```
:-student_of(peter,maria)
    |               student_of(peter,maria):-
                        teaches(peter,cs),follows(maria,cs)
    |                           /
:-(teaches(peter,cs),follows(maria,cs))
    |               teaches(peter,cs):-true
    |                           /
:-follows(maria,cs)
    |               follows(maria,cs):-true
    |                           /
                []
```

```
:-student_of(peter,paul)
        |                   student_of(peter,paul):-
        |                       teaches(peter,ai),follows(paul,ai)
        |                                      /
:-(teaches(peter,ai),follows(paul,ai))
        |                   teaches(peter,ai):-true
        |                                  /
:-follows(paul,ai)
        |                   follows(paul,ai):-true
        |                                  /
                        []
```

Note that these are propositional proof trees, in the sense that all substitutions needed for the proof have already been applied. If we want to collect the uninstantiated program clauses in the proof tree then we should make a copy of each clause, before it is used in the proof:

```
prove_p((A,B),[p((A,B),Clause)|Proof]):-!,
    clause(A,C),
    copy_term((A:-C),Clause),   % make copy of the clause
    conj_append(C,B,D),
    prove_p(D,Proof)
```

The predicate `copy_term/2` makes a copy of a term, with all variables replaced by new ones. It is a built-in predicate in many Prolog interpreters, but could be defined by means of `assert/2` and `retract/2` (see Appendix A.2 for details).

3.9 A methodology of Prolog programming

At the end of this chapter, we spend a few words on the *methodology* of writing Prolog programs. Given a problem to solve, how do I obtain the program solving the problem? This is the fundamental problem of software engineering. Here, we can only scratch the surface of this question: we will concentrate on the subtask of writing relatively simple predicates which use no more than two other predicates.

Consider the following problem: define a predicate which, given a number *n*, partitions a list of numbers into two lists: one containing numbers smaller than *n*, and the other containing the rest. So we need a predicate `partition/4`:

```
% partition(L,N,Littles,Bigs) <- Littles contains numbers
%                                 in L smaller than N,
%                                 Bigs contains the rest
```

Since the only looping structure of Prolog is recursion, simple predicates like this will typically be recursive. This means that
  (*i*)   there is a *base case*, and one or more recursive clauses;
  (*ii*) there is a *recursion argument* distinguishing between the base case and the recursive clauses.

For list predicates, the recursion argument is typically a list, and the distinction is typically between empty and non-empty lists. For the `partition/4` predicate, the recursion argument is the first list. The base case is easily identified: the empty list is partitioned in two empty lists, no matter the value of N. This gives us the following *skeleton*:

```
partition([],N,[],[]).
partition([Head|Tail],N,?Littles,?Bigs):-
    /* do something with Head */
    partition(Tail,N,Littles,Bigs).
```

The question marks denote *output arguments*, whose relation to the variables in the recursive call still has to be decided. It should be noted that not all predicates are tail recursive, so it is not yet known whether the recursive call will be last indeed. Notice also that the output arguments in the recursive call have been given meaningful names, which is, in general, a good idea.

Once we have 'chopped off' the first number in the list, we have to do something with it. Depending on whether it is smaller than N or not, it has to be added to the `Littles` or the `Bigs`. Suppose `Head` is smaller than N:

```
partition([Head|Tail],N,?Littles,?Bigs):-
    Head < N,
    partition(Tail,N,Littles,Bigs)
```

Thus, `Head` must be added to `Littles`. In this case, it does not matter in which position it is added: obviously, the most simple way is to add it to the head of the list:

```
?Littles = [Head|Littles]
```

In such cases, where output arguments are simply constructed by unification, the unification is performed implicitly in the head of the clause (the fourth argument remains unchanged):

```
partition([Head|Tail],N,[Head|Littles],Bigs):-
    Head < N,
    partition(Tail,N,Littles,Bigs)
```

A second recursive clause is needed to cover the case that `Head` is larger than or equal to N, in which case it must be added to `Bigs`. The final program looks as follows:

```
% partition(L,N,Littles,Bigs) <- Littles contains numbers
%                                 in L smaller than N,
%                                 Bigs contains the rest
partition([],N,[],[]).
partition([Head|Tail],N,[Head|Littles],Bigs):-
    Head < N,
    partition(Tail,N,Littles,Bigs).
partition([Head|Tail],N,Littles,[Head|Bigs]):-
    Head >= N,
    partition(Tail,N,Littles,Bigs).
```

The approach taken here can be formulated as a general strategy for writing Prolog predicates. The steps to be performed according to this strategy are summarised below:

(*i*)   write down a declarative specification;
(*ii*)   identify the recursion argument, and the output arguments;
(*iii*) write down a skeleton;
(*iv*)   complete the bodies of the clauses;
(*v*)   fill in the output arguments.

Notice that step (*iv*) comprises most of the work, while the other steps are meant to make this work as easy as possible.

Exercise 3.18. Implement a predicate `permutation/2`, such that `permutation(L,P)` is true if P contains the same elements as the list L but (possibly) in a different order, following these steps. (One auxiliary predicate is needed.)

As a second example, consider the problem of sorting a list of numbers. The declarative specification is as follows:

```
% sort(L,S) <- S is a sorted permutation of list L
```

Note that this specification can immediately be translated to Prolog:

```
sort(L,S):-
    permutation(L,S),
    sorted(S).
```

This program first guesses a permutation of L, and then checks if the permutation happens to be sorted. Declaratively, this program is correct; procedurally, it is extremely inefficent since there are *n*! different permutations of a list of length *n*. Thus, we have to think of a more efficient algorithm.

The recursion and output arguments are easily identified as the first and second argument, respectively. The base case states that the empty list is already sorted, while the recursive clause states that a non-empty list is sorted by sorting its tail separately:

```
sort([],[]).
sort([Head|Tail],?Sorted):-
    /* do something with Head */
    sort(Tail,Sorted).
```

It remains to decide what the relation is between `?Sorted`, `Head` and `Sorted`. Obviously, `Head` cannot be simply added to the front of `Sorted`, but has to be inserted in the proper place. We thus need an auxiliary predicate `insert/3`, to add `Head` at the proper position in `Sorted`. Note that tail recursion is not applicable in this case, since we have to insert `Head` in an already sorted list. We thus arrive at the following definition:

```
sort([],[]).
sort([Head|Tail],WholeSorted):-
    sort(Tail,Sorted),
    insert(Head,Sorted,WholeSorted).
```

In order to implement `insert/3`, we follow the same steps. The second argument is the recursion argument, and the third is the output argument. This gives the following skeleton:

```
insert(X,[],?Inserted).
insert(X,[Head|Tail],?Inserted):-
        /* do something with Head */
        insert(X,Tail,Inserted).
```

The base case is simple: `?Inserted = [X]`. In the recursive clause, we have to compare X and Head. Suppose X is greater than Head:

```
insert(X,[Head|Tail],?Inserted):-
        X > Head,
        insert(X,Tail,Inserted)
```

We have to construct the output argument `?Inserted`. Since X has already been properly inserted to `Tail`, it remains to add Head to the front of `Inserted`:

```
?Inserted = [Head|Inserted]
```

A third clause is needed if X is not greater than Head (note that this clause, being non-recursive, is a second base case):

```
insert(X,[Head|Tail],?Inserted):-
        X =< Head
```

In this case, X should be added before Head:

```
?Inserted = [X,Head|Tail]
```

The complete program is given below:

```
insert(X,[],[X]).
insert(X,[Head|Tail],[Head|Inserted]):-
        X > Head,
        insert(X,Tail,Inserted).
insert(X,[Head|Tail],[X,Head|Tail]):-
        X =< Head.
```

Exercise 3.19. Implement an alternative to this sorting method by using the `partition/4` predicate.

Further reading

There are many introductory and advanced textbooks on Prolog programming. (Bratko, 1990) is a particularly practical introduction. (Sterling & Shapiro, 1986) offers a slightly more advanced presentation. (Nilsson & Maluszynski, 1990) is one of the few books dealing with both the theoretical and practical aspects of programming in Prolog. (Ross, 1989) and (O'Keefe, 1990) discuss advanced issues in the practice of Prolog programming.

Those eager to learn more about the implementation of Prolog interpreters are referred to (Maier & Warren, 1988). (Bowen & Kowalski, 1982) is an early source on meta-programs in Logic Programming. The slogan Algorithm = Logic + Control was put forward by Kowalski (1979). A discussion of the relation between declarative and procedural programming can be found in (Kowalski, 1993).

K.A. BOWEN & R.A. KOWALSKI (1982), 'Amalgamating language and metalanguage in Logic Programming'. In *Logic Programming*, K.L. Clark & S. Tärnlund (eds.), Academic Press.

I. BRATKO (1990), *Prolog Programming for Artificial Intelligence*, Addison-Wesley, second edition.

R.A. KOWALSKI (1979), 'Algorithm = Logic + Control', *Communications of the ACM* **22**(7): 424-436.

R.A. KOWALSKI (1993), 'Logic Programming'. In *Encyclopedia of Computer Science*, A. Ralston & E.D. Reilly (eds), pp. 778-783, Van Nostrand Reinhold, third edition.

D. MAIER & D.S. WARREN (1988), *Computing with Logic: Logic Programming with Prolog*, Benjamin/Cummings.

U. NILSSON & J. MALUSZYNSKI (1990), *Logic, Programming and Prolog*, John Wiley.

R.A. O'KEEFE (1990), *The Craft of Prolog*, MIT Press.

P. ROSS (1989), *Advanced Prolog: Techniques and Examples*, Addison-Wesley.

L.S. STERLING & E.Y. SHAPIRO (1986), *The Art of Prolog*, MIT Press.

II

Reasoning with structured knowledge

A physical object is *structured* if it consists of several components having certain spatial relationships to each other. Likewise, knowledge is structured if its components have certain logical relationships. For instance, a description of the London underground system consists of a list of stations (the components) plus a list of connections between stations (the relationships). As can be seen in fig. 1.1 in Chapter 1, such structured knowledge has a convenient graphical representation, in which components are represented by points or *nodes*, and relationships are represented by lines or *arcs* between nodes. In mathematics, such graphical structures are called *graphs*.

A characteristic property of structured knowledge is the distinction that is made between *explicit* and *implicit* relationships. For instance, in the underground example the direct connections which exist between two stations are the explicit relationships. All other relationships (i.e. connections between stations that are further apart) are only implicitly represented, and must be reconstructed from the explicit relationships. Therefore, *reasoning* forms an integral part of any form of structured knowledge.

Other examples of structured knowledge, encountered in Part I, include Prolog terms, proof trees, and SLD-trees. Among these, SLD-trees constitute a special case, since they are not given *a priori* as part of the knowledge describing a certain Universe of Discourse, but are instead *derived* from problem specifications of the form 'given program P, find all answers to query Q'. By means of SLD-trees, such problems are translated to problems of the form 'given SLD-tree T, find all paths from the root of the tree to the empty clause'. Problems of the latter kind are called *search problems*, and the graph being searched is called

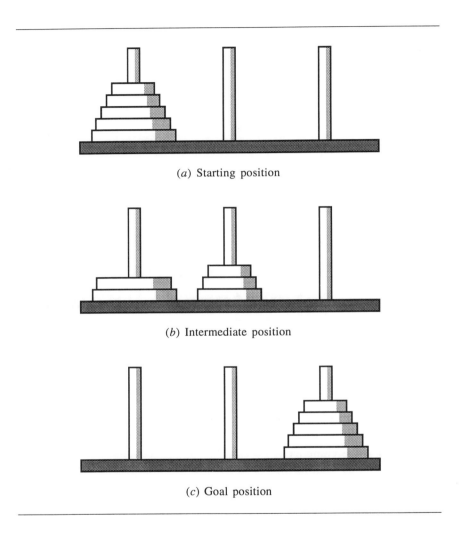

(*a*) Starting position

(*b*) Intermediate position

(*c*) Goal position

Figure II.1. The Towers of Hanoi.

a *search space*. Most problems in intelligent reasoning are search problems of one kind or the other.

In principle, any given problem can be defined as a search problem. To this end, we must identify:

(*i*) the nodes in the search space;
(*ii*) the arcs between nodes;
(*iii*) the starting node;
(*iv*) the goal node.

An analytic solution to the Towers of Hanoi

In the case of the Towers of Hanoi, there is a simple analytic solution based on the following observation: suppose we are able to solve the problem for $n-1$ disks, then we can solve it for n disks also: move the upper $n-1$ disks from the left to the middle peg[12], move the remaining disk on the left peg to the right peg, and move the $n-1$ disks from the middle peg to the right peg. Since we are able to solve the problem for 0 disks, it follows by complete induction that we can solve the problem for any number of disks. The inductive nature of this argument is nicely reflected in the following recursive program:

```
:-op(900,xfx,to).
% hanoi(N,A,B,C,Moves) <- Moves is the list of moves to
%                         move N disks from peg A to peg C,
%                         using peg B as intermediary peg
hanoi(0,A,B,C,[]).
hanoi(N,A,B,C,Moves):-
        N1 is N-1,
        hanoi(N1,A,C,B,Moves1),
        hanoi(N1,B,A,C,Moves2),
        append(Moves1,[A to C|Moves2],Moves).
```

For instance, the query `?-hanoi(3,left,middle,right,M)` yields the answer

```
M = [ left to right, left to middle, right to middle,
      left to right,
      middle to left, middle to right, left to right ]
```

The first three moves move the upper two disks from the left to the middle peg, then the largest disk is moved to the right peg, and again three moves are needed to move the two disks on the middle peg to the right peg.

For instance, when searching for an answer to a query by means of SLD-resolution, the nodes in the search space are resolvents, the arcs are resolution steps by means of a program clause, the starting node is the query, and the goal node is the empty clause. As another example, we consider the puzzle known as *The Towers of Hanoi*. This puzzle consists of three pegs and n disks of decreasing size. Initially, all the disks are on the left peg, such that no disk is placed on a smaller one. This rule is to be obeyed throughout the game. The goal is to move all the disks to the right peg by moving one disk at a time. This problem is easily reformulated as a search problem, where nodes are allowed positions, and arcs are moves of the upper disk on one peg to another. Starting node and goal node are as in fig. II.1.

Since the number of allowed positions is 3^n, the search space for the Towers of Hanoi grows exponentially with the number of disks. In practice, this means that the problem will be unsolvable for large n, no matter how efficient the search program, or how powerful the computer. *This is a common characteristic of search problems.* Search is a problem solving

---

[12]The remaining disk on A can safely be ignored, since it is the largest.

method which, although applicable to almost any problem, has considerable practical limitations. Therefore, search is only applied to problems for which no analytic solutions are known.

For many problems in intelligent reasoning such analytic solutions simply do not exist, and search is the best we can do. In Chapters 5 and 6, we will present and analyse various methods for searching graphs. Since graphs are not only important for search problems, but for all forms of structured knowledge, Chapter 4 is devoted to a discussion of various ways to represent structured knowledge in clausal logic.

4
Representing structured knowledge

In this chapter we will discuss various ways to represent structured knowledge in Prolog. The central notion is that of a *graph*, which is the mathematical abstraction of the graphical representation of structured knowledge. A graph consists of *nodes*, and *arcs* between nodes. Nodes are identified by their name, and arcs are identified by the pair of nodes they connect. By convention, arcs are taken to be *directed*, which means that an arc from n_1 to n_2 is not the same as an arc from n_2 to n_1. Undirected arcs (as in the London Underground example of Chapter 1) can be viewed as consisting of two directed arcs, one in each direction. If an arc is directed from n_1 to n_2, then n_1 is called the *parent* of n_2, and n_2 is called the *child* of n_1.

A *path* in a graph is a sequence of nodes, such that for each consecutive pair n_i, n_j in the sequence the graph contains an arc from n_i to n_j. If there is a path from n_k to n_l, then n_k is called an *ancestor* of n_l, and n_l is called a *descendant* of n_k. A *cycle* is a path from a node to itself. Obviously, when a path from n_i to n_j passes through a node which is also on a cycle, there are infinitely many different paths from n_i to n_j. Thus, a graph consisting of a limited number of nodes and arcs can generate infinite behaviour. This is something to keep in mind when searching such cyclic graphs!

A *tree* is a special kind of graph which contains a *root* such that there is a **unique** path from the root to any other node. From this it follows that for any two nodes in a tree, either there is no path between them, or there is exactly one. Thus, trees are necessarily non-cyclic or *acyclic*. A *leaf* is a node without children. Often, leaves are goal nodes in search spaces like SLD-trees. Strictly speaking, an SLD-tree is not a tree, because there might be several ways to construct the same resolvent. By convention, however, resolvents constructed in a different way are considered to be distinct nodes in the SLD-tree. Usually, trees are drawn upside down, with the root node at the top; arcs are implicitly understood to be directed from top to bottom. Note that, if n is the root of a tree, each of its children is the root of a *subtree* (fig. 4.1).

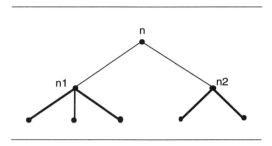

Figure 4.1. A tree with two subtrees.

4.1　Trees as terms

Recall from section 1.3 that complex Prolog terms like

```
route(tottenham_court_road,route(leicester_square,noroute))
```

can be viewed as a tree, with the functor `route` acting as the root of (sub)trees, and `tottenham_court_road`, `leicester_square`, and `noroute` as leaves (fig. 1.6). Conversely, trees can be represented by Prolog terms.

Exercise 4.1. Draw the tree represented by the term `1(2(4),3(5,6))`.

A tree is traversed by first visiting its root, and then recursively traversing all of its subtrees. A list of subtrees is obtained by decomposing the complex term by means of the `=..` predicate (see section 3.7):

```
% term_tree(T,R,S) <- term T represents a tree with root R
%                     and list of subtrees S
term_tree(Tree,Root,Subtrees):-
    Tree=..[Root|Subtrees].

% term_root(T,R) <- R is the root of tree T
term_root(Tree,Root):-
    term_tree(Tree,Root,S).

% term_subtree(T,S) <- S is a subtree of tree T
term_subtree(Tree,Subtree):-
    term_tree(Tree,R,S),
    element(Subtree,S).
```

Data abstraction

The principle of *data abstraction* prescribes to keep datastructures local to specific predicates such as `term_tree`, `term_root` and `term_subtree`, and to access the datastructures only through these predicates. The main advantage of this design principle is *modularity*: if we choose to change the representation of a tree, we just have to modify these specific predicates, but the predicates which call them need not be changed. In contrast, if we unfold `term_tree`, `term_root` and `term_subtree` into the definition of `term_arc`, we get the following piece of code:

```
term_arc(Tree,[Root,R]):-
        Tree=..[Root|Subtrees].
        element(Subtree,Subtrees),
        Subtree=..[R|S].
term_arc(Tree,Arc):-
        Tree=..[Root|Subtrees].
        element(Subtree,Subtrees),
        term_arc(Subtree,Arc).
```

This program fragment is badly designed, because `term_arc` explicitly mentions the way trees are represented by Prolog terms. Consequently, if we change this representation, `term_arc` needs to be changed as well. This illustrates that the design of good datastructures is as important in Prolog as it is in any other programming language.

By means of these simple predicates, we can write a program for finding arcs and paths in a tree. Paths are represented as lists of nodes, and an arc is simply a path consisting of two nodes:

```
% term_arc(T,A) <- T is a tree, and A is an arc in T
term_arc(Tree,[Root,SR]):-      % Arc from Root to Subtree
    term_root(Tree,Root),
    term_subtree(Tree,Subtree),
    term_root(Subtree,SR).
term_arc(Tree,Arc):-            % Arc in Subtree
    term_subtree(Tree,Subtree),
    term_arc(Subtree,Arc).

% term_path(T,P) <- T is a tree, and P is a path in T
term_path(Tree,Arc):-           % consisting of one arc
    term_arc(Tree,Arc).
term_path(Tree,[Node1,Node2|Nodes]):-  % several arcs
    term_arc(Tree,[Node1,Node2]),
    term_path(Tree,[Node2|Nodes]).
```

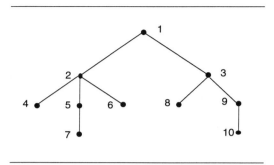

Figure 4.2. Which are the paths
through this tree?

Exercise 4.2. Give a term `Tree`, such that it contains the tree of exercise 4.1, and
such that `Path=[1,2,7,8]` is an answer to the query
                    `?-term_path(Tree,Path).`

Consider the tree in fig. 4.2. The following query lists all the paths in this tree:

```
?-term_path(1(2(4,5(7),6),3(8,9(10))),Path).
  Path = [1,2];
  Path = [1,3];
  Path = [2,4];
  Path = [2,5];
  Path = [2,6];
  Path = [5,7];
  Path = [3,8];
  Path = [3,9];
  Path = [9,10];
  Path = [1,2,4];
  Path = [1,2,5];
  Path = [1,2,6];
  Path = [1,2,5,7];
  Path = [1,3,8];
  Path = [1,3,9];
  Path = [1,3,9,10];
  Path = [2,5,7];
  Path = [3,9,10];
  No more solutions
```

Exercise 4.3. Explain the order in which these paths are found.

It would be convenient to have a program for printing Prolog terms which represent trees in a tree-like way. The nicest way to do this is to print from the root down; however, this requires a rather elaborate program[13]. A reasonable alternative is to print the tree rotated at 90 degrees, from the root to the right. A program to do this is given below.

```
term_write(Tree):-
    term_write(0,Tree),nl.

% write a Tree at position Pos
term_write(Pos,Tree):-
    term_tree(Tree,Root,Subtrees),    % decompose Tree
    term_write_node(Pos,Pos2,Root),   % write Root
    term_writes(Pos2,Subtrees).       % new position

% write a list of trees at position Pos
term_writes(Pos,[]).
term_writes(Pos,[Tree]):-!,           % no newline here
    term_write(Pos,Tree).
term_writes(Pos,[Tree|Subtrees]):-
    term_write(Pos,Tree),
    nl,tab(Pos),                      % skip to position Pos
    term_writes(Pos,Subtrees).

% write a Node from Begin to End
term_write_node(Begin,End,Node):-
    name(Node,L),length(L,N),         % N is length of Nodename
    End is Begin+10,
    N1 is End-Begin-N,                % N1 is length of line
    write_line(N1),
    write(Node).

% write a line of given length
write_line(0).
write_line(N):-
    N>0,N1 is N-1,
    write('-'),
    write_line(N1).
```

name/2[14] is a built-in predicate, converting an atom into a list of ASCII-codes. In combination with length/2, it is used to determine the number of characters in an atom.

---

[13]Such a program should perform breadth-first search; see Exercise 5.2.
[14]From now on, we denote a Predicate with Arity as Predicate/Arity. This is because predicates with different arity are different predicates, even if they share the same predicate name.

The query `?-term_write(1(2(4,5(7),6),3(8,9(10))))` displays the tree as follows:

```
---------1---------2---------4
                   ---------5---------7
                   ---------6
         ---------3---------8
                   ---------9--------10
```

4.2 Graphs generated by a predicate

In the preceding section, a tree was represented by a Prolog term. This is convenient for relatively small trees such as proof trees, that are processed and passed around as a unit. However, for bigger trees it is a better idea not to represent them explicitly by a Prolog term, but implicitly by a set of ground facts, listing the arcs in the graph. An additional advantage of this representation is the possibility of representing graphs that are not trees.

As an example of this representation, the tree in fig. 4.2 would be represented by the following facts:

```
arc(1,2).
arc(1,3).
arc(2,4).
arc(2,5).
arc(2,6).
arc(5,7).
arc(3,8).
arc(3,9).
arc(9,10).
```

The predicate for finding a path in a graph now needs a few minor adjustments: the graph is not passed on as an argument, and `arc/2` is used rather than `term_arc/2`:

```
% path(P) <- P is a path in the graph given by arc/2
path([Node1,Node2]):-
    arc(Node1,Node2).
path([Node1,Node2|Nodes]):-
    arc(Node1,Node2),
    path([Node2|Nodes]).
```

Exercise 4.4. Draw the SLD-tree for the query `?-path([1|Path])`.

`path/2` will generate paths between any two connected nodes. When searching a graph such as an SLD-tree, we are normally only interested in paths which start at a given node (for instance, the root of a tree), and end in a leaf. The following program will do the job.

Note that this program differs from the previous one in that it allows for paths consisting of one node only.

```
% path_leaf(N,P) <- P is a path starting at node N, ending
%                    in a leaf in the graph given by arc/2
path_leaf(Leaf,[Leaf]):-
    leaf(Leaf).
path_leaf(Node1,[Node1|Nodes]):-
    arc(Node1,Node2),
    path_leaf(Node2,Nodes).

leaf(Leaf):-
    not arc(Leaf,SomeNode).
```

The query ?-path_leaf(1,Path) will lead to the following answers:

```
Path = [1,2,4];
Path = [1,2,5,7];
Path = [1,2,6];
Path = [1,3,8];
Path = [1,3,9,10];
No more solutions
```

Exercise 4.5. Draw the SLD-tree for this query.

Notice the order in which the paths to the leafs are found — the longer path [1,2,5,7] is found before the shorter path [1,2,6]. This kind of search is called *depth-first search*, because the deepest unvisited nodes are preferred. In contrast, *breadth-first search* tries all nodes on a given level before going one level deeper; consequently, shortest paths are found first. Of course, the order in which nodes are visited can only be understood procedurally — logically speaking, there is nothing in the program which prescribes such an order. It is only because Prolog itself searches the SLD-tree in a depth-first fashion, that programs like the above perform depth-first search.

In real life, graphs are often infinite. For instance, many SLD-trees are infinite, even for very simple programs such as ('br' abbreviates brother):

```
br(X,Y):-br(X,Z),br(Z,Y).
br(paul,peter).
```

Exercise 4.6. Sketch the SLD-tree for the query ?-br(paul,B).

SLD-trees are graphs, with resolvents as nodes. Representing a resolvent by the list of its literals, we would need an infinite number of facts to represent SLD-trees, for instance:

```
arc([br(paul,B)],[br(paul,Z),br(Z,B)]).
arc([br(paul,B)],[]).
arc([br(paul,Z),br(Z,B)],[br(paul,Z1),br(Z1,Z),br(Z,B)]).
arc([br(paul,Z),br(Z,B)],[br(peter,B)]).
arc([br(paul,Z),br(Z,B)],[br(paul,paul)]).
...
arc([br(peter,B)],[br(peter,Z),br(Z,B)]).
...
arc([br(paul)],[br(paul,Z),br(Z,paul)]).
...
```

In such cases, it is a better idea to write a program which **generates** these facts. In other words, we need a logical definition of `arc/2`.

Now, `arc(A,B)` is true if A and B are lists of negative literals interpreted as resolvents, and one resolution step applied to A and a clause for `br/2` yields B. We can write this down by means of the predicate `resolve/3`, which performs one resolution step, and the two clauses for `br/2` in the appropriate representation. This gives the following program:

```
arc(A,B):- resolve(A,(br(X,Y):-[br(X,Z),br(Z,Y)]),B).
arc(A,B):- resolve(A,(br(paul,peter):-[]),B).

% resolve(G,C,NewG) <- the goal G (a list of atoms)
%                      resolves with the clause C (body
%                      is a list) to yield the goal NewG
resolve([H1|T],(H2:-Body),B):-
    H1=H2,  % literal in goal unifies with head of clause
    append(Body,T,B).
resolve([H|T],Clause,[H|B]):-
    resolve(T,Clause,B).     % try next literal
```

The query `?-arc([br(paul,B)],N)` results in the answers

```
B = Y
N = [br(paul,Z),br(Z,Y)];

B = peter
N = []
```

as expected.

Note that a query of the form `?-arc(R,[])` asks for a path from R to a success branch in the SLD-tree, thus simulating a query `:-R`. That is, the above program for `arc/2` is simply a meta-interpreter (with the object-level program hardwired in its clauses). In section 5.3, we encounter a similar meta-interpreter for full clausal logic.

4.3 Inheritance hierarchies

In the foregoing sections, we studied two kinds of graphs: trees represented by Prolog terms, and graphs generated by predicate definitions. In both cases, the main inference step is to

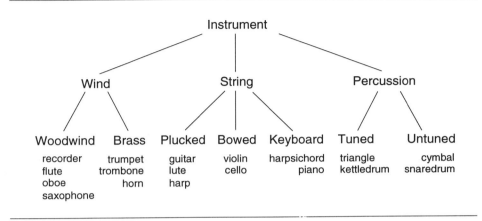

Figure 4.3. An inheritance hierarchy of musical instruments. Nodes in the tree denote classes; at the bottom, instances for each class are listed.

search for a path satisfying certain conditions. In this section, we study a type of structured knowledge called an *inheritance hierarchy*, which differs from the previous cases in that it requires a more elaborate kind of reasoning. Basically, this is because a node in such a hierarchy is a more complex entity with various kinds of properties. Lower nodes in the hierarchy *inherit* properties from ancestor nodes, unless they are assigned a property of their own. Thus, reasoning about inheritance hierarchies not only requires searching for a path, but also collecting properties found along a path.

Fig. 4.3 displays an inheritance hierarchy of a variety of musical instruments. The topmost node represents the *class* of all instruments in the Universe of Discourse, which has three *subclasses*: wind instruments, string instruments, and percussion instruments. In turn, wind instruments are divided into woodwinds and brass instruments, and so on. At the bottom of the figure, *instances* are listed for each most specific subclass. Thus, guitar, lute and harp are instances of the class 'plucked instruments', and thus also of the classes 'string instruments' and 'instruments'.

If we want to represent such hierarchies in Prolog, we have to choose a representation for instances and classes. By far the most natural choice is to represent an instance by a constant, and a class by a unary predicate. A class–superclass relation is then expressed by a clause, and an instance–class relation is expressed by a ground fact:

```
% Classes
instrument(X):-wind(X).
instrument(X):-string(X).
instrument(X):-percussion(X).
wind(X):-woodwind(X).
wind(X):-brass(X).
string(X):-plucked(X).
```

```
string(X):-bowed(X).
string(X):-keyboard(X).
percussion(X):-tuned(X).
percussion(X):-untuned(X).

% Instances
woodwind(recorder).            woodwind(flute).
woodwind(oboe).                woodwind(saxophone).
brass(trumpet).                brass(trombone).
brass(horn).                   plucked(guitar).
plucked(lute).                 plucked(harp).
bowed(violin).                 bowed(cello).
keyboard(harpsichord).         keyboard(piano).
tuned(triangle).               tuned(kettledrum).
untuned(cymbal).               untuned(snaredrum).
```

With these clauses, it is possible to ask questions about instances and (super)classes. For example, we can find out what instruments there are by means of the query

```
?-instrument(X).
```

As was remarked above, nodes (and instances) in an inheritance hierarchy can be assigned properties, where a *property* is an attribute–value pair. For instance, the material an instrument is made of can be an attribute, with possible values 'wood' and 'metal'. The statement 'saxophones are made of metal' is represented by the ground fact

```
material(saxophone,metal)
```

The statement 'instances of the class of string instruments are made of wood' is represented by the clause

```
material(X,wood):-string(X).
```

Since `string(piano)` is a logical consequence of the previous clauses expressing the hierarchy, we can now prove `material(piano,wood)`. Thus, the chosen representation takes care of the inheritance of properties, as required.

In our musical Universe of Discourse, we consider three attributes: the `function` of an instrument (all instruments have a musical function), the `material` of an instrument (wood or metal), and the way the instrument produces sound, expressed by the attribute `action`:

```
function(X,musical):-instrument(X).
```

```
material(flute,metal).
material(saxophone,metal).
material(X,wood):-woodwind(X).
material(X,metal):-brass(X).
material(X,wood):-string(X).
material(X,metal):-percussion(X).
```

```
action(oboe,reed(double)).
action(saxophone,reed(single)).
action(harpsichord,plucked).
action(piano,hammered).
action(X,reed(lip)):-brass(X).
action(X,plucked):-plucked(X).
action(X,bowed):-bowed(X).
action(X,hammered):-percussion(X).
```

For instance, all brass instruments have lip-reeds, while some woodwinds have a double reed (oboes, for example) or a single reed (saxophones).

Note that there is a potential conflict in the above clauses: woodwinds are generally made of wood, but flutes and saxophones are made of metal. Thus, the query

```
?-material(flute,M)
```

has two answers:

```
M = metal;
M = wood
```

The order in which these answers are found is, of course, determined by the order of the clauses above. Since we put the ground facts listing properties of instances before the clauses listing properties assigned to classes (and the clauses pertaining to classes before those pertaining to superclasses), the answers are found by climbing the inheritance hierarchy from bottom to top, and the first property found is the desired one. It should be noted, however, that things are not always that simple. If more sophisticated *inheritance strategies* are needed, alternative representations, like the ones to be discussed later in this section, are to be preferred.

A typical thing one would like to know regarding an inheritance hierarchy is: what are the properties of a given instance? In principle, this requires a second-order query

```
?-Attr(Inst,Value)
```

which is not allowed in Prolog if `Attr` is not instantiated. We can get around this by maintaining a list of all attributes, and constructing the appropriate goal for each attribute by means of the predicate `get_value/3`:

```
properties(Inst,Props):-
    attributes(Attrs),
    properties(Attrs,Inst,Props).

properties([],Inst,[]).
properties([Attr|Attrs],Inst,[Attr=Value|Props]):-
    get_value(Attr,Inst,Value),!, % only first answer
    properties(Attrs,Inst,Props).

attributes([function,material,action]).

get_value(A,B,C):-
    Goal =.. [A,B,C],
    call(Goal).
```

> ### Instance–class vs. class–superclass
>
> In this representation there appears to be no difference between instance–class relations and class–superclass relations. Indeed, we could have treated instances just as classes, and use the `isa/2` predicate for both. However, this obscures the semantic difference between instances and classes, which can lead to problems. For example, instances of one class can be *composed* of instances of other classes (a bycicle is composed of two wheels and a frame), but this is not true for classes (the class of bycicles is not composed of the class of wheels and the class of frames).

For instance, the query `?-properties(saxophone,P)` yields the answer

```
P = [function=musical,material=metal,action=reed(single)]
```

Only the most specific property regarding material is found, because of the cut in the recursive clause of `properties/3`.

As indicated above, the representation of inheritance hierarchies by means of clauses only allows a relatively simple inheritance strategy. Moreover, since classes are represented by predicates, reasoning about classes becomes a second-order logical inference. For example, the question 'what are the subclasses of the class of instruments' is not easily handled in the above representation. Both shortcomings can be alleviated if classes and attributes are represented by terms instead of predicates. In effect, this will result in a clearer separation of declarative knowledge describing the hierarchy, and procedural knowledge describing the inheritance strategy. This can be done in several ways; two possibilities are worked out below.

The first idea is to represent the tree in fig. 4.3 according to the first method in section 4.2, i.e. by a set of ground facts listing the arcs in the tree. Thus, nodes (classes) are represented by constants, and arcs (class–superclass relations) are represented by means of the predicate `isa/2`:

```
% Classes
isa(wind,instrument).              isa(string,instrument).
isa(percussion,instrument).        isa(woodwind,wind).
isa(brass,wind).                   isa(plucked,string).
isa(bowed,string).                 isa(keyboard,string).
isa(tuned,percussion).             isa(untuned,percussion).
```

Instances are listed by means of the predicate `inst/2`:

```
% Instances
inst(recorder,woodwind).           inst(flute,woodwind).
inst(oboe,woodwind).               inst(saxophone,woodwind).
```

```
inst(trumpet,brass).            inst(trombone,brass).
inst(horn,brass).               inst(guitar,plucked).
inst(lute,plucked).             inst(harp,plucked).
inst(violin,bowed).             inst(cello,bowed).
inst(harpsichord,keyboard).     inst(piano,keyboard).
inst(triangle,tuned).           inst(kettledrum,tuned).
inst(cymbal,untuned).           inst(snaredrum,untuned).
```

The difference between inheritance hierarchies and ordinary graphs lies in the additional meaning assigned to classes and instances by means of properties. Therefore, a graph extended with properties is commonly called a *semantic network*. Properties are represented by means of the predicate `prop/3`:

```
% Class properties
prop(instrument,function,musical).
prop(string,material,wood).
prop(percussion,material,metal).
prop(percussion,action,hammered).
prop(woodwind,material,wood).
prop(brass,material,metal).
prop(brass,action,reed(lip)).
prop(plucked,action,plucked).
prop(bowed,action,bowed).

% Instance properties
prop(flute,material,metal).
prop(oboe,action,reed(double)).
prop(saxophone,material,metal).
prop(saxophone,action,reed(single)).
prop(harpsichord,action,plucked).
prop(piano,action,hammered).
```

Since we will be using a more sophisticated inheritance strategy, the order of these facts is now immaterial.

The inheritance strategy is to collect the properties of instances before properties inherited from classes:

```
properties_sn(Inst,Props):-
    props(Inst,InstProps),    % properties of instance
    inst(Inst,Class),
    inherit_sn(Class,InstProps,Props). % inherit the rest

props(IC,Props):-
    findall(Attr=Value,prop(IC,Attr,Value),Props).
```

In turn, inherited properties are collected from bottom to top in the hierarchy, so that specific properties are found before general properties:

```
inherit_sn(top,Props,Props).
inherit_sn(Class,SpecificProps,AllProps):-
    props(Class,GeneralProps),  % properties of this class
    override(SpecificProps,GeneralProps,Props),
    isa(Class,SuperClass),      % climb hierarchy
    inherit_sn(SuperClass,Props,AllProps). % inherit rest
```

`top` refers to the root of the universal inheritance hierarchy, which should be added as the root of any sub-hierarchy:

```
isa(instrument,top).
```

The predicate `override/3` checks for every general property whether a more specific property has already been found. If so, we say that the specific property *overrides* the general property:

```
override(Props,[],Props).
override(Specific,[Attr=Val|General],Props):-
    element(Attr=V,Specific),           % overriding
    override(Specific,General,Props).
override(Specific,[Attr=Val|General],[Attr=Val|Props]):-
    not element(Attr=V,Specific),       % no overriding
    override(Specific,General,Props).
```

Again, the query `?-properties_sn(saxophone,P)` yields the answer

```
P = [function=musical,material=metal,action=reed(single)]
```

What we gained with this representation, however, is a declarative specification of the inheritance strategy, which is therefore also amenable to change. For instance, if the inheritance hierarchy is not a tree, a class could be a subclass of two or more other classes. In this case, different values for the same attribute could be inherited along different paths; this is called *multiple inheritance*. Such conflicts need to be resolved (or at least signalled) by the inheritance strategy.

Exercise 4.7. Implement a multiple inheritance strategy.

A slightly different but related representation is obtained if we group all information about one class or instance together in a socalled *frame*. A frame representation is obtained from the semantic network representation by adding a list of properties to each arc in the network. Below, class frames are defined by the predicate `class/3`, and instance frames are defined by the predicate `instance/3`:

```
% Classes
class(instrument,top,[]).
class(wind,instrument,[function=musical]).
class(string,instrument,[material=wood]).
```

```
class(percussion,instrument,[material=metal,
                            action=hammered]).
class(woodwind,wind,[material=wood]).
class(brass,wind,[material=metal,action=reed(lip)]).
class(plucked,string,[action=plucked]).
class(bowed,string,[action=bowed]).
class(keyboard,string,[]).
class(tuned,percussion,[]).
class(untuned,percussion,[]).

% Instances
instance(recorder,woodwind,[]).
instance(flute,woodwind,[material=metal]).
instance(oboe,woodwind,[action=reed(double)]).
instance(saxophone,woodwind,[material=metal,
                             action=reed(single)]).
/* etcetera... */
instance(cymbal,untuned,[]).
instance(snaredrum,untuned,[]).
```

Inheritance is as easily implemented as in the semantic network representation:

```
properties_fr(Inst,Props):-
    instance(Inst,Class,InstProps), % instance properties
    inherit_fr(Class,InstProps,Props).  % inherit the rest

inherit_fr(top,Props,Props).
inherit_fr(Class,SpecificProps,AllProps):-
    class(Class,SuperClass,GeneralProps),  % this class
    override(SpecificProps,GeneralProps,Props),
    inherit_fr(SuperClass,Props,AllProps). % inherit rest
```

Historically, semantic network and frame-based representations were proposed in quite different contexts. We see that their representation in Prolog is very similar.

Further reading

An introduction to Knowledge Representation can be found in (Ringland & Duce, 1989). (Brachman & Levesque, 1985) is a collection of papers discussing various aspects of Knowledge Representation, such as the difference between isa-links and instance-of-links in semantic networks. Papers about inheritance hierarchies can be found in (Lenzerini *et al.*, 1991). LOGIN is an extension of Prolog in which inheritance is represented by terms rather than clauses (Aït-Kaci & Nasr, 1986).

H. AÏT-KACI & R. NASR (1986), 'LOGIN: a logic programming language with built-in inheritance', *Journal of Logic Programming* **1986**(3): 185-215.

R.J. BRACHMAN & H.J. LEVESQUE (eds) (1985), *Readings in Knowledge Representation*, Morgan Kaufmann.

M. LENZERINI, D. NARDI & M. SIMI (eds) (1991), *Inheritance Hierarchies in Knowledge Representation and Programming Languages*, John Wiley.

G.A. RINGLAND & D.A. DUCE (eds) (1989), *Approaches to Knowledge Representation: an Introduction*, Research Studies Press.

5
Searching graphs

As explained earlier, a *search problem* is defined by a *search space*, which is a graph with one or more *starting nodes* and one or more *goal nodes*. Given a search space, a *solution* is a path from a starting node to a goal node . A *cost function c* assigns a number to each arc from n_1 to n_2, specifying the *cost* of moving from n_1 to n_2. The cost of a path is the sum of the costs of the arcs in the path. Given a search space and a cost function, an *optimal solution* is a solution with minimal cost. A trivial example of a cost function is $c(a)=1$ for each arc a, in which case the cost of a path equals the length of the path, and an optimal solution is a shortest path. For SLD proofs, such a cost function would measure the depth of the proof tree.

In this chapter, we will discuss and implement some basic techniques for finding solutions in search spaces. Their common denominator is that they are *exhaustive*: that is, in the worst case they will eventually visit every node in the search space along every possible path, before finding a solution. On the other hand, they differ with regard to:
- *completeness* — will a solution always be found?
- *optimality* — will shorter paths be found before longer ones?
- *efficiency* — what are the runtime and memory requirements?

We start with a general discussion of the problem of search. Then, we will discuss the basic exhaustive search strategies: depth-first search, breadth-first search, and forward chaining.

5.1 A general search procedure

Imagine a visit with a friend to the Staatsgalerie in Stuttgart. It is very crowded in this beautiful art museum, and while admiring the Mondriaan works you lose sight of each other. Having been through situations like this before, you had made the agreement that she would stay where she was, while you would go looking for her. What strategy would you employ?

First of all, to make sure that you don't miss any room, you have to visit them in some systematic way. You don't have a global map of the building, so you decide to never leave a room through the door through which you entered. Thinking about it, you recognise that this procedure won't fully work, because a room might have just one door: the one

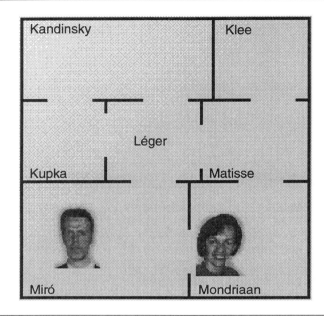

Figure 5.1. Searching for a friend.

through which you entered. Assuming that there are still rooms not yet visited, you **have** to leave such a room through the same door through which you entered, and find a room you've visited before, with a door not yet taken. Such a procedure, however, requires that, for each room you visit, you remember the door through which you entered the room (in order to go back to a room you've been in before), and the doors you tried already (in order to try a remaining door).

Luckily enough, you carry a piece of paper and a pencil with you, so you can stick little papers saying 'entrance' or 'exit' on the appropriate doors. However, the amount of paper you have is limited, so a better idea is to mark the doors *not yet* tried, and to remove the paper when you try a door, so that you can use the paper again. By reusing those pieces of paper that become obsolete, you minimise the amount of paper needed. Similarly, if you return to a room in which there are no remaining doors, you will never return to that room, so you might want to remove the paper saying 'entrance' as well. On the other hand, leaving one paper might be a good idea, just in case you return to the room later via a 'circular' route; you are then able to see that you already tried all the doors in that room.

So you decide to employ the following procedure:

1.   mark every door in the starting room as 'exit';
2.   examine the current room;
3.   if you find your friend, stop;

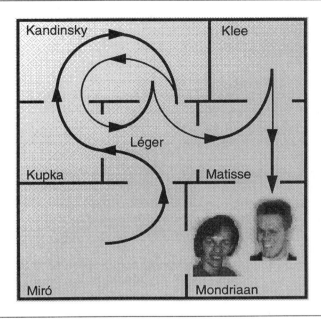

Figure 5.2. You find her by systematically searching the rooms,
backtracking when all the rooms reachable from the room you're in
have been visited already (thin lines).

4.   otherwise, if there are any doors marked 'exit' in the room,
      4a.   choose one of them;
      4b.   remove the mark 'exit';
      4c.   go through it;
      4d.   if one of the doors in this room is already marked 'entrance', go
           back to the previous room, and go to step 4;
      4d.   otherwise, mark the door you just came through as 'entrance';
      4e.   mark all other doors as 'exit';
      4f.   go to step 2;
5.   otherwise, take the door marked 'entrance', and go to step 4.

Steps 1-3 are obvious enough. In step 4, you check whether there are any untried doors left;
if not, you have to go back to a previously visited room, and do the same there (step 5).
This process of reconsidering previous decisions is called *backtracking*. It is an essential step
in any exhaustive search procedure. If there are any alternatives left, you have to check
whether you have been there already via some other route (step 4d). This step is called *loop
detection*, and is only needed for cyclic search spaces. If you omit this step in such cases,

you risk walking in circles forever. If you are in a yet unvisited room, you do some bookkeeping and proceed in the same way.

How does this search procedure work in practice? Suppose you are in the Miró room (fig. 5.1). You decide to try the doors in that room in a clockwise order. You first check the Léger room, then the Kupka room, and finally the Kandinsky room. When you enter the Léger room again from Kandinsky, you realise that you've been there before, because there's a door marked 'entrance'. So you backtrack to Léger (because there are no alternatives left in Kandinsky and Kupka), and try the next door. This one leads you straight to Kandinsky again, and your little papers remind you that you have been there already. You backtrack again to Léger, and try the Matisse room. From there, Klee is a dead end, so you backtrack and finally find your friend still admiring the Mondriaan paintings! The route you walked is shown in fig. 5.2, (thin lines denote backtracking).

In a computer implementation of such a search procedure, you don't walk from room to room. Instead of marking nodes and returning to them later, the search program stores a description of those nodes in memory. In the above example, the number of marks needed corresponds to the amount of memory required during search, and just as marks can be used several times, memory space can be reclaimed once all the children of a node have been put on the list. This list of nodes to be tried next is called the *agenda*; this is an important concept, which can be used to describe any backtracking search procedure. Such a general-purpose agenda-based search algorithm operates as follows (for simplicity, we have omitted loop detection):

1. take the next node from the agenda;
2. if it is a goal node, stop;
3. otherwise,
      3a. generate its children;
      3b. put them on the agenda;
      3c. go to step 1.

This procedure can be almost directly translated into a Prolog program:

```
% search(Agenda,Goal) <- Goal is a goal node, and a
%                        descendant of one of the nodes
%                        on the Agenda
search(Agenda,Goal):-
    next(Agenda,Goal,Rest),
    goal(Goal).
search(Agenda,Goal):-
    next(Agenda,Current,Rest),
    children(Current,Children),
    add(Children,Rest,NewAgenda),
    search(NewAgenda,Goal).
```

In this program, we have abstracted from the way the agenda is represented. Furthermore, as remarked above, by specifying the order in which nodes are added to and removed from the agenda, we obtain specific search strategies. In the Staatsgalerie example, doors marked most recently are tried first. In other words, the agenda is a *last in–first out* datastructure, or a *stack*. In this example, it seems the most reasonable approach, because it minimises the amount of walking needed to backtrack to another room. The result is a *depth-first* search procedure, moving away as quickly as possible from the initial room, only coming closer again when backtracking.

On the other hand, the shortest path between your initial position and your friend is Miró-Mondriaan, while you finally reach your friend along the path Miró-Léger-Matisse-Mondriaan[15]. You would have found your friend sooner if you would have examined all rooms next to Miró first. But suppose your friend was two rooms away, e.g. in the Matisse room? Well, in that case you would have gone to the rooms next to Miró (Léger and Mondriaan), and then to all rooms next to those (Kupka, Kandinsky and Matisse). That is, doors marked most recently are tried last: a *first in–first out* strategy, implemented by a datastructure called a *queue*. Thus you would have found your friend along one of the two shortest paths (Miró-Léger-Matisse). This second method is an example of *breadth-first* search.

Finally, a third approach called *best-first* search orders the doors to be tried next according to some criterion called a *heuristic*. For instance, suppose you saw your friend last in the Mondriaan room. In this case it would be wise to overrule the default clockwise ordering, and to try Mondriaan before Léger. Consequently, you would have found your friend along the path Miró-Mondriaan-Matisse. In the following sections, we will take a closer look at depth-first and breadth-first search. The use of heuristics will be studied in Chapter 6.

5.2 Depth-first search

We obtain a depth-first search strategy if the agenda is implemented as a last in–first out datastructure. The obvious way to do this in Prolog is to represent the agenda by a list of nodes, and to add and remove nodes from the front of the list:

```
% depth-first search
search_df([Goal|Rest],Goal):-
    goal(Goal).
search_df([Current|Rest],Goal):-
    children(Current,Children),
    append(Children,Rest,NewAgenda),
    search_df(NewAgenda,Goal).
```

The `children/2` predicate finds all children of a given node. If arcs in the search space are defined as before by the `arc/2` predicate, we could define `children/2` as

```
children(Node,Children):-
    findall(C,arc(Node,C),Children).
```

In this way, all children of the current node are generated and stored on the agenda before examining the next node.

This depth-first search program can be refined in several ways, of which we will consider two: returning a path to the goal, and loop detection. In the above implementation,

---

[15]Here, we refer to the resultant path, ignoring backtracking.

it is impossible to return a path if we discover a goal node on the agenda, because we do not know how that goal node was reached. Instead of putting a single node on the agenda, we will store a complete path to that node. This is simply accomplished by changing the `children/2` predicate as follows:

```
children([Node|Path],Children):-
    findall([C,Node|Path],arc(Node,C),Children).
```

Of course, the `goal/1` predicate must be changed accordingly, because its argument is now a path instead of a single node. A query now takes the form

```
?-search_df([[InitialNode]],PathToGoal).
```

The second refinement concerns loop detection. In order to check whether a node has been investigated before, we must maintain a list of visited nodes. We only add nodes to the agenda which do not already occur on this list (or on the agenda):

```
% depth-first search with loop detection
search_df_loop([Goal|Rest],Visited,Goal):-
    goal(Goal).
search_df_loop([Current|Rest],Visited,Goal):-
    children(Current,Children),
    add_df(Children,Rest,Visited,NewAgenda),
    search_df_loop(NewAgenda,[Current|Visited],Goal).

add_df([],Agenda,Visited,Agenda).
add_df([Child|Rest],OldAgenda,Visited,[Child|NewAgenda]):-
    not element(Child,OldAgenda),
    not element(Child,Visited),
    add_df(Rest,OldAgenda,Visited,NewAgenda).
add_df([Child|Rest],OldAgenda,Visited,NewAgenda):-
    element(Child,OldAgenda),
    add_df(Rest,OldAgenda,Visited,NewAgenda).
add_df([Child|Rest],OldAgenda,Visited,NewAgenda):-
    element(Child,Visited),
    add_df(Rest,OldAgenda,Visited,NewAgenda).
```

Note that the combination of loop detection and path construction allows the following optimisation: instead of maintaining complete paths to a node on the agenda and the list of visited nodes, we only store a node together with its parent. Once we encounter a goal, all its parents are on the list of visited nodes, which allows us to reconstruct the path.

Exercise 5.1. Modify the predicate `search_df_loop/3` such that it reconstructs the path to a goal in this way.

We now analyse depth-first search with respect to completeness, optimality and efficiency. A search strategy is *complete* if it is guaranteed to find every goal. Obviously, any exhaustive strategy is complete for finite search spaces. However, in an infinite search space depth-first search might get trapped in an infinite branch before having found all the solutions. For instance, reconsider the infinite SLD-tree in fig. 3.2. A left-to-right depth-first search strategy would dive deeper and deeper into the tree, taking the left branch at every node, and never find the goals in the branches to the right. So, *depth-first search is, in general, incomplete*. Since Prolog itself employs depth-first search, Prolog is also incomplete. Often, however, the incompleteness of Prolog can be avoided by reordering the clauses such that goals are found before infinite branches (for instance, by putting the recursive clause last), and to cut away the infinite parts of the search space.

If there is no cost function, a search strategy is optimal if it is guaranteed to reach any goal along the shortest path possible. The Staatsgalerie example already showed that this is not true for depth-first search: you found your friend but, while she was in a room next to your initial position, you finally reached that room through two other rooms. Thus, *depth-first search does not always find a shortest solution path*. Finally, we can estimate the memory requirements for depth-first search as follows. Suppose we are searching a tree in which each node has, on the average, B children. The number B is known as the *branching factor*. Generating the children of a node adds B nodes to the agenda. We are interested in the following question: if a goal is found at depth n (i.e. the path from the root to the goal has length n), how many nodes are there on the agenda? Since at each level only the children of a single node are generated, the size of the agenda is of the order $B \times n$, that is, a linear function of the depth of the tree. The time complexity of depth-first search is of the order B^n, since the runtime is proportional to the number of nodes searched, and in the worst case the goal is found in the last branch, after searching B^n nodes. Of course, we cannot hope to achieve any better for blind exhaustive search!

In practice, depth-first search is only implemented as above if loop detection is an absolute must. Otherwise, the agenda is represented *implicitly* by means of Prolog's internal goal stack. Children of a given node are generated one at a time, by means of Prolog's backtracking mechanism, and examined immediately upon generation:

```
% depth-first search by means of backtracking
search_bt(Goal,Goal):-
    goal(Goal).
search_bt(Current,Goal):-
    arc(Current,Child),
    search_bt(Child,Goal).
```

If there is a chance that the search program gets trapped in an infinite loop, it might be a good idea to employ a predefined *depth bound*:

```
% backtracking depth-first search with depth bound
search_d(D,Goal,Goal):-
    goal(Goal).
search_d(D,Current,Goal):-
    D>0, D1 is D-1,
    arc(Current,Child),
    search_d(D1,Child,Goal).
```

In this way the search process is guaranteed to halt, but solutions which appear beyond the depth bound are missed.

Iterative deepening is a form of depth-first search which employs a depth bound that is increased on each iteration. That is, after performing a depth-first search with depth bound d, search starts all over again from the starting nodes with an increased depth bound $d+n$. The predicate `search_id/2` implements iterative deepening for $n=1$.

```
% iterative deepening
search_id(First,Goal):-
    search_id(1,First,Goal).            % start with depth 1

search_id(D,Current,Goal):-
    search_d(D,Current,Goal).
search_id(D,Current,Goal):-
    D1 is D+1,                          % increase depth
    search_id(D1,Current,Goal).
```

A big advantage of iterative deepening over simple depth-first search is that iterative deepening is complete: it will find all the goals at depth d and less before proceeding to depth $d+n$. Moreover, if we set the depth increment n to 1, iterative deepening is also optimal: it will find shorter paths first. A disadvantage of iterative deepening is that upper parts of the search space are searched more than once (and goals in those upper parts are found more than once as well).

5.3 Breadth-first search

Breadth-first search is realised by implementing the agenda as a first in–first out datastructure. That is, while removing nodes from the front of the list, they are added at the end:

```
% breadth-first search
search_bf([Goal|Rest],Goal):-
    goal(Goal).
search_bf([Current|Rest],Goal):-
    children(Current,Children),
    append(Rest,Children,NewAgenda),
    search_bf(NewAgenda,Goal).
```

Exercise 5.2. Implement the predicate `term_write_bf/1`, which writes the tree represented by a term from the root downward (as opposed to the predicate `term_write/1` of section 4.1, which writes from left to right). Employ breadth-first search with two agendas, one for nodes at depth n and the other for nodes at depth $n+1$.

In breadth-first search, the agenda is implemented as a queue. This means that the nodes on the agenda are ordered according to increasing depth: all the nodes on depth n occur before the nodes on depth $n+1$. This has profound consequences with regard to the properties of breadth-first search. First of all, *breadth-first search is complete*, even for infinite search spaces. This is so because every goal on depth n will be found before descending to depth $n+1$. Secondly, *breadth-first search always finds a shortest solution path*. It may seem that breadth-first search is much better than depth-first search. However, like every coin this one has a reverse side also: the number of nodes at depth n is B^n, such that breadth-first search requires much more memory than depth-first search.

We will now show how to change Prolog into a *complete* SLD prover, by employing breadth-first search. We start from the meta-interpreter `prove_r/1` given in section 3.8:

```
prove_r(true):-!.
prove_r((A,B)):-!,
    clause(A,C),
    conj_append(C,B,D),
    prove_r(D).
prove_r(A):-
    clause(A,B),
    prove_r(B).
```

As explained in that section, this meta-interpreter operates on the complete resolvent, which is exactly what we need. This predicate is turned into an agenda-based depth-first search procedure as follows:

```
% agenda-based version of prove_r/1
prove_df(Goal):-
    prove_df_a([Goal]).

prove_df_a([true|Agenda]).
prove_df_a([(A,B)|Agenda]):-!,
    findall(D,(clause(A,C),conj_append(C,B,D)),Children),
    append(Children,Agenda,NewAgenda),
    prove_df_a(NewAgenda).
prove_df_a([A|Agenda]):-
    findall(B,clause(A,B),Children),
    append(Children,Agenda,NewAgenda),
    prove_df_a(NewAgenda).
```

The changes are relatively straightforward: all solutions to the calls in the bodies of the second and third `prove_r` clauses are collected by means of the predicate `findall/3`, and added to the front of the agenda.

In order to search in a breadth-first fashion, we swap the first two arguments of the `append/3` literals. One additional improvement is required, since `prove_df/1` succeeds for every proof that can be found, but it does not return an answer substitution for the variables in the query. This is because the call `findall(X,G,L)` creates new variables for the unbound variables in the instantiation of X before putting it in the list L. In order to obtain an answer substitution, we should maintain the agenda as a list of pairs

```
a(Literals,OrigGoal)
```

where `OrigGoal` is a copy of the original goal. To illustrate this, suppose the following clauses are given:

```
likes(peter,Y):-student(Y),friendly(Y).
likes(X,Y):-friend(Y,X).
student(maria).
student(paul).
friendly(maria).
friend(paul,peter).
```

Below, the agenda obtained after each breadth-first search iteration is given for the query
?-likes(X,Y):

```
[ a((student(Y1),friendly(Y1)), likes(peter,Y1)),
  a(friend(Y2,X2), likes(X2,Y2)) ]
```

```
[ a(friend(Y2,X2), likes(X2,Y2))
  a(friendly(maria), likes(peter,maria)),
  a(friendly(paul), likes(peter,paul)) ]
```

```
[ a(friendly(maria), likes(peter,maria)),
  a(friendly(paul), likes(peter,paul)),
  a(true, likes(peter,paul)) ]
```

```
[ a(friendly(paul), likes(peter,paul)),
  a(true, likes(peter,paul)),
  a(true, likes(peter,maria)) ]
```

```
[ a(true, likes(peter,paul)),
  a(true, likes(peter,maria)) ]
```

Here, Y1, X2 and Y2 denote new variables introduced by findall/3. It can be clearly
seen that for each item a(R,G) on the agenda, R and G share the right variables — thus,
whenever the resolvent gets more instantiated during the proof, the corresponding copy of
the goal is instantiated correspondingly. In particular, if the empty clause is found on the
agenda in the form of a term a(true,Goal), then Goal will contain the correct answer
substitutions.

The final, complete SLD prover looks as follows:

```
% breadth-first version of prove_r/1 + answer substitution
prove_bf(Goal):-
    prove_bf_a([a(Goal,Goal)],Goal).

prove_bf_a([a(true,Goal)|Agenda],Goal).
prove_bf_a([a((A,B),G)|Agenda],Goal):-!,
    findall(a(D,G),
            (clause(A,C),conj_append(C,B,D)),
            Children),
    append(Agenda,Children,NewAgenda),    % breadth-first
    prove_bf_a(NewAgenda,Goal).
prove_bf_a([a(A,G)|Agenda],Goal):-
    findall(a(B,G),clause(A,B),Children),
    append(Agenda,Children,NewAgenda),    % breadth-first
    prove_bf_a(NewAgenda,Goal).
```

Notice that this program is able to find alternative solutions, since it will backtrack from the first clause into the third and, being unable to find a clause for the predicate `true/0`, `findall/3` will generate an empty list of children and search will proceed with the rest of the agenda.

Exercise 5.3. Consider the following program:

```
brother(peter,paul).
brother(adrian,paul).
brother(X,Y):-brother(Y,X).
brother(X,Y):-brother(X,Z),brother(Z,Y).
```

Compare and explain the behaviour of `prove_bf/1` and Prolog on the query `?-brother(peter,adrian)`. Can you re-order the clauses, such that Prolog succeeds?

As a second, related example of a breadth-first search program, we give a program for finding refutation proofs in full clausal logic. Object-level clauses are given by the predicate `cl/1`. Note that `true` denotes the empty body, while `false` denotes the empty head; thus, `false:-true` denotes the empty clause.

```
% refute_bf(Clause) <- Clause is refuted by clauses
%                      defined by cl/1
%                      (breadth-first search strategy)
refute_bf(Clause):-
    refute_bf_a([a(Clause,Clause)],Clause).

refute_bf_a([a((false:-true),Clause)|Rest],Clause).
refute_bf_a([a(A,C)|Rest],Clause):-
    findall(a(R,C),(cl(Cl),resolve(A,Cl,R)),Children),
    append(Rest,Children,NewAgenda),     % breadth-first
    refute_bf_a(NewAgenda,Clause).

% resolve(C1,C2,R) <- R is the resolvent of C1 and C2.
resolve((H1:-B1),(H2:-B2),(ResHead:-ResBody)):-
    resolve(H1,B2,R1,R2),
    disj_append(R1,H2,ResHead),
    conj_append(B1,R2,ResBody).
resolve((H1:-B1),(H2:-B2),(ResHead:-ResBody)):-
    resolve(H2,B1,R2,R1),
    disj_append(H1,R2,ResHead),
    conj_append(R1,B2,ResBody).

resolve((A;B),C,B,E):-
    conj_remove_one(A,C,E).
resolve((A;B),C,(A;D),E):-
    resolve(B,C,D,E).
resolve(A,C,false,E):-
    conj_remove_one(A,C,E).
```

```
%%% disj_append/3, conj_remove_one/3: see Appendix A.2
```

For instance, given the following clauses:

```
cl((bachelor(X);married(X):-man(X),adult(X))).
cl((has_wife(X):-man(X),married(X))).
cl((false:-has_wife(paul))).
cl((man(paul):-true)).
cl((adult(paul):-true)).
```

and the query `?-refute_bf((false:-bachelor(X)))` (refute that no-one is a bachelor), the program answers `X=paul`. Note that there are many proofs for this answer!

Exercise 5.4. Extend the meta-interpreter, such that it returns a proof tree (see section 3.8). In order to ensure correct variable substitutions, each item on the agenda must be extended with a partial proof tree.

As a search program, the above program is complete. As a theorem prover, however, the program is incomplete. This is due to the resolution strategy used, in which every resolvent has at least one given clause as its parent. This strategy is called *input* resolution; it is refutation complete for definite clauses, but not for indefinite clauses.

5.4 Forward chaining

Search programs involving if-then rules, such as meta-interpreters and theorem provers, can use these rules in either of two directions: from body to head or forward, and from head to body or backward. The meta-interpreters we encountered up till now apply clauses backward, just like Prolog; they are said to perform *backward chaining*. For checking if a given formula follows logically from a given theory, this is usually the best strategy.

However, in some cases we must rather perform *forward chaining*, because we do not have a goal to start from. For instance, consider the problem of constructing a model of a given theory. It would not be feasible to generate all the ground atoms in the Herbrand base and follow the chains back to the theory. Rather, we would generate the model incrementally by forward chaining. The procedure is as follows:

  (*i*)   search for a violated clause of which the body is true in the current model,
          but the head is not (such a clause is said to *fire*);
  (*ii*) add a literal from the head to the model[16].

By step (*ii*), the head (a disjunction) is made true in the model, so that this clause is no longer violated. The procedure iterates back to step (*i*); if no violated clauses remain, the model is complete.

The program for model generation by forward chaining is given below. It is a fairly simple forward chainer, in the sense that it simply chooses the first clause which fires. More

---

[16]We will assume for the moment that the head literals are ground by the substitution which makes the body true; a more detailed discussion follows below.

sophisticated forward chainers use *conflict resolution* strategies in order to choose among the rules which fire at a certain stage.

```
% model(M) <- M is a model of the clauses defined by cl/1
model(M):-
     model([],M).

model(M0,M):-
     is_violated(Head,M0),!,  % instance of violated clause
     disj_element(L,Head),    % L: ground literal from head
     model([L|M0],M).         % add L to the model
model(M,M).                   % no more violated clauses

is_violated(H,M):-
     cl((H:-B)),
     satisfied_body(B,M),     % grounds the variables
     not satisfied_head(H,M).

satisfied_body(true,M).       % body is a conjunction
satisfied_body(A,M):-
     element(A,M).
satisfied_body((A,B),M):-
     element(A,M),
     satisfied_body(B,M).

satisfied_head(A,M):-         % head is a disjunction
     element(A,M).
satisfied_head((A;B),M):-
     element(A,M).
satisfied_head((A;B),M):-
     satisfied_head(B,M).

%%% disj_element/2: see Appendix A.2
```

Given the following clauses:

```
cl((married(X);bachelor(X):-man(X),adult(X))).
cl((has_wife(X):-married(X),man(X))).
cl((man(paul):-true)).
cl((adult(paul):-true)).
```

and the query ?-model(M), the program constructs the following models (on backtracking):

```
M = [has_wife(paul),married(paul),adult(paul),man(paul)];

M = [bachelor(paul),adult(paul),man(paul)]
```

Notice that these are the two minimal models of the program.

Exercise 5.5. Give the remaining models of the program.

Not every model generated by `model/1` is minimal. Consider the following set of clauses:

```
cl((likes(peter,maria):-true)).
cl((student(maria):-true)).
cl((teacher(X);friendly(Y):-likes(X,Y),student(Y))).
cl((friendly(Y):-teacher(X),likes(X,Y))).
```

`is_violated/2` will first succeed for the third clause, returning the instantiated head `teacher(peter);friendly(maria)`. The first literal in this head will be added to the model. Next, the fourth clause is violated, and `friendly(maria)` is added to the model. This results in the following model:

```
[friendly(maria),teacher(peter),
 student(maria),likes(peter,maria)]
```

However, this is not a minimal model since `teacher(peter)` can be removed from it, yielding the model

```
[friendly(maria),student(maria),likes(peter,maria)]
```

which will be returned as the second answer.

Exercise 5.6. Are all minimal models always constructed by `model/1`?

It should be noted that the program only works properly for a restricted class of clauses, namely those clauses for which grounding the body also grounds the head. Otherwise, a head literal from a violated clause might still contain variables. Adding a non-ground literal to the model could result in incorrect behaviour. Consider the following set of clauses:

```
cl((man(X);woman(X):-true)).
cl((false:-man(maria))).
cl((false:-woman(peter))).
```

Since the first clause is violated by the empty model, the program will attempt to add `man(X)` to the model. This leads to the second clause being violated, and since this clause has an empty head, it cannot be satisfied by adding a literal to the model. Upon backtracking `woman(X)` is tried instead, but this leads to a similar problem with the third clause. Consequently, `model/1` will fail to construct a model, although there exists one, namely `{man(peter),woman(maria)}`.

The solution is to add a literal to the body of the first clause, which serves to enumerate the possible values for X:

```
cl((man(X);woman(X):-person(X))).
cl((person(maria):-true)).
cl((person(peter):-true)).
cl((false:-man(maria))).
cl((false:-woman(peter))).
```

In this way, the first clause is violated only under the substitutions {X→peter} and {X→maria}. Thus, all literals which are added to the model are ground, and the program constructs the correct model

```
[man(peter),person(peter),woman(maria),person(maria)]
```

Clauses of which all variables in the head occur also in the body are called *range-restricted*. Every set of clauses can be transformed into a set of range-restricted clauses by adding domain predicates enumerating the domains of variables, as above. The two sets of clauses are equivalent in the sense that there exists a one-to-one correspondence between their models:

- any model of the original clauses provides an enumeration of all the domains;
- any model of the range-restricted clauses can be transformed to a model of the original clauses by dropping the domain literals.

Obviously, model/1 loops if the model being constructed is infinite. This will happen, for instance, with the following set of clauses, representing a range-restricted version of the append predicate:

```
cl((append([],Y,Y):-list(Y))).
cl((append([X|Xs],Ys,[X|Zs]):-thing(X),append(Xs,Ys,Zs))).
cl((list([]):-true)).
cl((list([X|Y]):-thing(X),list(Y))).
cl((thing(a):-true)).
cl((thing(b):-true)).
cl((thing(c):-true)).
```

Instead of the complete, infinite model, we might be interested in a subset over a universe of lists up to a given length. Such a 'submodel' can be computed by a forward chaining procedure which stops after a prespecified number of steps. In this way, the procedure gets more of a 'breadth-first' flavour. The program is given below:

```
% model_d(D,M) <- M is a submodel of the clauses
%                 defined by cl/1
model_d(D,M):-
    model_d(D,[],M).

model_d(0,M,M).
model_d(D,M0,M):-
    D>0,D1 is D-1,
    findall(H,is_violated(H,M0),Heads),
    satisfy_clauses(Heads,M0,M1),
    model_d(D1,M1,M).

satisfy_clauses([],M,M).
satisfy_clauses([H|Hs],M0,M):-
    disj_element(D,H),
    satisfy_clauses(Hs,[D|M0],M).
```

model/1 is replaced by model_d/2, which has an additional depth parameter. On each iteration, all the violated clauses are generated and satisfied.

Below, we illustrate the operation of the program on the above set of clauses, setting the depth to 4:

```
?-model_d(4,M)
M = [ list([a,c,a]), list([a,c,b]), list([a,c,c]),    % D=4 %
        list([a,b,a]), list([a,b,b]), list([a,b,c]),
        list([a,a,a]), list([a,a,b]), list([a,a,c]),
        list([b,c,a]), list([b,c,b]), list([b,c,c]),
        list([b,b,a]), list([b,b,b]), list([b,b,c]),
        list([b,a,a]), list([b,a,b]), list([b,a,c]),
        list([c,c,a]), list([c,c,b]), list([c,c,c]),
        list([c,b,a]), list([c,b,b]), list([c,b,c]),
        list([c,a,a]), list([c,a,b]), list([c,a,c]),
        append([a],[a],[a,a]), append([a],[b],[a,b]),
        append([a],[c],[a,c]), append([a,c],[],[a,c]),
        append([a,b],[],[a,b]), append([a,a],[],[a,a]),
        append([b],[a],[b,a]), append([b],[b],[b,b]),
        append([b],[c],[b,c]), append([b,c],[],[b,c]),
        append([b,b],[],[b,b]), append([b,a],[],[b,a]),
        append([c],[a],[c,a]), append([c],[b],[c,b]),
        append([c],[c],[c,c]), append([c,c],[],[c,c]),
        append([c,b],[],[c,b]), append([c,a],[],[c,a]),
        append([],[c,a],[c,a]), append([],[c,b],[c,b]),
        append([],[c,c],[c,c]), append([],[b,a],[b,a]),
        append([],[b,b],[b,b]), append([],[b,c],[b,c]),
        append([],[a,a],[a,a]), append([],[a,b],[a,b]),
        append([],[a,c],[a,c]),
        list([a,c]), list([a,b]), list([a,a]),         % D=3 %
        list([b,c]), list([b,b]), list([b,a]),
        list([c,c]), list([c,b]), list([c,a]),
        append([a],[],[a]), append([b],[],[b]),
        append([c],[],[c]), append([],[c],[c]),
        append([],[b],[b]), append([],[a],[a]),
        list([a]), list([b]), list([c]),               % D=2 %
        append([],[],[]),
        thing(c), thing(b), thing(a),                  % D=1 %
        list([])   ]
```

At depth 1, only domain clauses are satisfied; at depth 2 the first `append` literal appears. Depths 3 and 4 add `list` literals for all lists of length 2 and 3, and `append` literals for all lists of length 1 and 2, respectively.

Further reading

Korf (1987) gives a comprehensive overview of search methods in Artificial Intelligence. He is also the originator of the iterative deepening search strategy (Korf, 1985). The model generation program in section 5.4 is adapted from (Manthey & Bry, 1988).

R.E. KORF (1985), 'Depth-first iterative deepening: an optimal admissible tree search', *Artificial Intelligence* **27**: 97-109.

R.E. KORF (1987), 'Search'. In *Encyclopedia of Artificial Intelligence*, S.C. Shapiro (ed.), pp. 994-998, John Wiley.

R. MANTHEY & F. BRY (1988), 'SATCHMO: a theorem prover implemented in Prolog'. In E. Lusk & R. Overbeek (eds), *Proc. 9th International Conference on Automated Deduction*, Lecture Notes in Computer Science 310, pp. 415-434, Springer-Verlag.

6
Informed search

The search strategies of the previous chapter do not make any assumptions about the plausibility of a certain node in the search space leading to a goal. Such a form of search is called *blind* search. Alternatively, search strategies which **do** make such assumptions are called *informed* search strategies. The extra information which is incorporated in the search process is provided by an evaluation function *h* called a *heuristic*, which estimates how far a given node is from a goal. This information can be used in several ways. If we use it to order the nodes on the agenda, such that most promising nodes are tried first, the resulting search method is called *best-first* search. In section 6.2, we will discuss a complete variant of best-first search called the *A algorithm*, and investigate the conditions under which this algorithm is optimal. In section 6.3, we will discuss non-exhaustive informed search strategies, that can be derived from best-first search by limiting the size of the agenda.

6.1 Best-first search

We will assume that a predicate `eval/2` is defined, which returns for a given node in the search space an estimate of the distance between that node and a goal node. The children of the current node are added to the agenda according to their heuristic evaluation (lowest values first). Thus, the agenda will always be sorted.

```
% best-first search
% goal/1, children/2 and eval/2 depend on
% the search problem at hand
search_bstf([Goal|Rest],Goal):-
    goal(Goal).
search_bstf([Current|Rest],Goal):-
    children(Current,Children),
    add_bstf(Children,Rest,NewAgenda),
    search_bstf(NewAgenda,Goal).
```

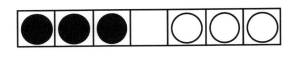

Figure 6.1. Initial board position.

```
% add_bstf(A,B,C) <- C contains the elements of A and B
%                    (B and C sorted according to eval/2)
add_bstf([],Agenda,Agenda).
add_bstf([Child|Children],OldAgenda,NewAgenda):-
    add_one(Child,OldAgenda,TmpAgenda),
    add_bstf(Children,TmpAgenda,NewAgenda).

% add_one(S,A,B) <- B is A with S inserted acc. to eval/2
add_one(Child,OldAgenda,NewAgenda):-
    eval(Child,Value),
    add_one(Value,Child,OldAgenda,NewAgenda).

add_one(Value,Child,[],[Child]).
add_one(Value,Child,[Node|Rest],[Child,Node|Rest]):-
    eval(Node,V),
    Value<V.
add_one(Value,Child,[Node|Rest],[Node|NewRest]):-
    eval(Node,V),
    Value>=V,
    add_one(Value,Child,Rest,NewRest).
```

add_bstf/3 operates by inserting the new children one by one in the current agenda. Note that if the list of children were already sorted, it could more efficiently be **merged** with the current agenda.

Exercise 6.1. Suppose the call children(Current,Children) results in an ordered list of children. Write a predicate merge/3 which directly merges this list with the current agenda.

As an application of best-first search, consider the following puzzle. We have a board consisting of seven consecutive squares, three black tiles and three white tiles, initially placed on the board as in fig. 6.1. The goal is to move the tiles in such a way that the black tiles are to the right of the white tiles (the position of the empty square is immaterial). Each move consists of moving one tile into the empty square, which is allowed if there are at

When not to use lists

Recall (section 1.3) that [b,b,b,e,w,w,w] is an alternative notation for the term
.(b,.(b,.(b,.(e,.(w,.(w,.(w,[]))))))). This term contains, besides the
seven constants in the linear notation, one additional constant ('[]') and seven
functors ('.'), each with two arguments. In contrast, a 'flat' term
p(b,b,b,e,w,w,w) contains only one additional functor, with seven arguments.
Recursive datastructures like lists are useful if the number of items to be stored is
not fixed, but they require significantly more storage space. In general, if the
number of items is fixed, a non-recursive datastructure is preferred as far as memory
is concerned. Given a term T holding the items, the call arg(N,T,A) retrieves the
Nth argument A. However, arg/3 requires N to be instantiated, and cannot be used
to generate all arguments on backtracking. Therefore, lists are sometimes used
even if the nature of the data is non-recursive.

most two other tiles in between. The cost of such a move is 1 if there are no tiles in
between, and equals the number of tiles jumped over otherwise.

This puzzle defines a search space, in which nodes are board positions and arcs are single
moves. We choose a simple list representation for board positions: e.g.
[b,b,b,e,w,w,w] represents the starting position of fig. 6.1. The following predicates
examine and manipulate board positions:

```
% get_tile(P,N,T) <- pos. P contains tile T at square N
get_tile(Pos,N,T):-
    get_tile(Pos,1,N,T).

get_tile([X|Xs],N,N,X).
get_tile([X|Xs],N0,N,Y):-
    N1 is N0+1,
    get_tile(Xs,N1,N,Y).

% replace(P,N,T,P1) <- P1 is P with tile T at square N
replace([X|Xs],1,Y,[Y|Xs]).
replace([X|Xs],N,Y,[X|Zs]):-
    N>1, N1 is N-1,
    replace(Xs,N1,Y,Zs).
```

We use the above best-first search procedure, with a number of changes. First, rather
than returning the goal position found, the program should construct a sequence of moves by
which the goal position is reached. Therefore, nodes that are examined during the search
process are collected in the list Visited. After a goal position has been found, the
solution path and its total cost are reconstructed from the list Visited by means of the
predicate construct_moves/6.

Secondly, the items on the agenda are represented as pairs v(Value,Move), where
Value is the heuristic evaluation of the position reached by Move. Children of the current
position are generated by means of the setof/3 predicate, which yields a **sorted** list. By

putting the heuristic `Value` as the first argument of the functor `v`, the list `Children` is therefore sorted according to increasing heuristic value. Therefore, this list can be simply merged with the current agenda to yield the new agenda. The program thus looks as follows:

```
% tiles(M,C) <- moves M lead to a goal position at cost C
%                (best-first search strategy)
tiles(Moves,Cost):-
    start(Start),
    eval(Start,Value),
    tiles_a([v(Value,Start)],Final,[],Visited),
    construct_moves(Final,Visited,[],Moves,0,Cost).

% tiles_a(A,M,V0,V) <- goal position can be reached from
%                      one of the positions on A with last
%                      move M (best-first strategy)
tiles_a([v(V,LastMove)|Rest],LastMove,Visited,Visited):-
    goal(LastMove).
tiles_a([v(V,LastMove)|Rest],Goal,Visited0,Visited):-
    show_move(LastMove,V),
    setof0(v(Value,NextMove),
           ( move(LastMove,NextMove),
             eval(NextMove,Value) ),
           Children),
    merge(Children,Rest,NewAgenda),    % best-first
    tiles_a(NewAgenda,Goal,[LastMove|Visited0],Visited).

%%% merge/3: see exercise 6.1
```

`setof0/3` is a variant of `setof/3` which succeeds with the empty list if no solutions can be found (see Appendix A.2).

A move from `OldPos` to `NewPos` is represented by a triple

```
m(OldPos,NewPos,Cost)
```

where `Cost` specifies the cost of the move. According to the principle of data abstraction, this representation is kept local to the following predicates:

```
% move(m(X,P,Y),m(P,NP,C)) <- position NP can be reached
%                             from position P in one move
%                             at cost C
move(m(OldPos,Pos,OldCost),m(Pos,NewPos,Cost)):-
    get_tile(Pos,Ne,e),get_tile(Pos,Nbw,BW),not(BW=e),
    Diff is abs(Ne-Nbw),Diff<4,
    replace(Pos,Ne,BW,Pos1),
    replace(Pos1,Nbw,e,NewPos),
    ( Diff=1     -> Cost=1
    ; otherwise -> Cost is Diff-1 ).

start(m(noparent,[b,b,b,e,w,w,w],0)).
```

```
% reconstruct total cost and path from visited nodes
construct_moves(m(noparent,Start,0),V,Ms,[Start|Ms],C,C).
construct_moves(m(P,Pos,C),Visited,Ms0,Ms,C0,C):-
    on(m(GP,P,C1),Visited),   % GP is parent of P
    C1 is C0+C,
    construct_moves(m(GP,P,C1),Visited,[Pos|Ms0],Ms,C1,C).

show_move(m(P,Pos,C),Value):-
    write(Pos-Value),nl.
```

Finally, we have to choose a heuristic evaluation function. A first idea is to count, for each white tile, the number of black tiles to the left of it:

```
goal(Pos):-
    eval(Pos,0).

eval(Pos,Value):-
    bLeftOfw(Pos,Value).

bLeftOfw(Pos,Value):-
    findall((Nb,Nw),
            (get_tile(Pos,Nb,b),get_tile(Pos,Nw,w),Nb<Nw),
            L),
    length(L,Value).
```

Note that this program actually *counts* the number of solutions to the query

```
?-get_tile(Pos,Nb,b),get_tile(Pos,Nw,w),Nb<Nw.
```

by determining the length of the list that is returned by the second-order predicate `findall/3`.

Exercise 6.2. Rewrite `bLeftOfw/2` such that it uses only first-order predicates.

The program writes every move it considers on the screen, together with its heuristic evaluation. For instance, the query

```
?-tiles([b,b,b,e,w,w,w],M,C).
```

results in the following output:

```
[b,b,b,e,w,w,w]-9
[b,b,b,w,e,w,w]-9
[b,b,e,w,b,w,w]-8
[b,b,w,w,b,e,w]-7
[b,b,w,w,b,w,e]-7
[b,b,w,w,e,w,b]-6
[b,e,w,w,b,w,b]-4
```

```
[b,w,e,w,b,w,b]-4
[e,w,b,w,b,w,b]-3
[w,w,b,e,b,w,b]-2
[w,w,b,w,b,e,b]-1
M = [[b,b,b,e,w,w,w],[b,b,b,w,e,w,w],[b,b,e,w,b,w,w],
     [b,b,w,w,b,e,w],[b,b,w,w,b,w,e],[b,b,w,w,e,w,b],
     [b,e,w,w,b,w,b],[b,w,e,w,b,w,b],[e,w,b,w,b,w,b],
     [w,w,b,e,b,w,b],[w,w,b,w,b,e,b],[w,w,e,w,b,b,b]]
C = 15
```

Since the only moves that are considered are those that are on the final solution path, there is no backtracking. This seems to suggest that the heuristic works quite well. On the other hand, the first few moves seem a bit awkward: in particular, the first and the fourth move are relatively expensive.

Let's try another heuristic, which counts the number of tiles out of place: a wrong tile on the first or seventh square gives 3, on the second or sixth square 2, and on the third or fifth square 1.

```
eval(Pos,Value):-
    outOfPlace(Pos,1,0,Value).

outOfPlace(Pos,8,N,N).
outOfPlace(Pos,K,N0,N):-
    K<8, K1 is K+1,
    ( K<4,get_tile(Pos,K,b) -> N1 is N0-(K-4)
    ; K>4,get_tile(Pos,K,w) -> N1 is N0+(K-4)
    ; otherwise -> N1=N0 ),
    outOfPlace(Pos,K1,N1,N).
```

We get the following result:

```
[b,b,b,e,w,w,w]-12
[b,b,b,w,w,w,e]-9
[e,b,b,b,w,w,w]-9
[b,b,b,w,w,e,w]-10
[b,b,b,w,w,w,e]-9
[b,b,e,w,w,b,w]-9
[e,b,b,w,w,b,w]-7
[w,b,b,e,w,b,w]-7
[w,b,b,w,w,b,e]-4
[w,b,b,w,w,e,b]-4
[w,b,e,w,w,b,b]-3
[w,b,w,w,e,b,b]-2
M = [[b,b,b,e,w,w,w],[b,b,b,w,w,e,w],[b,b,e,w,w,b,w],
     [e,b,b,w,w,b,w],[w,b,b,e,w,b,w],[w,b,b,w,w,b,e],
     [w,b,b,w,w,e,b],[w,b,e,w,w,b,b],[w,b,w,w,e,b,b],
     [w,e,w,w,b,b,b]]
C = 14
```

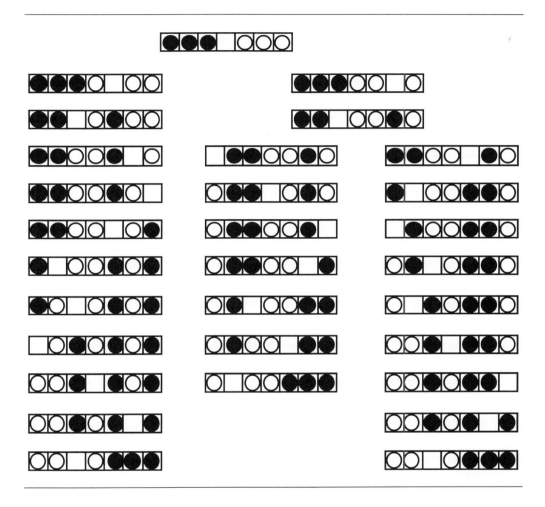

Figure 6.2. Solutions found for different heuristics.

We observe a couple of differences with the previous heuristic. First of all, there is backtracking: the first, second and fourth moves are not pursued any further. Furthermore, the solution found requires two moves less, and is also cheaper.

This improvement seems to suggest that an increased punishment for wrongly placed tiles might lead to an even cheaper solution. For instance, we could increase the punishment to 4, 3 and 2, respectively, by adapting the predicate `outOfPlace/4` (try it!). This leads to the following sequence of moves:

```
[b,b,b,e,w,w,w]-18
[b,b,b,w,w,w,e]-14
[e,b,b,b,w,w,w]-14
[b,b,b,w,w,e,w]-15
[b,b,e,w,w,b,w]-13
[b,b,w,w,e,b,w]-11
[b,e,w,w,b,b,w]-8
[e,b,w,w,b,b,w]-7
[w,b,e,w,b,b,w]-7
[w,e,b,w,b,b,w]-6
[e,w,b,w,b,b,w]-6
[w,w,b,e,b,b,w]-6
[w,w,b,w,b,b,e]-2
[w,w,b,w,b,e,b]-2
M = [[b,b,b,e,w,w,w],[b,b,b,w,w,e,w],[b,b,e,w,w,b,w],
     [b,b,w,w,e,b,w],[b,e,w,w,b,b,w],[e,b,w,w,b,b,w],
     [w,b,e,w,b,b,w],[w,e,b,w,b,b,w],[w,w,b,e,b,b,w],
     [w,w,b,w,b,b,e],[w,w,b,w,b,e,b],[w,w,e,w,b,b,b]]
C = 15
```

Obviously, this heuristic works no better than the previous two: it does not find an optimal solution, and it investigates more moves than the first heuristic. In fig. 6.2, the solutions found by the three heuristics are compared. In the next section, we will investigate the conditions under which a heuristic is guaranteed to find an optimal solution.

6.2 Optimal best-first search

Best-first search is an exhaustive search strategy, with a possible behaviour ranging from depth-first search to breadth-first search, depending on the heuristic used. By itself, best-first search is not complete: the heuristic might consistently assign lower values to the nodes on an infinite path. This is because the heuristic evaluation only takes into account an estimate of the distance to a goal, while we are actually interested in minimising the **total cost** of reaching a goal along a particular path. In order to obtain a complete best-first search algorithm, we use an evaluation function f consisting of two components:

$$f(n) = g(n) + h(n)$$

Here, $h(n)$ is the heuristic estimate of the cost of reaching a goal node from node n, as it was introduced before. $g(n)$ is the actual cost of reaching n from the starting node. Their sum $f(n)$ is used to order the nodes on the agenda.

A best-first search algorithm which uses such an evaluation function f to estimate the total cost of a path is called an *A algorithm*. An A algorithm is complete, since the depth count $g(n)$ will prevent search from getting trapped in an infinite path. In effect, the depth count will give the search strategy more of a breadth-first flavour. Indeed, breadth-first search is a special case of an A algorithm, with $h(n)=0$ for every node n. A disadvantage of A algorithms is the decreased efficiency associated with this breadth-first flavour.

Exercise 6.3. Change the `tiles` program into an A algorithm, by associating with each move the *g*-value of the position reached by that move (i.e. the cost of the path leading to that position, instead of the cost of the last move). Demonstrate the decreased efficiency of the search.

Breadth-first search is not only complete, it is also optimal: it always returns a shortest solution path[17]. Do A algorithms inherit this property from breadth-first search? Obviously, this depends on the function *h*: if a node n_1 on the cheapest path gets an *h*-estimate that is too high, other nodes will be tried instead, and a solution along a non-optimal path may be found first. We say that the heuristic was too *pessimistic* regarding n_1. Conversely, a heuristic which never assigns a value to a node that is higher than the actual cost of reaching a goal state from that node is called *optimistic*.

For instance, consider the first heuristic for the puzzle in the previous section, which counts for each white tile the number of black tiles to the left of it. Suppose one black tile has *w* white tiles to its right, which adds *w* to the heuristic value for that position. In order to reach a goal position, the black tile has to jump over some of the white tiles, while the remaining white tiles have to jump over the black tile; this has a cost of at least *w*. Therefore, this heuristic is optimistic. The second heuristic, calculating a weighted sum of tiles out of place, is also optimistic. For instance, suppose that a black tile is at the first square, then there are three white tiles to its right, over which it must jump. Analogously, if it is on the second square, then there are at least two white tiles to jump over. In contrast, the weights used in the third heuristic are too high.

Exercise 6.4. Find a position for which the third heuristic is too pessimistic.

It is possible to prove the following important result: *an A algorithm with an optimistic heuristic h always results in an optimal solution*. The resulting algorithm is called *A** (A star); both A* search and optimistic heuristics are said to be *admissible*. This should not be mistaken to suggest that better heuristics are more optimistic! On the contrary, a good heuristic is as pessimistic as possible, without becoming non-admissible. In general, if $h_1(n) \geq h_2(n)$ for any node *n*, then we call heuristic h_1 at least as *informed* as h_2. It can be shown that a more informed heuristic indeed searches a smaller part of the search space.

As a small example, consider the search space in fig. 6.3. The *h*-values for each node are as indicated; the cost per arc is 1. The heuristic is optimistic, so A* search will return the shortest path *start-r-s-goal*. However, this path is not found immediately: since both *p* and *q* have a lower *f*-value than *r*, they are investigated first. After *q* has been investigated, *s* is put on the agenda with *f*-value 3+1=4. Since *r* has a lower *f*-value of 3, it is the next one to be investigated. Now *s* will again be added to the agenda, this time with *f*-value 2+1=3! In fact, it is this latter *s* which, being on the optimal path, leads to the goal.

---

[17]If arcs can have different costs, breadth-first search does not necessarily return the **cheapest** solution path.

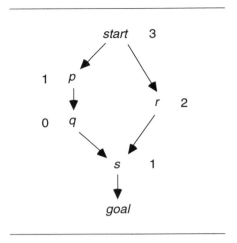

Figure 6.3. A heuristic which is not
monotonic.

Thus, although admissible search leads to optimal solutions, it is not necessarily the case that every node on an optimal path is immediately reached along that optimal path. In fig. 6.3, this is caused by 'local pessimism' of the heuristic, which estimates the cost of moving from *start* to *p* as 3–1=2, while the actual cost is 1. Indeed, if *p* would have an *h*-value of 2, *s* would have been reached the first time along the shortest path. This is true in general: if the heuristic estimates the cost of moving from one node to another optimistically, then any node is reached along the cheapest path first. This property is called *monotonicity*, since one can show that the *f*-values are monotonically non-decreasing along a path.

The first heuristic of the previous section is monotonic, while the second is not. This can be concluded from the following two evaluations:

    [b,b,e,w,w,b,w]-9
    [e,b,b,w,w,b,w]-7

The heuristic estimates the cost of this move as 9–7=2, while the actual cost is 1. Since monotonicity implies admissibility, the third heuristic is not monotonic either.

Exercise 6.5. Implement a Prolog meta-interpreter which employs an A search algorithm. Use *h*(*R*)= |*R*| (the number of literals in resolvent *R*) as heuristic. Is this heuristic admissible and monotonic?

6.3 Non-exhaustive informed search

The search strategies discussed until now are all *exhaustive*: they will all search the complete search space in the worst case. This is so because **all** children of a certain node will be put on the agenda, in some order. Exhaustive search is often impractical, since the size of the agenda grows exponentially with the search depth. The use of a heuristic offers the possibility of keeping only a selection of best nodes on the agenda. Such non-exhaustive search strategies are, of course, not guaranteed to be complete, and should only be applied in combination with a reasonably informed heuristic.

Beam search is a form of best-first search in which the number of nodes on the agenda is limited. In its most simple form, the agenda is of fixed size. Alternatively, one could allow the agenda to grow polynomially (instead of exponentially) with the search depth. The effect of this strategy is, that only a 'beam' of the search space is searched:

```
search_beam(Agenda,Goal):-
    search_beam(1,Agenda,[],Goal).

search_beam(D,[],NextLayer,Goal):-
    D1 is D+1,
    search_beam(D1,NextLayer,[],Goal).
search_beam(D,[Goal|Rest],NextLayer,Goal):-
    goal(Goal).
search_beam(D,[Current|Rest],NextLayer,Goal):-
    children(Current,Children),
    add_beam(D,Children,NextLayer,NewNextLayer),
    search_beam(D,Rest,NewNextLayer,Goal).
```

In this program, two agendas are maintained, one for the current level, and one for the children of the nodes on the current level. Once the current level is exhausted, the agenda's are swapped and the depth count is increased. The depth count is passed on to the predicate add_beam/4, in order to decide how many children to add to the agenda for the next level.

Exercise 6.6. Extend the program of exercise 6.3 with beam search with fixed agenda size. Demonstrate the non-optimality of the search strategy.

If we limit the size of the agenda to 1, we arrive at a search strategy called *hill-climbing*. It is also callled *greedy* search, since there is no backtracking involved. Hill-climbing is the type of search employed by a wanderer who wants to reach the top of a hill by always moving in the steepest direction. Clearly, she will reach the top of a hill (and never get off it), but it is not necessarily the highest one.

The predicate search_hc/2 below implements a hill-climbing search strategy. Instead of maintaining an agenda of nodes yet to be investigated, it maintains a single node in its first argument. Therefore, hill-climbing has some similarity with depth-first search with implicit agenda:

```
search_hc(Goal,Goal):-
    goal(Goal).
search_hc(Current,Goal):-
    children(Current,Children),
    select_best(Children,Best),
    search_hc(Best,Goal).
```

The predicate `select_best/2` selects the best child of the current node, according to the heuristic value to be optimised. To stress that backtracking is not needed after the best child has been selected, one can place a cut before the recursive call in the second clause.

Further reading

Nilsson (1980) gives a gentle introduction to the use of heuristics and their properties. (Pearl, 1984) is the main source for mathematical results on heuristics. The sliding tiles puzzle was taken from (Luger & Stubblefield, 1993).

G.F. LUGER & W.A. STUBBLEFIELD (1993), *Artificial Intelligence: Structures and Strategies for Complex Problem Solving*, Benjamin/Cummings, second edition.

N.J. NILSSON (1980), *Principles of Artificial Intelligence*, Tioga Press.

J. PEARL (1984), *Heuristics: Intelligent Search Strategies for Computer Problem Solving*, Addison-Wesley.

III

Advanced
reasoning techniques

In Part I, we introduced the formalism of clausal logic and showed how it can be used in practice to perform logical inferences. In Part II, we discussed the basic issues one encounters when writing a program to solve some reasoning task: how to represent the knowledge needed to solve the task, and how to search the space of possible solutions. In Part III, we will go beyond the power of clausal logic in a number of ways.

Why would one want to have a formalism more powerful than first-order clausal logic? One reason could be that we want to perform inferences that are simply not expressible in first-order clausal logic. We might want to express knowledge such as 'he inherited all his father's bad characteristics', which is a second-order statement (section 2.5). We might want to express statements like 'Peter believes his boss knows he is writing a book', where 'Peter's boss knows' is a *modality* of the formula 'Peter is writing a book', and 'Peter believes' is a modality of the formula 'Peter's boss knows Peter is writing a book'. We might want to reason about sequences of events happening over time. Each of these examples requires a specialised logic extending the syntax of first-order logic. Needless to say, this increased expressiveness also requires more powerful semantics and proof theory.

There are also reasoning tasks which use the language of clausal logic, but differ nonetheless from standard clausal logic in the validity of the conclusions drawn. For instance, the truth of a conclusion might not be guaranteed but only plausible, given the premises. Alternatively, a conclusion might be a general theory derived from a number of specific observations, a theory which might be falsified by new contradicting evidence.

Typically, such non-standard reasoning tasks require a more elaborate semantic and proof-theoretic characterisation than required for standard logical inference.

Thirdly, the knowledge required for the reasoning task might be available in non-logical form only: think of pictures, spoken or written text, or video images. In such cases, the reasoning task requires pre- and postprocessing stages, in which the non-logical data are converted to and from logical formulas.

In the following three chapters, we will encounter each of these three types of reasoning. Chapter 7 is devoted to reasoning with knowledge expressed in natural language. We demonstrate how to translate sentences like 'Socrates is human' and 'all humans are mortal', and questions like 'is Socrates mortal?' into clausal logic, and how to obtain a natural language sentence as the answer. In Chapter 8, we discuss a number of approaches to reasoning with incomplete information. Most of these approaches are of the second type, extending semantics and proof theory but not syntax of clausal logic; one approach extends syntax as well. We provide a detailed discussion of how these approaches are related. Finally, inductive reasoning is discussed in Chapter 9. Induction aims at completing partial knowledge about specific instances of a theory, and is therefore, although related to, much harder than the forms of reasoning with incomplete knowledge discussed in Chapter 8. We give an in-depth analysis of the problem, and develop two Prolog programs that can inductively infer simple predicate definitions from exampes.

7
Reasoning with natural language

A language which is used for communication between humans is commonly called a *natural language*, in order to distinguish it from an artificial computer language. Despite their apparent differences, artificial and natural language can be described by the same tools, some of which will be studied in this chapter.

Natural language can be described on a number of different levels:

(*i*)   *Prosody*: rhythm and intonation of spoken language;
(*ii*) *Phonology*: how to combine simple sounds (*phonemes*) in spoken language;
(*iii*) *Morphology*: how to build words from meaningful components (*morphemes*);
(*iv*) *Syntax*: how to build sentences from words;
(*v*)   *Semantics*: how to assign meaning to words and sentences;
(*vi*) *Pragmatics*: how to use sentences in communication.

Here, we are mainly concerned with written language, so we will not talk about prosody and phonology. Morphology tells us, for instance, that in English the plural of many nouns can be obtained by adding the suffix -s (house–houses, chair–chairs). Syntax allows us to distinguish well-formed sentences (like 'I sleep') from ill-formed ones (like 'me sleeps'), and to discover their grammatical structure. Semantics allows us to understand sentences like 'time flies like an arrow, but fruit flies like a banana'. Pragmatics tells us that 'yes' is in general not a very helpful answer to questions of the form 'do you know ...?'.

It should be noted that this distinction between different levels is not as clear-cut as it may seem. For instance, the sentences 'time flies like an arrow' and 'fruit flies like a banana' look very similar; yet, semantic analysis shows that they have a different grammatical structure: 'time (noun) flies (verb) like an arrow' in the first case, and 'fruit flies (noun) like (verb) a banana (noun phrase)' in the second. That is, both sentences have at least two possible grammatical structures, and we need semantics to prefer one over the other.

Without doubt, the language level which has been formalised most successfully is the syntactic level. The process of deriving the grammatical structure of a sentence is called *parsing*. The outcome of the parsing process is a *parse tree*, showing the grammatical constituents of the sentence, like verb phrase and noun phrase. This grammatical structure can be further used in the semantic analyis of the sentence. The reverse process, starting from a semantic representation and producing a sentence, is called *sentence generation*. It is applied in dialogue systems, where answers to queries must be formulated in natural language.

7.1   Grammars and parsing

The syntax of a language is specified by a *grammar*, which is a set of *grammar rules* of the form

```
Category1 --> Category2,Category3
Category2 --> [Terminal]
```

Here, `CategoryX` denotes a *syntactic category*, specifying the type of a sentence part (e.g. noun, noun phrase, etc.). The first rule states that a `Category2` followed by a `Category3` is a `Category1`. For instance, the fact that a sentence may consist of a noun phrase followed by a verb phrase is expressed by the rule

```
sentence --> noun_phrase,verb_phrase
```

A *terminal* is any word which occurs in the language. The second rule above assigns a syntactic category to a word. For instance:

```
noun --> [bicycle]
```

Syntactic categories are also called *non-terminals*.

A grammar which specifies a tiny bit of the English language is given below. As in clausal logic, grammar rules are separated by periods.

```
sentence              --> noun_phrase,verb_phrase.
noun_phrase           --> proper_noun.
noun_phrase           --> article,adjective,noun.
noun_phrase           --> article,noun.
verb_phrase           --> intransitive_verb.
verb_phrase           --> transitive_verb,noun_phrase.
article               --> [the].
adjective             --> [lazy].
adjective             --> [rapid].
proper_noun           --> [achilles].
noun                  --> [turtle].
intransitive_verb     --> [sleeps].
transitive_verb       --> [beats].
```

Some sentences generated by this grammar are: 'the lazy turtle sleeps', 'Achilles beats the turtle', and 'the rapid turtle beats Achilles'. The grammatical structure of these sentences can be described by a *parse tree*, which is a tree containing the words of the sentence as leaves, and the syntactic categories assigned to parts of the sentence as nodes (fig. 7.1).

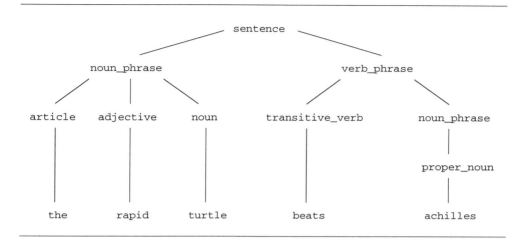

Figure 7.1. Parse tree for the sentence 'the rapid turtle beats Achilles'.

Exercise 7.1. Redraw this parse tree in the manner of an SLD proof tree, where 'resolvents' are partially parsed sentences such as
[the],[rapid],noun,verb_phrase
and 'clauses' are grammar rules.

Such a parse tree can be constructed by starting with the non-terminal sentence, and repeatedly replacing non-terminals by the righthand side of an applicable rule, until the given sentence is obtained as a sequence of terminals. This method is called *top-down parsing*. Alternatively, we could start with the sentence and look for parts of it which occur on the righthand side of a rule, and replace that part of the sentence with the non-terminal on the lefthand side of the rule, until we obtain the single non-terminal sentence. This procedure is called *bottom-up parsing*. It should be noted that both methods require search: at any stage, several rules might be applicable.

Exercise 7.2. Draw the search space generated by the above grammar for a top-down parse, if grammar rules are applied to sentences from left to right. Discuss the similarities and differences with SLD-trees.

In general, grammar rules are allowed to be recursive. For instance, a noun phrase can contain several adjectives, as described by the following rules:

```
noun_phrase              --> article,noun_phrase2.
noun_phrase2             --> noun.
noun_phrase2             --> adjective,noun_phrase2.
```

This set of rules allows 'the lazy rapid turtle' as a noun phrase. Recursion extends the descriptive power of a grammar considerably, by allowing repetitive structures.

Grammars like the ones we have seen are called *context-free grammars*. This name derives from the fact that only one non-terminal is allowed on the left of a grammar rule. A grammar rule which contains several non-terminals on its lefthand side is called *context-sensitive*: some of those non-terminals act as a *context* for the others, allowing the rule to be used only when that context is present. As an example, consider a grammar which would rule out sentences like 'the turtles sleeps', in which the 'plurality' (singular, plural) of noun and verb disagree. A candidate would be:

```
sentence                 --> noun_phrase,plurality,verb_phrase.
noun_phrase              --> article,noun.
plurality                --> singular.
plurality                --> plural.
verb_phrase              --> intransitive_verb.
article                  --> [the].
noun,singular            --> [turtle],singular.
noun,plural              --> [turtles],plural.
singular,intransitive_verb     --> [sleeps].
plural,intransitive_verb       --> [sleep].
```

In this grammar, the non-terminal `plurality` creates a context for the applicability of the rewrite rules for noun and intransitive verb. Procedural programming languages like Pascal are also, to some extent, context-sensitive: statements like `X:=10` can only be parsed in the context created by the declaration of the variable `X` (if it is declared to be a Boolean, the statement is illegal). Apart from this, such programming languages are context-free: each statement can be parsed without referring to its context.

Context-sensitive grammars greatly increase the complexity of the parsing task; moreover, the grammatical structure of sentences cannot be simply described by a parse tree. In this chapter, we will restrict attention to context-free grammars, extended with some Prolog-specific features. The resulting grammars are called *Definite Clause Grammars*, and will be introduced in the next section.

7.2 Definite Clause Grammars

If we want to build a parser in Prolog, we need a representation for sentences. Ignoring capitals and punctuation marks, a sentence can simply be represented by the list of its words in the same order, for instance

```
[the,rapid,turtle,beats,achilles]
```

Given this representation, a grammar rule like

```
sentence --> noun_phrase,verb_phrase
```

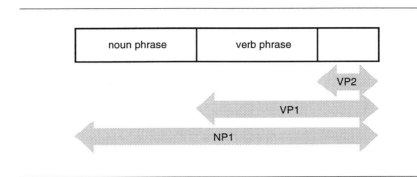

Figure 7.2. The use of difference lists in grammar rules.

has the following meaning: a list of words representes a sentence, if some first part of it represents a noun phrase, and the rest represents a verb phrase. This statement can easily be expressed as a Prolog clause:

```
sentence(S):-
    noun_phrase(NP),
    verb_phrase(VP),
    append(NP,VP,S)
```

Similarly, a grammar rule containing a terminal

```
verb --> [sleeps]
```

means: a list of words represents a verb if it is the list consisting of the single word 'sleeps'. Translated to Prolog:

```
verb([sleeps])
```

Obviously, there is a very close relationship between context-free grammar rules and definite clauses, and any context-free grammar can easily be translated to a set of Prolog clauses. The exciting thing about this is that these Prolog clauses are nothing less than a parsing program: for instance, we could ask the query

```
?-sentence([the,rapid,turtle,beats,achilles]).
```

and get an affirmative answer.

We can actually push the correspondence between grammar rules and definite clauses further by employing difference lists (section 3.6). This allows us to get rid of the `append` literals:

```
sentence(NP1-VP2):-
    noun_phrase(NP1-VP1),
    verb_phrase(VP1-VP2)
```

	GRAMMAR	PARSING
META-LEVEL	`s --> np,vp`	`?-phrase(s,L)`

OBJECT-LEVEL	`s(L,L0):-`
	`    np(L,L1),`
	`    vp(L1,L0)`
		`?-s(L,[])`

Figure 7.3. Meta-level and object-level in Definite Clause Grammars.

This clause should be read as follows: `NP1` is a sentence followed by `VP2`, if `NP1` is a noun phrase followed by `VP1`, and `VP1` is a verb phrase followed by `VP2` (fig. 7.2). Queries now should take the form

```
?-sentence([the,rapid,turtle,beats,achilles]-[])
```

(after parsing the initial part of the list as a sentence, nothing should be left).

We have shown that there is a one-to-one correspondence between context-free grammars and Prolog programs interpreting those grammars. In fact, the translation from the first to the second is so straightforward that it is built into Prolog. That is, meta-level grammar rules like

```
sentence --> noun_phrase,verb_phrase
```

are allowed in Prolog programs. When interpreting these rules, Prolog will invisibly convert them to object-level program clauses like

```
sentence(L,L0):-
    noun_phrase(L,L1),
    verb_phrase(L1,L0)
```

in which the additional variable is an accumulator rather than the minus list of a difference list (section 3.6). Furthermore, Prolog provides the meta-level predicate `phrase/2`, such that the object-level query `?-sentence(L,[])` can be replaced by the meta-level query `?-phrase(sentence,L)` (fig. 7.3).

These Prolog grammars are known as *Definite Clause Grammars* (DCG's). They are an excellent illustration of the power of declarative programming: *specifying a grammar gives you the parser for free*. That is, a grammar is a declarative specification of the corresponding parser, and Prolog directly converts this specification into an executable parser. Moreover, since a grammar is purely declarative, the program is also a sentence **generator**: for instance, it is possible to generate every sentence starting with 'Achilles' by means of the query `?-phrase(sentence,[achilles|Rest])`.

Definite Clause Grammars further extend the power of context-free grammars in two ways:

(*i*) arguments can be added to non-terminals;

(*ii*) Prolog goals can be added to the body of grammar rules.

As an illustration of the first feature, we show how plurality agreement can be achieved by means of a DCG instead of a context-sensitive grammar:

```
sentence                        --> noun_phrase(N),verb_phrase(N).
noun_phrase(N)                  --> article(N),noun(N).
verb_phrase(N)                  --> intransitive_verb(N).
article(singular)               --> [a].
article(singular)               --> [the].
article(plural)                 --> [the].
noun(singular)                  --> [turtle].
noun(plural)                    --> [turtles].
intransitive_verb(singular)     --> [sleeps].
intransitive_verb(plural)       --> [sleep].
```

The first rule states that the pluralities of noun phrase and verb phrase should correspond. The second rule states that the plurality of a noun phrase is determined by both article and noun, which should have corresponding pluralities as well. The remaining rules assign pluralities to specific articles, nouns and verbs.

We can also use this feature to construct a parse tree while parsing a sentence. Parse trees can be represented by Prolog terms (section 4.1):

- a parse tree for a terminal `T` of syntactic category `S` is represented by the term `S(T)`;
- a parse tree for a sequence `N1...Nk` of non-terminals of syntactic category `S` is represented by the term `S(N1,...,Nk)`.

Thus, a parse tree for the verb 'sleeps' is represented by the term `verb(sleeps)`, and a parse tree for the sentence 'the turtle sleeps' is represented by the term

```
s(np(art(the),n(turtle)),vp(iv(sleeps)))
```

(for brevity, syntactic categories are abbreviated). The following grammar indicates how parse trees are built up from their constituents.

```
sentence(s(NP,VP))              --> noun_phrase(NP),
                                    verb_phrase(VP).
noun_phrase(np(N))              --> proper_noun(N).
noun_phrase(np(Art,Adj,N))      --> article(Art),
                                    adjective(Adj),
                                    noun(N).
noun_phrase(np(Art,N))          --> article(Art),noun(N).
verb_phrase(vp(IV))             --> intransitive_verb(IV).
```

```
verb_phrase(vp(TV,NP))          --> transitive_verb(TV),
                                    noun_phrase(NP).
article(art(the))               --> [the].
adjective(adj(lazy))            --> [lazy].
adjective(adj(rapid))           --> [rapid].
proper_noun(pn(achilles))       --> [achilles].
noun(n(turtle))                 --> [turtle].
intransitive_verb(iv(sleeps))   --> [sleeps].
transitive_verb(tv(beats))      --> [beats].
```

In the query, the argument of the non-terminal `sentence` will be instantiated to the final parse tree:

```
?-phrase(sentence(T),[achilles,beats,the,lazy,turtle]).
  T = s(np(pn(achilles)),
        vp(tv(beats),
           np(art(the),
              adj(lazy),
              n(turtle))))
```

If we use the predicate `term_write/1` given in section 4.1, a nice tree-like output is obtained:

```
?-phrase(sentence(T),[achilles,beats,the,lazy,turtle]),
  term_write(T).

---------s--------np--------pn--achilles
         --------vp--------tv-----beats
                 -------np-------art-------the
                         -------adj------lazy
                         --------n----turtle
```

These examples show one way to use arguments of non-terminals: to collect information coming out of the parsing process. In addition, we might want to express that arguments of different non-terminals in a rule are related in some way. To this end, we can add Prolog goals to the body of grammar rules, by enclosing them in curly brackets { }. For instance, suppose we have a grammar for English numerals like 'one hundred twenty three', and we want to calculate the number represented by such numerals during parsing. We could write the following DCG:

```
numeral(N)      --> n1_999(N).
numeral(N)      --> n1_9(N1),[thousand],n1_999(N2),
                    {N is N1*1000+N2}.
n1_999(N)       --> n1_99(N).
n1_999(N)       --> n1_9(N1),[hundred],n1_99(N2),
                    {N is N1*100+N2}.
n1_99(N)        --> n0_9(N).
n1_99(N)        --> n10_19(N).
n1_99(N)        --> n20_90(N).
n1_99(N)        --> n20_90(N1),n1_9(N2),{N is N1+N2}.
```

```
n0_9(0)         --> [].
n0_9(N)         --> n1_9(N).
n1_9(1)         --> [one].
n1_9(2)         --> [two].
                ...
n10_19(10)      --> [ten].
n10_19(11)      --> [eleven].
                ...
n20_90(20)      --> [twenty].
n20_90(30)      --> [thirty].
                ...
```

We could use this DCG for parsing a given numeral, but also for generating the numeral corresponding to a given number:

```
?-phrase(numeral(2211),N).
  N = [two,thousand,two,hundred,eleven]
```

Exercise 7.3. Write a DCG that parses time indications like 'twenty minutes to four', and converts them to terms like 3 : 40.

In this section, we have seen that writing parsers in Prolog is easy: just write the context-free grammar, possibly extended by arguments to non-terminals and Prolog goals in the body of grammar rules, and you have a program for parsing and sentence generation. However, parsing is not an end in itself: we want to assign an interpretation to a sentence. This is the topic of the following section.

7.3 Interpretation of natural language

Suppose we want to build a rulebase consisting of rules like 'every human is mortal' and 'Socrates is a human'. A small grammar for rules of this form is given below.

```
sentence        --> determiner,noun,verb_phrase.
sentence        --> proper_noun,verb_phrase.
verb_phrase     --> [is],property.
property        --> [a],noun.
property        --> [mortal].
determiner      --> [every].
proper_noun     --> [socrates].
noun            --> [human].
```

If the rulebase consists of Prolog clauses, then we need a way to convert natural language rules to clauses. For instance, 'every man is human' must be translated to the clause human(X):-man(X). The clause represents the *meaning* of the sentence, and assigning clauses to sentences can be seen as *interpreting* the sentences.

We will build such an interpreter by extending each non-terminal in the above grammar with one or more arguments, which give the meaning of that non-terminal. We start with the simplest case: the meaning of the proper noun 'Socrates' is the term `socrates`:

```
proper_noun(socrates) --> [socrates]
```

Proper nouns occur in the second rule for sentences:

```
sentence --> proper_noun,verb_phrase
```

which can be used to construct the sentence 'Socrates is a human'. The meaning of this sentence is the clause `human(socrates):-true`, which can be constructed as follows:

```
sentence((P(X):-true)) --> proper_noun(X),verb_phrase(P)
```

This rule states: `P(X):-true` is the meaning of a sentence if it is composed of a proper noun with meaning `X` followed by a verb phrase with meaning `P`.

However, there are several problems with this grammar rule. For one thing, not every Prolog interpreter allows a variable in functor position, as in `P(X)`. This could be solved by constructing the literal `P(X)` separately by means of a Prolog goal:

```
sentence((L:-true))  --> proper_noun(X),verb_phrase(P),
                            {L=..[P,X]}
```

A more serious problem, however, is that verb phrases are not necessarily interpreted as unary predicates. For instance, transitive verbs are interpreted as binary predicates, and the meaning of the verb phrase 'likes Achilles' is the literal `likes(X,achilles)`, where `X` is the meaning of the proper noun preceding the verb phrase.

In general, a verb phrase defines a *mapping* from a term `X` to a literal `L`:

```
sentence((L:-true))  --> proper_noun(X),verb_phrase(X=>L)
```

The declarative reading of this rule is: a sentence is interpreted as `L:-true` if it starts with a proper noun with meaning `X`, and it ends with a verb phrase whose meaning is *applied* to `X` to yield `L`. The meaning of the verb phrase is a mapping from terms to literals indicated as `X=>L`, where '`=>`' is a user-defined operator. In our case, the mapping is determined by the property in the verb phrase:

```
verb_phrase(M)              --> [is],property(M).
property(M)                 --> [a],noun(M).
property(X=>mortal(X))      --> [mortal].
noun(X=>human(X))           --> [human].
```

For instance, the declarative reading of the last rule is: the meaning of the noun 'human' is a mapping from `X` to `human(X)`.

Exercise 7.4. Extend the following grammar rules with arguments expressing their interpretation:

```
        verb_phrase      --> transitive_verb,proper_noun.
        transitive_verb  --> [likes].
```

It remains to consider the first rule for sentences:

```
sentence         --> determiner,noun,verb_phrase
```

which constructs sentences like 'every human is mortal'. As explained above, the meaning of the noun in this sentence is the mapping from X to human(X), and the meaning of the verb phrase is the mapping from X to mortal(X). These two mappings are 'glued together' by the non-terminal determiner:

```
sentence(C)      --> determiner(M1,M2,C),
                     noun(M1),verb_phrase(M2).
determiner(X=>B,X=>H,(H:-B))  --> [every].
```

One could say that the meaning of the determiner 'every' is a *second-order mapping* which, given the mappings defined by the noun and verb phrase, determines a clause. Note that the noun determines the body literal, while the verb phrase determines the head; note also that the variables in the two literals are unified in the determiner rule.

With this DCG, the query ?-phrase(sentence(C),S) now produces the following answers:

```
C = human(X):-human(X)
S = [every,human,is,a,human];
C = mortal(X):-human(X)
S = [every,human,is,mortal];
C = human(socrates):-true
S = [socrates,is,a,human];
C = mortal(socrates):-true
S = [socrates,is,mortal]
```

Note that this very simple language already allows some form of reasoning: for instance, given the second and third sentence, we could conclude the fourth. We will implement a program which performs this kind of reasoning, taking sentences and questions in natural language, converting them to clausal logic, and converting the answers back to natural language. In order to make the program a bit more interesting, we will extend the grammar with existentially quantified sentences.

Consider the sentence 'some living beings are mortal', where 'some' is a determiner. The meaning of this sentence is 'some things are living beings, and they are mortal', which can be expressed by two clauses:

```
living_being(sk):-true
mortal(sk):-true.
```

where sk is a Skolem constant introducing a new name for the things known to exist (see section 2.5). The two head literals in these clauses are determined by the noun and the verb phrase, and the only thing we have to do is to substitute the Skolem constant and add the empty body:

```
determiner(sk=>H1,sk=>H2,[(H1:-true),(H2:-true)]) -->
                                                    [some]
```

The complete DCG is given below. Since the determiner 'some' requires a plural form of noun and verb phrase, an argument for plurality (s for singular, p for plural) has been added to each non-terminal. Furthermore, since the determiner 'some' results in a list of clauses, the other rules for determiner and sentence have been changed accordingly.

```
:-op(600,xfy,'=>').
sentence(C)                       --> determiner(N,M1,M2,C),
                                      noun(N,M1),
                                      verb_phrase(N,M2).
sentence([(L:-true)])             --> proper_noun(N,X),
                                      verb_phrase(N,X=>L).
verb_phrase(s,M)                  --> [is],property(s,M).
verb_phrase(p,M)                  --> [are],property(p,M).
property(s,M)                     --> [a],noun(s,M).
property(p,M)                     --> noun(p,M).
property(N,X=>mortal(X))          --> [mortal].
determiner(s,X=>B,X=>H,[(H:-B)]) --> [every].
determiner(p,sk=>H1,sk=>H2,[(H1:-true),(H2:-true)]) -->
                                                    [some].
proper_noun(s,socrates)           --> [socrates].
noun(s,X=>human(X))               --> [human].
noun(p,X=>human(X))               --> [humans].
noun(s,X=>living_being(X))        --> [living],[being].
noun(p,X=>living_being(X))        --> [living],[beings].
```

In addition, we give a small grammar for allowable questions, which are of the form 'who is mortal?', 'is Socrates mortal?', and 'are some living beings mortal?':

```
question(Q)          --> [who],[is],property(s,X=>Q).
question(Q)          --> [is],proper_noun(N,X),
                         property(N,X=>Q).
question((Q1,Q2))    --> [are],[some],noun(p,sk=>Q1),
                         property(p,sk=>Q2).
```

The program below is a shell for interactively building up and querying a small rulebase. User inputs are handled by the predicate `handle_input/2`; possible inputs are 'stop', 'show', a new rule, or a question. For the latter to be answered, we use a simple depth-first meta-interpreter, which possibly instantiates variables in the query. For instance, the question 'who is mortal' is interpreted as the goal `mortal(X)`, which is instantiated by the meta-interpreter to `mortal(socrates)`.

Interestingly, for transforming this answer back to natural language we do not need a separate grammar for answers: we can use the existing grammar for sentences! For instance, we can **generate** the answer 'Socrates is mortal' by means of the query

```
?-phrase(sentence([(mortal(socrates):-true)]),Answer)
Answer = [socrates,is,mortal]
```

Therefore, the only thing we have to do after the meta-interpreter has found an answer is to transform the instantiated query (a conjunction of literals) to a list of clauses with empty body (see predicate `transform/2`). Again, we encounter the declarative power of DCG's, which can at the same time be used for interpreting natural language sentences, and for constructing sentences that express a certain logical meaning.

```
% natural language shell
nl_shell(Rulebase):-
    get_input(Input),
    handle_input(Input,Rulebase).

% handle input from user
handle_input(stop,Rulebase):-!.
handle_input(show,Rulebase):-!,
    show_rules(Rulebase),
    nl_shell(Rulebase).
handle_input(Sentence,Rulebase):-
    phrase(sentence(Rule),Sentence),!,  % new rule
    nl_shell([Rule|Rulebase]).
handle_input(Question,Rulebase):-
    phrase(question(Query),Question),    % question
    prove_rb(Query,Rulebase),!,          % it can be solved
    transform(Query,Clauses),            % transform to
    phrase(sentence(Clauses),Answer),    % answer
    show_answer(Answer),
    nl_shell(Rulebase).
handle_input(Question,Rulebase):-   % illegal sentence or
    show_answer('No'),              % no answer found
    nl_shell(Rulebase).

% show current rulebase
show_rules([]).
show_rules([Rule|Rules]):-
    phrase(sentence(Rule),Sentence),
    show_answer(Sentence),
    show_rules(Rules).

% meta-interpreter
prove_rb(true,Rulebase):-!.
prove_rb((A,B),Rulebase):-!,
    prove_rb(A,Rulebase),
    prove_rb(B,Rulebase).
prove_rb(A,Rulebase):-
    find_clause((A:-B),Rulebase),
    prove_rb(B,Rulebase).

% find applicable clause in rulebase
find_clause(Clause,[Rule|Rules]):-
    copy_element(Clause,Rule).   % don't instantiate Rule
find_clause(Clause,[Rule|Rules]):-
    find_clause(Clause,Rules).
```

```
%%% copy_element/2: see Appendix A.2

% transform query to answer
transform((A,B),[(A:-true)|Rest]):-!,
    transform(B,Rest).
transform(A,[(A:-true)]).

% get input from user
get_input(Input):-
    write('? '),read(Input).

% show answer to user
show_answer(Answer):-
    write('! '),write(Answer),nl.
```

A conversation with this program might proceed as follows (following ? is user input, following ! is program output):

```
? [every,human,is,mortal].
? [socrates,is,a,human].
? [who,is,mortal].
! [socrates,is,mortal]
? [some,living,beings,are,humans].
? show.
! [some,living,beings,are,humans]
! [socrates,is,a,human]
! [every,human,is,mortal]
? [are,some,living,beings,mortal].
! [some,living,beings,are,mortal]
? stop.
```

Exercise 7.5. The predicates for user-interaction nl_shell/1 and handle_input/2 are mutually recursive. This might cause memory problems in longer sessions. Rewrite the interactive loop into a so-called *failure-driven loop*:

```
        shell:-repeat,get_input(X),handle_input(X).
        handle_input(stop):-!.
        handle_input(X):- /* do something */,fail.
```

handle_input/1 is now a predicate which always fails, unless the loop should be terminated. Upon its failure, the first clause will backtrack to repeat, which is a built-in predicate which succeeds an indefinite number of times. Thus, get_input/1 will again be called.

(NB. Since it is impossible to pass arguments on to the next iteration, the changes to the rulebase have to be made through side-effects, i.e. by means of assert/1 and retract/1.)

Further reading

(Pereira & Warren, 1980) contains a detailed discussion of the DCG formalism. More Prolog programs for natural language processing can be found in (Gazdar & Mellish, 1989) and (Pereira & Shieber, 1987).

G. GAZDAR & C. MELLISH (1989), *Natural Language Processing in Prolog*, Addison-Wesley.

F.C.N. PEREIRA & D.H.D. WARREN (1980), 'Definite Clause Grammars for language analysis: a survey of the formalism and a comparison with Augmented Transition Networks', *Artificial Intelligence* **13**: 231-278.

F.C.N. PEREIRA & S.M. SHIEBER (1987), *Prolog and Natural-language Analysis*, Center for the Study of Language and Information, Menlo Park, CA.

8

Reasoning with incomplete information

In everyday life, we use a surprising number of different reasoning methods, exemplified by the following arguments:

— 'It is getting dark already, it must be after five.'
— 'If I push this button, the light in my room will switch on.'
— 'The light doesn't switch on!? The lightbulb must be broken!'

The first argument is based on general knowledge about the regular hours of sunset. This knowledge is reached after numerous observations, and it is embedded in a theory about the movements of the heavenly bodies. We are pretty confident that this theory is **true**; that is, it accurately describes the actual state of affairs. This justifies its use to predict events in the future. However, it should be noted that we can never be **absolutely** sure that the theory is true: tomorrow the sun may set at eleven in the morning, falsifying our theory. The theory is reached by *induction*: given a number of distinct but similar observations, conclude that they are governed by a general law. Induction is an important reasoning method in the natural sciences, and it also underlies some forms of learning, like *learning from examples*. Despite this common usage, it is surprisingly hard to formalise inductive reasoning: in particular, what it takes to *justify* an inductive hypothesis remains a largely unresolved question.

The second argument above seems perfectly alright, given knowledge about how the switch is connected to the lightbulb and the power supply. However, this argument requires a lot of implicit assumptions: the switch is not broken, the connections are in order, the lightbulb is not broken, there is a supply of power, and so on. The argument is not in general true, but it describes the normal case; there might be some exceptional circumstance, invalidating the argument. Typically, we assume things to be normal, unless there is evidence to the contrary. We call this *default reasoning*.

In the third argument, we give an *explanation* for the observation that the light doesn't switch on. It is a sort of reversed implication: we know that if the lightbulb is broken, the light won't switch on; we observe that the light doesn't work, so we conclude that the lightbulb must be broken. This is but one of several possible explanations, however: the switch might be broken, or the power supply might be down. This process of finding explanations for observed facts is called *abduction*.

The common characteristic of these three types of reasoning is that their conclusions, however plausible they may seem, are not guaranteed to be true in the intended interpretation, because the information we have is *incomplete*. In default reasoning, the conclusion might be false because the state of affairs is not so normal as it is assumed to be. In abduction, there might be several alternative explanations, and we do not know which one to choose. In induction, we typically base our conclusion on only a fraction of the possible observations. Thus, the general rule (e.g. all swans are white) might be invalidated by the next observation (a black swan).

In other words, such common-sense arguments are *unsound*. Recall that an inference rule is sound if the truth of its conclusion is guaranteed by the truth of its premises. Sound reasoning is also called *deduction*; it is the only allowed form of reasoning in fields where rigorous arguments are needed, like mathematics. However, deductive conclusions only make explicit what is already implicitly present in the premises (e.g. the mathematical axioms, or a logic program). In everyday reasoning we often want to reach conclusions which contain **new** information, information that is not present in the premises. In this chapter, we will take a closer look at various forms of reasoning with incomplete information, such as default reasoning, abduction, and diagnostic reasoning. Inductive reasoning is a subject which deserves a chapter of its own (Chapter 9).

8.1 Default reasoning

Consider the following argument:

> 'Tweety is a bird.'
> 'Normally, birds fly.'
> 'Therefore, Tweety flies.'

There are several ways to translate this argument into logic. One is to read the second statement as 'normal birds fly', such that the following clauses represent the premises of the argument:

```
bird(tweety).
flies(X):-bird(X),normal(X).
```

Can we draw the conclusion that Tweety flies? There are three models:

```
{bird(tweety)}
{bird(tweety),flies(tweety)}
{bird(tweety),flies(tweety),normal(tweety)}
```

In the first two models, Tweety is a bird but not normal; hence, it might or might not fly. In the third model, Tweety is a normal flying bird. Since `flies(tweety)` is not true in every model, it is not a logical consequence of the program.

If we want to conclude that Tweety flies, we must explicitly state that Tweety is a normal bird, thus ruling out the first two of the above models. However, in default reasoning we do not want to say that a case is normal: rather, we assume a case to be normal, unless it is known to be abormal. Therefore, it is more natural to use a predicate

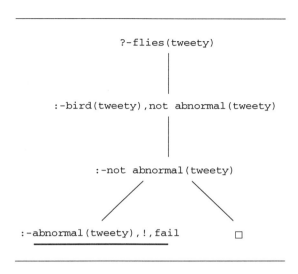

Figure 8.1. Tweety flies by negation as failure.

`abnormal/1` representing the negation of `normal/1`. Adding `abnormal(X)` to the head of the clause leads to the indefinite clause

```
flies(X);abnormal(X):-bird(X)
```

As has already been indicated in section 2.4, such indefinite clauses can be transformed into 'pseudo-definite' or *general clauses* by moving all but one of the positive literals to the body of the clause, preceded by the negation symbol `not`. This results in the following program:

```
bird(tweety).
flies(X):-bird(X),not abnormal(X).
```

Since general clauses extend the language of definite clauses, we must extend both proof theory and semantics to deal with the negation symbol `not`. A practical way to do this has been discussed in section 3.3, where we treated `not/1` as a Prolog meta-predicate, implemented by means of cut. Under this interpretation, we can prove that Tweety flies (fig. 8.1).

What happens if we learn that Tweety is an ostrich, and that ostriches are non-flying birds? We should add a clause which says that ostriches are abnormal (when it comes to flying):

```
bird(tweety).
ostrich(tweety).
flies(X):-bird(X),not abnormal(X).
abnormal(X):-ostrich(X).
```

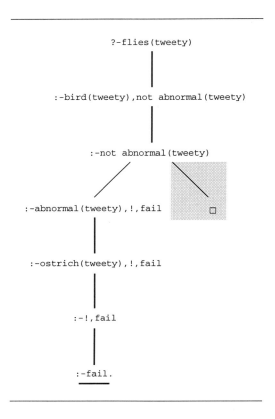

Figure 8.2. Tweety doesn't fly, since it is an ostrich.

As the SLD-tree in fig. 8.2 shows, Prolog is now unable to prove that Tweety flies, since Tweety is provably abnormal. We say that the *default rule* 'normally birds fly' is *cancelled* by a more *specific* rule (about ostriches).

Exercise 8.1. Give the models of this program (interpreting the general clause as the corresponding indefinite clause). Which one is the intended model (see section 2.4)?

This example shows that in default reasoning, *new information can invalidate previous conclusions*, if these conclusions are based on unprovable assumptions which are contradicted by the new information. This property clearly distinguishes default reasoning from deductive reasoning, which is *monotonic* in the following sense:

$$Theory \vdash Conclusion \quad \Rightarrow \quad Theory \cup \{AnyFormula\} \vdash Conclusion$$

That is, adding *AnyFormula* to a set of formulas *Theory* does not invalidate any *Conclusion* drawn from *Theory* alone. If we define the *deductive closure* of a theory as the set of conclusions that can be drawn from it:

$$Closure(Theory) = \{ Conclusion \mid Theory \vdash Conclusion \}$$

then the property of monotonicity can also be stated as a relation between theories and their closures:

$$Theory1 \subseteq Theory2 \quad \Rightarrow \quad Closure(Theory1) \subseteq Closure(Theory2)$$

This formulation clearly demonstrates the use of the term 'monotonic'. Since default reasoning lacks this property, it is often called *non-monotonic reasoning*.

Although Prolog's `not/1` meta-predicate can handle default arguments such as the above, there are a couple of problems. First of all, as has been shown in section 3.3, the implementation of `not/1` by means of cut may misbehave if the goal to be negated contains variables. The second problem is that, since cut is a procedural feature without declarative semantics, we likewise have no declarative semantics for `not` implemented by means of cut. Thus, even if we avoid the first problem by a clever re-ordering of literals in a clause, we do not know what we are computing! This problem will be addressed in the next section.

An alternative to handling possible exceptions to rules via negation as failure, is to distinguish between two possible types of rules, those with exceptions, and those without exceptions. For instance, the rule 'penguins are birds' is a rule without exceptions, whereas the rule 'birds fly' is a rule with exceptions. Let us call a rule with exceptions a *default* rule, or simply a *default*. Rules and defaults are then treated differently when trying to prove something: a rule is applied whenever possible, while a default is applied only when it does not lead to an inconsistency. So, if we only know that Tweety is a bird, the default 'birds fly' can be used to conclude that Tweety flies, but if we also know that Tweety is a penguin and that penguins don't fly, the default cannot be applied. Thus, instead of expressing our knowledge as a general program and using Prolog to derive conclusions, we will extend the syntax of clausal logic to distinguish between defaults and rules. We will develop a meta-interpreter which implements the inference rules for this extended logic.

The Tweety example can be expressed in terms of rules and defaults as follows.

```
default((flies(X):-bird(X))).
rule((not flies(X):-penguin(X))).
rule((bird(X):-penguin(X))).
rule((penguin(tweety):-true)).
rule((bird(opus):-true)).
```

In order to explain why Opus flies but Tweety doesn't, we use two meta-interpreters. One is the familiar `prove` meta-interpreter for definite clauses, extended with two arguments to collect the rules used in the proof. The other meta-interpreter applies a default whenever it does not lead to a contradiction.

```
% explain(F,E) <- E explains F from rules and defaults
explain(F,E):-
     explain(F,[],E).

% meta-interpreter for rules and defaults
explain(true,E,E):-!.
explain((A,B),E0,E):-!,
     explain(A,E0,E1),
     explain(B,E1,E).
explain(A,E0,E):-
     prove_e(A,E0,E).          % explain by rules only
explain(A,E0,[default((A:-B))|E]):-
     default((A:-B)),          % explain by default
     explain(B,E0,E),
     not contradiction(A,E).   % A consistent with E

% meta-interpreter for rules
prove_e(true,E,E):-!.
prove_e((A,B),E0,E):-!,
     prove_e(A,E0,E1),
     prove_e(B,E1,E).
prove_e(A,E0,[rule((A:-B))|E]):-
     rule((A:-B)),
     prove_e(B,E0,E).

% check contradiction against rules
contradiction(not A,E):-!,
     prove_e(A,E,E1).
contradiction(A,E):-
     prove_e(not A,E,E1).
```

The query ?-explain(flies(X),E) has only one answer:

```
X = polly
E = [ default((flies(polly):-bird(polly))),
      rule((bird(polly):-true)) ]
```

Tweety does not fly, since not flies(tweety) is provable from the rules:

```
?-explain(not flies(X), E)
X = tweety
E = [ rule((not flies(tweety):-penguin(tweety))),
      rule((penguin(tweety):-true)) ]
```

Sometimes, both a fact and its negation can be explained. Consider the following set of defaults and rules:

```
default((not flies(X):-mammal(X))).
default((flies(X):-bat(X))).
default((not flies(X):-dead(X))).
```

```
rule((mammal(X):-bat(X))).
rule((bat(dracula):-true)).
rule((dead(dracula):-true)).
```

Does Dracula fly or not? One explanation claims he does, because he is a bat, and bats typically fly:

```
?-explain(flies(dracula),E)
E = [ default((flies(dracula):-bat(dracula))),
      rule((bat(dracula):-true)) ]
```

However, there are also two explanations stating that Dracula doesn't fly; after all, he's not only a mammal, and mammals typically don't fly, but he's also dead, and dead things typically don't fly either:

```
?-explain(not flies(dracula), E)
E = [ default((not flies(dracula):-mammal(dracula))),
      rule((mammal(dracula):-bat(dracula))),
      rule((bat(dracula):-true)) ];
E = [ default((not flies(dracula):-dead(dracula))),
      rule((dead(dracula):-true)) ]
```

It seems that only the third of these explanations is acceptable. Thus, we need a way to cancel particular defaults in certain situations.

This can be done by attaching *names* to defaults, which are parametrised with the variables in the default. Then, we can refer to a default in the conclusion of a rule:

```
% default(Name,Rule)
default(mammals_dont_fly(X),(not flies(X):-mammal(X))).
default(bats_fly(X),(flies(X):-bat(X))).
default(dead_things_dont_fly(X),(not flies(X):-dead(X))).
rule((mammal(X):-bat(X))).
rule((bat(dracula):-true)).
rule((dead(dracula):-true)).
% bats are flying mammals
rule((not mammals_dont_fly(X):-bat(X))).
% dead bats don't fly
rule((not bats_fly(X):-dead(X))).
```

We change the fourth clause of the explain/3 predicate accordingly:

```
explain(A,E0,[default(Name)|E]):-
    default(Name,(A:-B)),        % explain by default rule
    explain(B,E0,E),
    not contradiction(Name,E).   % default applicable
    not contradiction(A,E).      % A consistent with E
```

There are two changes: (*i*) when applying a default, its name is tested for consistency with the rules, and (*ii*) the name of the default is added to the explanation, instead of the default itself. The above queries are now handled correctly:

```
?-explain(flies(dracula),E)
No.

?-explain(not flies(dracula), E)
E = [ default(dead_things_dont_fly(dracula)),
      rule((dead(dracula):-true)) ];
No more solutions.
```

We thus see that it is the programmer's responsibility to avoid inconsistencies by specifying appropriate cancellation rules.

8.2 The semantics of incomplete information

In this section, we present a way to interpret `not` as a logical symbol rather than a meta-predicate. In this way, it can be assigned a declarative semantics of its own, without reference to procedural features like cut. The basic idea is to transform the given program into an *intended* (possibly indefinite) program, which explicitly captures the intended meaning of the original general program. We will see that the intended program is *complete*, in the sense that for every ground fact in the Herbrand base, either that fact or its negation is a logical consequence of the intended program. Consequently, the intended program will have exactly one model, which is taken to be the intended model of the original program. We will discuss two methods to construct a complete program. The first, simple method is called the Closed World Assumption; it is simple in the sense that it only works for definite clauses without negation. The second method is called Predicate Completion; it can handle general programs with negated literals in the body of clauses.

Informally, the *Closed World Assumption* (CWA) states that *everything that is not known to be true, must be false*. Under the CWA, we need not say that something is not true: we simply say nothing about it. This is motivated by the assumption that, in general, there are many more false statements that can be made than true statements. Let us state the CWA more precisely. It suffices to know the truth or falsity of every ground atom in the Herbrand base, since this results in a single model from which the truth or falsity of any clause can be determined. Saying that such a ground atom A is false, is the same as saying that `:-A` is true. Thus, if P is a program and B is its Herbrand base, then we define the *CWA-closure* $CWA(P)$ of P as

$$CWA(P) = P \cup \{ \text{:-A} \mid A \in B \text{ and } P \not\models A \}$$

We refer to $CWA(P)-P$ as the *CWA-complement* of P. $CWA(P)$ is the *intended* program according to the Closed World Assumption.

For instance, if P is the program

```
likes(peter,S):-student_of(S,peter).
student_of(paul,peter).
```

then the ground atoms which are logical consequences of P are `likes(peter,paul)` and `student_of(paul,peter)`.

Exercise 8.2. Give the models of *P*.

The remaining ground atoms in the Herbrand base are not known to be true, and we add their negation to obtain *CWA(P)*:

```
likes(peter,S):-student_of(S,peter).
student_of(paul,peter).
:-student_of(paul,paul).
:-student_of(peter,paul).
:-student_of(peter,peter).
:-likes(paul,paul).
:-likes(paul,peter).
:-likes(peter,peter).
```

Note that *CWA(P)* has only one model:

```
{student_of(paul,peter),likes(peter,paul)}
```

That is, *CWA(P)* is a complete program, assigning **true** or **false** to every ground atom in the Herbrand base. While our original program had several, alternative models, the extended program has exactly one model. This model is then declared to be the *intended model* of the original program.

If we add the clause *C*=likes(paul,X) to *P*, we find that *CWA(P∪{C})* is

```
likes(peter,S):-student_of(S,peter).
student_of(paul,peter).
likes(paul,X).
:-student_of(paul,paul).
:-student_of(peter,paul).
:-student_of(peter,peter).
:-likes(peter,peter).
```

This example shows that extending the set of clauses results in a smaller CWA-complement, just as we would expect from a non-monotonic form of reasoning.

The CWA is limited to definite clauses: if it is applied to indefinite clauses, the resulting CWA-closure will be inconsistent. For instance, let *P* be

```
bird(tweety).
flies(X);abnormal(X):-bird(X).
```

then the Herbrand base is

```
{bird(tweety), abnormal(tweety), flies(tweety)}
```

of which only the first ground atom follows logically from *P*. Thus, *CWA(P)* is

```
bird(tweety).
flies(X);abnormal(X):-bird(X).
:-flies(tweety)
:-abnormal(tweety)
```

which is inconsistent: it does not have a model, since the first two clauses require that at least one of `abnormal(tweety)`, `flies(tweety)` is true. Since the Closed World Assumption is unable to handle indefinite clauses, it is equally unable to handle general clauses with negated literals in the body. The CWA originates from the field of databases, where all information is stored in the form of ground atoms, so that indefinite (disjunctive) information does not occur.

A more sophisticated way to construct complete programs is called *Predicate Completion*. The basic idea of Predicate Completion is to view each clause as part of the *definition* of a specific predicate. For instance, a clause like

```
likes(peter,S):-student_of(S,peter)
```

is seen as part of the definition of the `likes` predicate. Such a clause gives values for X and Y in which `likes(X,Y)` is true. In other words, it belongs to the *if* part of the definition: '*X* likes *Y* if ...'. This definition can be *completed* by adding the *only-if* parts, resulting in a full definition: '*X* likes *Y* if and only if ...'. Such a full definition is most easily expressed in Predicate Logic. For instance, the above clause could be completed to the following full definition:

$$\forall X \forall S: likes(X,S) \leftrightarrow X=peter \land student\_of(S,peter)$$

In words: '*X* likes *S* if and only if *X* is Peter, and *S* is a student of Peter', that is, Peter is the only one who likes people, and the people Peter likes are his students, and nobody else. We can translate this formula back to clausal form (see section 2.5), which yields a set of clauses

```
likes(peter,S):-student_of(S,peter).
X=peter:-likes(X,S).
student_of(S,peter):-likes(X,S).
```

The first clause was originally given; the other two are added by the Completion process.

In general, the procedure for completing a predicate definition consists of the following steps (a Prolog program which performs Predicate Completion is given in Appendix B.2):

(1)   make sure that every argument of the predicate in the head of each clause is a distinct variable, by adding literals of the form `Var=Term` to the body;
(2)   if there are several clauses, combine them into a single formula with a disjunctive body (this is possible since after step (1) each clause has the same head);
(3)   turn the implication in this formula into an equivalence.

Step (3) is the actual Completion step; the first two steps are preparatory.

As an example, consider the following set of clauses:

```
likes(peter,S):-student_of(S,peter).
likes(X,Y):-friend(Y,X).
```

The first step results in the clauses

```
likes(X,S):-X=peter,student_of(S,peter).
likes(X,Y):-friend(Y,X).
```

In the second step, these clauses are combined into a single formula in Predicate Logic:

```
∀X∀Y:likes(X,Y)←
              ((X=peter∧student_of(Y,peter))∨friend(Y,X))
```

This is a formula which is logically equivalent with the original set of clauses[18]. The Completion step is done by turning the implication into an equivalence.

Care should be taken if one of the original clauses contains variables in the body which do not occur in the head, for example

```
ancestor(X,Y):-parent(X,Y).
ancestor(X,Y):-parent(X,Z),ancestor(Z,Y).
```

Here, the second clause is equivalent with the formula

```
∀X∀Y∀Z:ancestor(X,Y)←(parent(X,Z)∧ancestor(Z,Y))
```

but also with the formula

```
∀X∀Y:ancestor(X,Y)←(∃Z:parent(X,Z)∧ancestor(Z,Y))
```

For this reason, variables which occur in the body of a clause but not in the head are often called *existential* variables. When performing Predicate Completion we must use the **second** formula, with explicit existential quantification in the body, because we want all clauses to have exactly the same head. The two original clauses are thus converted to

```
∀X∀Y:ancestor(X,Y)←
              (parent(X,Y)∨(∃Z:parent(X,Z)∧ancestor(Z,Y)))
```

A *program P* consisting of several predicate definitions is completed by completing each predicate definition separately; for those predicates P(X1,...,Xn) which occur in the body of clauses but are themselves not defined, a clause :-P(X1,...,Xn) is added. The resulting set of clauses is denoted *Comp(P)*. For instance, if *P* is

```
likes(peter,S):-student_of(S,peter).
student_of(paul,peter).
```

then *Comp(P)* is

```
likes(peter,S):-student_of(S,peter).
X=peter:-likes(X,S).
student_of(S,peter):-likes(X,S).
student_of(paul,peter).
X=paul:-student_of(X,Y).
Y=peter:-student_of(X,Y).
```

It is easily checked that the completed program has only one model:

```
{student_of(paul,peter), likes(peter,paul)}
```

---

[18]Ground literals of the form $t_1=t_2$ are **true** in an interpretation if and only if t_1 and t_2 are the same ground term. Thus, the predicate = (which represents, as usual, syntactical identity) is not explicitly represented in a model.

and is thus complete. As we saw earlier, this is also the single model of *CWA(P)*, which means that, in this case, *Comp(P)* and *CWA(P)* are logically equivalent. This is true in general, provided *P* is a set of definite clauses.

Predicate Completion extends the Closed World Assumption by also being able to handle programs containing general clauses, like

```
bird(tweety).
flies(X):-bird(X),not abnormal(X).
```

Predicate Completion produces the following formulas:

```
∀X:bird(X)↔X=tweety
∀X:flies(X)↔(bird(X)∧¬abnormal(X))
∀X:¬abnormal(X)
```

In words: Tweety is the only bird, something flies if and only if it is a bird which is not abnormal, and there are no abnormal birds. The last formula is added because there is no predicate definition for abnormal. The only model of this set of formulas is

```
{bird(tweety), flies(tweety)}
```

However, there are also general clauses which Predicate Completion cannot handle. One such a clause is the following:

```
friendly(peter):-not friendly(peter)
```

This clause states that the assumption that Peter is not friendly leads to a contradiction; therefore Peter must be friendly, and friendly(peter) should be a logical consquence of the intended program associated with this clause. Predicate Completion will construct the formula

```
∀X: friendly(X)↔(X=peter ∧ ¬friendly(peter))
```

It is easy to see that this formula is inconsistent.

Admittedly, the above clause is a bit awkward, since it is logically equivalent with

```
friendly(peter)
```

However, there are many programs which exhibit the same problem. Basically, the problem is caused by 'recursion through negation'. For instance, the completion of the following two clauses is also inconsistent:

```
wise(X):-not teacher(X).
teacher(peter):-wise(peter).
```

These clauses say 'anybody who is not a teacher is wise' and 'if Peter is wise, he is a teacher'. Assuming that Peter is not a teacher leads to a contradiction; therefore, he must be a teacher (and he may or may not be wise). However, Predicate Completion leads to inconsistencies.

Exercise 8.3. Apply Predicate Completion to this program.

A *stratified* program is a program without recursion through negation. One can prove that for stratified programs, Predicate Completion never results in inconsistencies.

8.3 Abduction and diagnostic reasoning

Abduction extends default reasoning by not only making assumptions about what is false, but also about what is true. For instance, in the lightbulb example given earlier, we know that if the lightbulb is broken, the light doesn't switch on. If we observe that the light doesn't switch on, a possible explanation is that the lightbulb is broken. Since this is only one of the possible explanations, it cannot be guaranteed to be true. For instance, there might be a problem with the power supply instead, or the switch might be broken.

The general problem of abduction can be stated as follows. Given a *Theory* and an *Observation*, find an *Explanation* such that

$$Theory \cup Explanation \models Observation$$

i.e. the *Observation* follows logically from the *Theory* extended with the *Explanation*. For instance, if *Theory* consists of the following clauses

```
likes(peter,S):-student_of(S,peter).
likes(X,Y):-friend(Y,X).
```

and we have the *Observation* likes(peter,paul), then possible *Explanations* are {student_of(paul,peter)} and {friend(paul,peter)}.

Other *Explanations* which satisfy the problem specification are {likes(X,paul)} and {likes(X,Y):-friendly(Y),friendly(paul)}. However, abductive explanations are usually restricted to ground literals with predicates that are undefined in *Theory* (such literals are called *abducibles*). Inferring general rules from specific observations is called induction, and is discussed in the next chapter.

Procedurally, we can construct an abductive explanation by trying to prove the *Observation* from the initial *Theory* alone: whenever we encounter a literal for which there is no clause to resolve with, we add the literal to the *Explanation*. This leads to the following abductive meta-interpreter.

```
% abduce(O,E) <- observation O follows by SLD-resolution
%                from the theory defined by clause/2,
%                extended with a list of unit clauses E
abduce(O,E) :-
    abduce(O,[],E).

% with accumulator for explanations
abduce(true,E,E):-!.
abduce((A,B),E0,E):-!,
    abduce(A,E0,E1),
    abduce(B,E1,E).
abduce(A,E0,E):-
    clause(A,B),
    abduce(B,E0,E).
```

```
abduce(A,E,E):-              % already assumed
    element(A,E).
abduce(A,E,[A|E]):-          % A can be added to E
    not element(A,E),        % if it's not already there,
    abducible(A).            % and if it's abducible

abducible(A):-
    not clause(A,B).
```

The last two clauses of `abduce/3` extend the original depth-first meta-interpreter. The program uses an accumulator containing the partial explanation found so far, such that literals are not unnecessarily duplicated in the final explanation. The query

```
?-abduce(likes(peter,paul),Explanation)
```

results in the answers

```
Explanation = [student_of(paul,peter)];
Explanation = [friend(paul,peter)]
```

Interestingly, this abductive meta-interpreter also works for general clauses, but it does not always produce correct explanations. For instance, suppose the initial *Theory* contains a general clause:

```
flies(X):-bird(X),not abnormal(X).
abnormal(X):-penguin(X).
bird(X):-penguin(X).
bird(X):-sparrow(X).
```

If asked to explain `flies(tweety)`, the above program will try to find a clause explaining `not(abnormal(tweety))`; since there is no such clause, this negated literal will be added to the explanation. As a result, the program will give the following explanations:

```
Explanation = [not abnormal(tweety),penguin(tweety)];
Explanation = [not abnormal(tweety),sparrow(tweety)]
```

There are two problems with these explanations. First of all, the first explanation is inconsistent with the theory. Secondly, `abnormal/1` is not an abducible predicate, and should not appear in an abductive explanation. For these reasons, we have to deal explicitly with negated literals in our abduction program.

As a first try, we can extend our abductive meta-interpreter with negation as failure, by adding the following clause (see also section 3.8):

```
abduce(not(A),E,E):-         % E explains not(A)
    not abduce(A,E,E).       % if E doesn't explain A
```

In order to prevent the query `abducible(not(A))` from succeeding, we change the definition of `abducible/1` to

```
abducible(A):-
    A \= not(X),
    not clause(A,B).
```

With this extended abductive meta-interpreter, the query

```
?-abduce(flies(tweety),Explanation).
```

now results in the following, correct answer:

```
Explanation = [sparrow(tweety)]
```

The explanation `[penguin(tweety)]` is found to be inconsistent, since

```
?-abduce(not(abnormal(tweety)),
        [penguin(tweety)],[penguin(tweety)])
```

will fail, as it should.

However, this approach relies on the fact that negated literals are checked **after** the abductive explanation has been constructed. To illustrate this, supppose that *Theory* is extended with the following clause:

```
flies1(X):-not abnormal(X),bird(X)
```

Since

```
?-abduce(not(abnormal(tweety)),[],[]).
```

succeeds, any explanation of `bird(tweety)` will also be an explanation of `flies1(tweety)`, which is of course wrong. The problem here is that the fact that `abnormal(tweety)` is considered to be **false** is not reflected in the explanation. Thus, we need a separate predicate `abduce_not/3` for building explanations for literals assumed to be false.

The full program is given below. There are two changes in `abduce/3`: in the fifth clause, an abducible `A` is only added to the explanation `E` if it is consistent with it; i.e. if `E` does not explain `not(A)`. In the sixth clause, an explicit explanation for `not(A)` is constructed.

```
% abduce(O,E0,E) <- E is abductive explanation of O, given
%                   E0 (works also for general programs)
abduce(true,E,E):-!.
abduce((A,B),E0,E):-!,
    abduce(A,E0,E1),
    abduce(B,E1,E).
abduce(A,E0,E):-
    clause(A,B),
    abduce(B,E0,E).
abduce(A,E,E):-
    element(A,E).          % already assumed
abduce(A,E,[A|E]):-
    not element(A,E),      % A can be added to E
    abducible(A),          % if it's not already there,
    not abduce_not(A,E,E). % if it's abducible,
abduce(not(A),E0,E):-      % and E doesn't explain not(A)
    not element(A,E0),     % find explanation for not(A)
    abduce_not(A,E0,E).    % should be consistent
```

The definition of abduce_not/3 closely mirrors the clauses for abduce/3:
- (*i*)   a negated conjunction not((A,B)) is explained by either explaining not(A) **or** not(B);
- (*ii*) if there are clauses for A, then not(A) is explained by constructing an explanation for not(B), for **every** body B;
- (*iii*) not(A) is explained if it is already part of the explanation;
- (*iv*) otherwise, not(A) is explained by itself, if A is abducible and not explained;
- (*v*)   not(not(A)) is explained by explaining A.

There is no clause for true, since not(true) cannot be explained.

```
% abduce_not(O,E0,E) <- E is abductive expl. of not(O)
abduce_not((A,B),E0,E):-!,
        abduce_not(A,E0,E);        % disjunction
        abduce_not(B,E0,E).
abduce_not(A,E0,E):-
        setof(B,clause(A,B),L),
        abduce_not_l(L,E0,E).
abduce_not(A,E,E):-
        element(not(A),E).         % not(A) already assumed
abduce_not(A,E,[not(A)|E]):-  % not(A) can be added to E
        not element(not(A),E),     % if it's not already there,
        abducible(A),              % if A is abducible
        not abduce(A,E,E).         % and E doesn't explain A
abduce_not(not(A),E0,E):-     % find explanation for A
        not element(not(A),E0),    % should be consistent
        abduce(A,E0,E).

abduce_not_l([],E,E).
abduce_not_l([B|Bs],E0,E):-
        abduce_not(B,E0,E1),
        abduce_not_l(Bs,E1,E).
```

We illustrate the program on the following set of clauses. Notice that there are several explanations for abnormal(tweety).

```
flies(X):-bird(X),not abnormal(X).
flies1(X):-not abnormal(X),bird(X).
abnormal(X):-penguin(X).
abnormal(X):-dead(X).
bird(X):-penguin(X).
bird(X):-sparrow(X).
```

The following queries show that the order of unnegated and negated literals in a clause only influences the order in which abducibles are added to the explanation, but not the explanation itself:

```
?-abduce(flies(tweety),Explanation).
Explanation =
    [not penguin(tweety),not dead(tweety),sparrow(tweety)]

?-abduce(flies1(tweety),Explanation).
Explanation =
    [sparrow(tweety),not penguin(tweety),not dead(tweety)]
```

Exercise 8.4. The abductive meta-interpreter will loop on the program
> wise(X):-not teacher(X).
> teacher(peter):-wise(peter).

with the query ?-abduce(teacher(peter),E) (see section 8.2). Change the interpreter such that this query is handled correctly, by adding **all** literals collected in the proof to the abductive explanation.

Abduction can be used for formulating hypotheses about faulty components in a malfunctioning system. Here, the *Theory* is a description of the operation of the system, an *Observation* is a combination of input values and the observed output values, and *Explanation* is a *diagnosis*, telling us which components are malfunctioning. As an example we consider a logical circuit for adding three binary digits. Such a circuit can be built from two XOR-gates, two AND-gates, and an OR-gate (fig. 8.3). Its behaviour can be described logically as follows:

```
adder(X,Y,Z,Sum,Carry):-
    xor(X,Y,S),
    xor(Z,S,Sum),
    and(X,Y,C1),
    and(Z,S,C2),
    or(C1,C2,Carry).
```

```
xor(0,0,0).     and(0,0,0).     or(0,0,0).
xor(0,1,1).     and(0,1,0).     or(0,1,1).
xor(1,0,1).     and(1,0,0).     or(1,0,1).
xor(1,1,0).     and(1,1,1).     or(1,1,1).
```

These clauses describe the normal operation of the system. However, since diagnosis deals with faulty operation of components, we have to extend the system description with a so-called *fault model*. Such a fault model describes the behaviour of each component when it is in a faulty state. We distinguish two faulty states: the output of a component can be stuck at 0, or it can be stuck at 1. Faulty states are expressed by literals of the form fault(Name=State), where State is either s0 (stuck at 0) or s1 (stuck at 1). The Name of a component is given by the system that contains it. Since components might be nested (e.g. the adder might itself be part of a circuit that adds two 8-bits binary numbers), the names of the components of a sub-system are prefixed by the name of that sub-system. This results in the following system description:

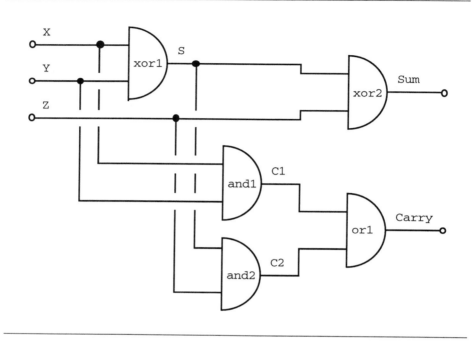

Figure 8.3. A 3-bit adder.

```
adder(N,X,Y,Z,Sum,Carry):-
    xorg(N-xor1,X,Y,S),
    xorg(N-xor2,Z,S,Sum),
    andg(N-and1,X,Y,C1),
    andg(N-and2,Z,S,C2),
    org(N-or1,C1,C2,Carry).

xorg(N,X,Y,Z):-xor(X,Y,Z).
xorg(N,0,0,1):-fault(N=s1).
xorg(N,0,1,0):-fault(N=s0).
xorg(N,1,0,0):-fault(N=s0).
xorg(N,1,1,1):-fault(N=s1).

andg(N,X,Y,Z):-and(X,Y,Z).
andg(N,0,0,1):-fault(N=s1).
andg(N,0,1,1):-fault(N=s1).
andg(N,1,0,1):-fault(N=s1).
andg(N,1,1,0):-fault(N=s0).
```

```
org(N,X,Y,Z):-or(X,Y,Z).
org(N,0,0,1):-fault(N=s1).
org(N,0,1,0):-fault(N=s0).
org(N,1,0,0):-fault(N=s0).
org(N,1,1,0):-fault(N=s0).
```

Such a fault model, which includes all possible faulty behaviours, is called a *strong* fault model.

In order to diagnose the system, we declare `fault/1` as the (only) abducible predicate, and we make a call to `abduce/2`:

```
diagnosis(Observation,Diagnosis):-
    abduce(Observation,Diagnosis).

abducible(fault(X)).
```

For instance, suppose the inputs `X=0`, `Y=0` and `Z=1` result in the outputs `Sum=0` and `Carry=1` (a double fault). In order to diagnose this behaviour, we formulate the following query:

```
?-diagnosis(adder(a,0,0,1,0,1),D).
D = [fault(a-or1=s1),fault(a-xor2=s0)];
D = [fault(a-and2=s1),fault(a-xor2=s0)];
D = [fault(a-and1=s1),fault(a-xor2=s0)];
D = [fault(a-and2=s1),fault(a-and1=s1),fault(a-xor2=s0)];
D = [fault(a-xor1=s1)];
D = [fault(a-or1=s1),fault(a-and2=s0),fault(a-xor1=s1)];
D = [fault(a-and1=s1),fault(a-xor1=s1)];
D = [fault(a-and2=s0),fault(a-and1=s1),fault(a-xor1=s1)];
No more solutions
```

The first diagnosis is very obvious: it states that `or1` (which calculates `Carry`) is stuck at 1, and `xor2` (which calculates `Sum`) is stuck at 0. But the fault in the output of `or1` might also be caused by `and2` or `and1`, and even by both! The fifth diagnosis is an interesting one: if `xor1` is stuck at 1, this accounts for **both** faults in the outputs of the adder. The remaining three diagnoses are considerably less interesting, since each of them makes unnecessary assumptions about additional faulty components.

The predicate `diagnosis/2` generates every possible diagnosis; it does not make any assumptions about the relative plausibility of each of them. Several such assumptions can be made. For instance, we might be interested in the diagnoses with the least number of faulty components (there is only one smallest diagnosis in the example, but there may be several in general). Alternatively, we might want to consider only non-redundant or *minimal* diagnoses: those of which no proper subset is also a diagnosis. This is readily expressed in Prolog:

```
min_diagnosis(O,D):-
    diagnosis(O,D),
    not((diagnosis(O,D1),proper_subset(D1,D))).

%%% proper_subset/2: see Appendix A.2
```

```
?-min_diagnosis(adder(a,0,0,1,0,1),D).
D = [fault(a-or1=s1),fault(a-xor2=s0)];
D = [fault(a-and2=s1),fault(a-xor2=s0)];
D = [fault(a-and1=s1),fault(a-xor2=s0)];
D = [fault(a-xor1=s1)];
No more solutions
```

It should be noted that the predicate `min_diagnosis/2` is quite inefficient, since it needs time quadratic in the number of diagnoses (for each possible diagnosis, it generates in the worst case each possible diagnosis to see if the second is a proper subset of the first). In turn, the number of diagnoses is exponential in the number of components. More efficient ways of generating minimal diagnoses can be found in the literature; they fall outside the scope of this book.

8.4 The complete picture

In this chapter we studied several ways of dealing with imcomplete information. Incompleteness occurs whenever there is a ground fact in the Herbrand base of which we do not know the truth value. In order to extend our knowledge, we need to make assumptions about the truth value of such ground facts. The simplest approach is to assume that everything that is not known to be true must be false. The procedural equivalent of this is *negation as failure*: everything that is not **provable** is assumed to be false. Thus, a negated literal `not` L in the body of a general clause is assumed to be proved if a proof of L fails. The resulting proof procedure is called *SLDNF-resolution*[19].

If we strengthen our proof procedure, we must strengthen the semantics accordingly. Since the original program is incomplete it has several models, one of which we need to choose. One way to do this is to transform the original program into a new, complete program, which we declare to be the *intended* program. The only model of this complete program is taken as the intended model of the original program. The *Closed World Assumption* is a rather naive way to achieve this, while *Predicate Completion* can also handle a restricted subclass of the class of general programs (so-called *stratified* programs).

The relation between SLDNF-resolution and Predicate Completion is as follows. Let P be a general program, let $Comp(P)$ denote the completion of P, and let $\vdash_{\text{SLDNF}}$ denote provability by SLDNF-resolution, treating negated literals in the body of clauses by negation as failure; then the following relation holds:

$$P \vdash_{\text{SLDNF}} q \quad \Rightarrow \quad Comp(P) \models q$$

This is a *soundness* result for SLDNF-resolution. The corresponding completeness result is not so easily proved, and holds only for specific sub-classes of programs.

Default reasoning is reasoning with typical cases and exceptions. A practical approach to default reasoning is by explicitly listing the exceptions to a rule by means of *abnormality predicates*. The rule describing the typical case is represented by a general clause, containing the negation of the abnormality predicate. An alternative approach is to distinguish between

---

[19]In SLDNF resolution, `not` is treated as belonging to the language of general clauses, rather than as a meta-predicate.

rules which always hold, and rules which typically hold (so-called *defaults*). A default is *applicable* whenever it does not lead to inconsistencies. In order to prevent the applicability of defaults in certain cases, they are assigned *names*. These names can then be used in other rules to refer to a specific default.

There is a close relation between abnormality predicates and names of defaults, demonstrated by the following translation of default rules to general clauses. The default rule

```
default(bats_fly(X),(flies(X):-bat(X)))
```

is first translated to a clause

```
flies(X):-bat(X),bats_fly(X)
```

after which the predicate `bats_fly/1`, indicating the normal case, is converted to a negated abnormality predicate:

```
flies(X):-bat(X),not nonflying_bat(X)
```

Furthermore, for each negated conclusion in a rule like

```
default(dead_things_dont_fly(X),(not flies(X):-dead(X)))
```

a new predicate is introduced:

```
notflies(X):-dead(X),not flying_deadthing(X)
```

Thus, the complete set of rules and defaults about Dracula is translated to the following general program:

```
notflies(X):-mammal(X),not flying_mammal(X).
flies(X):-bat(X),not nonflying_bat(X).
notflies(X):-dead(X),not flying_deadthing(X)
mammal(X):-bat(X).
bat(dracula).
dead(dracula).
flying_mammal(X):-bat(X).
nonflying_bat(X):-dead(X).
```

Exercise 8.5. Draw the SLD-trees for the queries `?-flies(X)` and `?-notflies(X)`.

What this shows is the close relationship between assuming that something is false unless the opposite can be proved (negation as failure), and assuming that a default rule is applicable unless this leads to inconsistencies.

Abduction generalises negation as failure by formulating assumptions about either truth or falsity of specific literals (*abducibles*). For instance, the Dracula example can be handled by the abductive meta-interpreter of section 8.3 without any problem, if we declare the abnormality predicates as abducibles:

```
abducible(flying_mammal(X)).
abducible(nonflying_bat(X)).
abducible(flying_deadthing(X)).

?-abduce(flies(X),E)
No.

?-abduce(notflies(X),E)
X = dracula
E = [not flying_deadthing(dracula)];
No more solutions.
```

Exercise 8.6. Remove the last two clauses from the program, and again determine the answers to the queries ?-abduce(flies(X),E) and
?-abduce(notflies(X),E).

This shows that negation as failure is a special case of abduction. Moreover, it shows that making assumptions about the applicability of a default rule is a form of abduction. We can therefore conclude that abduction is the most general form of reasoning with incomplete information among the ones discussed in this chapter. However, inductive reasoning extends abduction by hypothesising complete predicate definitions rather than sets of ground literals. This will be the subject of the next chapter.

Further reading

Negation as failure and Predicate Completion are discussed by Clark (1978). In the same volume, the Closed World Assumption was formally introduced by Reiter (1978). The approach to default reasoning by means of defaults and rules is due to Poole (1988). In (Poole, 1991), a more elaborate Prolog implementation of this approach is presented. (Sombé, 1990) gives a detailed comparison of formalisms for reasoning with incomplete information, using a single example.

An extensive overview of different approaches to abduction and their relation to other forms of reasoning with incomplete information can be found in (Kakas *et al.*, 1992). The abductive meta-interpreter in section 8.3 is based on ideas from the same paper, as well as parts of the analysis in section 8.4. (Mozetič, 1992) presents an efficient algorithm for the computation of minimal diagnoses.

K.L. CLARK (1978), 'Negation as failure'. In *Logic and Databases*, H. Gallaire & J. Minker (eds), pp. 293-322, Plenum Press.

A.C. KAKAS, R.A. KOWALSKI & F. TONI (1992), 'Abductive Logic Programming', *Journal of Logic and Computation* **2**(6): 719-770.

I. MOZETIČ (1992), 'A polynomial-time algorithm for model-based diagnosis'. In *Proc. Tenth European Conference on Artificial Intelligence, ECAI'92*, B. Neumann (ed.), pp. 729-733, John Wiley.

D. POOLE (1988), 'A logical framework for default reasoning', *Artificial Intelligence* **36**: 27-47.

D. POOLE (1991), 'Compiling a default reasoning system into Prolog', *New Generation Computing* **9**: 3-38.

R. REITER (1978), 'On closed world databases'. In *Logic and Databases*, H. Gallaire & J. Minker (eds), pp. 55-76, Plenum Press.

LÉA SOMBÉ (1990), *Reasoning under Incomplete Information in Artificial Intelligence*, John Wiley. Also *International Journal of Intelligent Systems* **5**(4).

9
Inductive reasoning

Induction is a form of reasoning which infers general rules from specific observations. For instance, given the following *Theory*

```
bird(tweety).              bird(polly).
has_feathers(tweety).      has_beak(polly).
```

we might want to infer a *Hypothesis* explaining why both Tweety and Polly fly:

```
flies(X):-bird(X)
```

There is a strong similarity between induction and abduction: if the *Examples*, which induction seeks to explain, are the ground facts `flies(tweety)` and `flies(polly)` then the following relation holds:

$$Theory \cup Hypothesis \models Examples$$

The main difference with abduction is that *Hypothesis* is allowed to be a set of clauses, rather than a set of ground facts as in abduction.

Given this similarity, we will try to adopt the abductive meta-interpreter developed in section 8.3 to perform induction. We assume that the set of possible hypotheses is given by means of the predicate `inducible/1`.

```
% induce(E,H) <- H is inductive explanation of E
induce(E,H):-
    induce(E,[],H).

induce(true,H,H).
induce((A,B),H0,H):-
    induce(A,H0,H1),
    induce(B,H1,H).
induce(A,H0,H):-
    clause(A,B),
    induce(B,H0,H).
```

```
induce(A,H0,H):-
    element((A:-B),H0),        % already assumed
    induce(B,H0,H).            % proceed with body of rule
induce(A,H0,[(A:-B)|H]):-      % A:-B can be added to H
    inducible((A:-B)),         % if it's inducible, and
    not element((A:-B),H0),    % if it's not already there
    induce(B,H0,H).            % proceed with body of rule
```

Whenever a clause is added to the inductive hypothesis, we proceed by constructing an inductive explanation of its body.

Suppose `inducible/1` is defined as follows:

```
inducible((flies(X):-bird(X),has_feathers(X),has_beak(X))).
inducible((flies(X):-has_feathers(X),has_beak(X))).
inducible((flies(X):-bird(X),has_beak(X))).
inducible((flies(X):-bird(X),has_feathers(X))).
inducible((flies(X):-bird(X))).
inducible((flies(X):-has_feathers(X))).
inducible((flies(X):-has_beak(X))).
inducible((flies(X):-true)).
```

These facts state that every clause with `flies/1` in its head and some of the predicates in *Theory* in its body is a possible inductive hypothesis. We can use `induce/2` to find out which of these clauses account for the fact that Tweety and Polly fly:

```
?-induce(flies(tweety),H).
H = [(flies(tweety):-bird(tweety),has_feathers(tweety))];
H = [(flies(tweety):-bird(tweety))];
H = [(flies(tweety):-has_feathers(tweety))];
H = [(flies(tweety):-true)];
No more solutions

?-induce(flies(polly),H).
H = [(flies(polly):-bird(polly),has_beak(polly))];
H = [(flies(polly):-bird(polly))];
H = [(flies(polly):-has_beak(polly))];
H = [(flies(polly):-true)];
No more solutions
```

We can combine the answers to these queries in order to find a single clause which explains **both** `flies(tweety)` and `flies(polly)`. One way to do this is by *generalisation*, as will be explained later. Another way is to process all the examples at once.

Exercise 9.1. Change `induce/3` so that it handles a list of examples rather than a single example. Moreover, the inductive hypothesis should contain uninstantiated clauses, so that the same clause can be used to explain several examples.

However, a serious problem with this approach is the impracticality of listing every possible hypothesis by means of the predicate `inducible/1`. In general, the inductive hypothesis can consist of several clauses, and might be recursive. The *hypothesis space* of possible sets of clauses is typically very large, and even infinite when functors are involved. This space needs to be searched in a systematic manner. Another complication is the possibility of *overgeneralisations* like the clause `flies(X):-true`. In order to prevent overgeneralisation, *negative examples* need to be included in the induction process (here: non-flying objects). For these reasons, induction requires a more sophisticated search strategy than abduction. We will take a closer look at the structure of the search space in the next section. Then, we will develop two programs that can induce definitions for predicates like `append/3` from examples.

9.1 Generalisation and specialisation

An *example* is a ground fact for the predicate of which a definition is to be induced. A *positive* example is true in the intended interpretation, while a *negative* example is false. Consequently, the inductive *Hypothesis* should be such that for every positive example *p*

$$Theory \cup Hypothesis \models p$$

while for every negative example *n*

$$Theory \cup Hypothesis \not\models n$$

We say that *p* is *covered* by *Hypothesis*, given *Theory*. For instance, if *Hypothesis* is the standard recursive definition of `element/2`:

```
element(X,[X|Z]).
element(X,[Y|Z]):-element(X,Z).
```

then the example `element(b,[a,b])` is covered (with empty *Theory*). This can be demonstrated by a simple meta-interpreter for definite clauses. Note that this proof requires **both** of the above clauses. Alternatively, if `element(b,[b])` is also known to be a positive example, we can say that `element(b,[a,b])` is covered by the second, recursive clause alone. The first definition of coverage, which refers to the complete hypothesis, is called *intensional* coverage, while the second, referring to single clauses plus the rest of the examples, is called *extensional* coverage. In the induction programs to be developed, we will employ both notions of coverage; for the moment, however, the distinction is immaterial.

Exercise 9.2. Write a predicate `covers_ex/3` which, given a clause, an example, and a list of positive examples, tests whether the clause extensionally covers the example.

If *Hypothesis1* covers at least all the examples covered by *Hypothesis2*, we say that *Hypothesis1* is at least as *general* as *Hypothesis2*, or that *Hypothesis2* is at least as *specific* as *Hypothesis1*. From the definition of coverage, one can see that *Hypothesis2* must be a logical consequence of *Hypothesis1*, given *Theory*:

$$Theory \cup Hypothesis1 \models Hypothesis2$$

Suppose p is a positive example covered by *Hypothesis1* but not by *Hypothesis2*. This means that *Hypothesis2* is too specific; if it is our current hypothesis, it needs to be *generalised*, for instance to *Hypothesis1*. Similarly, if a hypothesis covers a negative example, it needs to be *specialised*. Generalisation and specialisation are the basic operations of induction.

Although we defined generality between hypotheses being **sets** of clauses, practical approaches to induction usually generalise or specialise single clauses. For instance, the following are clauses of increasing generality:

```
element(X,[Y|Z]):-element(X,Z).
element(X,V):-element(X,Z).
element(X,V).
```

This shows that a more specific clause can be constructed by adding a literal, by applying a substitution, or both. This relation of generality between clauses is called θ-subsumption. Formally, `Clause1` *θ-subsumes* `Clause2` if there is a substitution θ that can be applied to `Clause1`, such that every literal in the resulting clause occurs in `Clause2`.

Notice that θ only replaces variables in `Clause1`, not in `Clause2`. One way to test if such a θ exists is to ground all variables in `Clause2`, and then unify the ground version of `Clause2` with `Clause1`. Grounding the variables in a term can be done by means of the built-in predicate `numbervars/3`, which unifies different variables with terms of the form `'$VAR(N)'`.

```
theta_subsumes1((H:-B1),(H:-B2)):-
    ground(B2),
    subset(B1,B2).

ground(Term):-
    numbervars(Term,0,N).

%%% subset/2: see Appendix A.2
```

This approach has the disadvantage that one or both clauses are changed after a call to `theta_subsumes1/2`. To avoid this, we apply the following little programming trick:

```
theta_subsumes((H1:-B1),(H2:-B2)):-
    not((H1=H2,ground(B2),
        not subset(B1,B2))).
```

`theta_subsumes/2` succeeds exactly when `theta_subsumes1/2` does, but by means of the double negation unifications are 'undone' after the call succeeds.

Next, we turn to the issue of how to construct generalisations of clauses. First we consider the simpler case of generalising two atoms. Consider the following two ground facts:

```
element(1,[1])
element(z,[z,y,x])
```

The following atom θ-subsumes both of them:

```
element(X,[X|Y])
```

Note that this atom θ-subsumes every other possible generalisation (such as element(X,[Y|Z]) or element(X,Y)). For this reason, it is called a *least general generalisation under θ-subsumption* or *θ-LGG*. θ-LGG's of atoms can be computed by means of *anti-unification*. This operation is the dual of unification. It operates by comparing the terms occurring at the same position in the two atoms, and replacing them by a new variable if they are different. The terms which have already been replaced by a variable are collected in two lists, because if the same pair of terms is encountered again, it should be replaced by the same variable (see 1 and z in the example above). For obvious reasons, such lists are called *inverse substitutions*.

```
:-op(600,xfx,'<-'). % operator for inverse substitution

% anti_unify(T1,T2,T) <-  T is the anti-unification
%                          of T1 and T2
anti_unify(Term1,Term2,Term):-
    anti_unify(Term1,Term2,Term,[],S1,[],S2).

% anti-unification with inverse subst.s and accumulators
anti_unify(Term1,Term2,Term1,S1,S1,S2,S2):-
    Term1 == Term2,!.                        % same terms
anti_unify(Term1,Term2,V,S1,S1,S2,S2):-      % already
    subs_lookup(S1,S2,Term1,Term2,V),!.      % substituted
anti_unify(Term1,Term2,Term,S10,S1,S20,S2):-
    nonvar(Term1),nonvar(Term2),
    functor(Term1,F,N),functor(Term2,F,N),!, % same
    functor(Term,F,N),                       % functor
    anti_unify_args(N,Term1,Term2,Term,S10,S1,S20,S2).
anti_unify(T1,T2,V,S10,[T1<-V|S10],S20,[T2<-V|S20]).

anti_unify_args(0,Term1,Term2,Term,S1,S1,S2,S2).
anti_unify_args(N,Term1,Term2,Term,S10,S1,S20,S2):-
    N>0,N1 is N-1,
    arg(N,Term1,Arg1),
    arg(N,Term2,Arg2),
    arg(N,Term,Arg),
    anti_unify(Arg1,Arg2,Arg,S10,S11,S20,S21),
    anti_unify_args(N1,Term1,Term2,Term,S11,S1,S21,S2).

subs_lookup([T1<-V|Subs1],[T2<-V|Subs2],Term1,Term2,V):-
    T1 == Term1,
    T2 == Term2,!.  % no alternative solutions needed
subs_lookup([S1|Subs1],[S2|Subs2],Term1,Term2,V):-
    subs_lookup(Subs1,Subs2,Term1,Term2,V).
```

The following query illustrates the operation of the program, including the use of inverse substitutions:

```
?-anti_unify(2*2=2+2,2*3=3+3,T,[],S1,[],S2)
  T = 2*X=X+X
  S1 = [2<-X]
  S2 = [3<-X]
```

Note that the inverse substitution [2<-X] does not indicate which occurrences of 2 should be replaced by X. This means that S1 applied to the first term does not yield T (the inverse of S1 applied to T yields the first term, however). Therefore, a proper definition of inverse substitution should include the positions of terms which are to be replaced by variables. We will not elaborate this any further here.

The construction of the θ-LGG of two clauses makes use of, but is more complicated than anti-unification. The basic difference with anti-unification is that the body of a clause is logically speaking unordered, whereas subterms within a term have fixed positions. Therefore, we cannot just compare the literals occurring at the same position in the respective bodies, but should consider all pairs of literals, one from each body. For instance, the θ-LGG of the following two clauses

```
element(c,[b,c]):-element(c,[c])
element(d,[b,c,d]):-element(d,[c,d]),element(d,[d])
```

is the clause

```
element(X,[b,c|Y]):-element(X,[c|Y]),element(X,[X])
```

The head of this clause is simply obtained by anti-unifying the heads of the original clauses, and the body is obtained by anti-unification of element(c,[c]) and element(d,[c,d]), giving element(X,[c|Y]), and anti-unification of element(c,[c]) and element(d,[d]), giving element(X,[X]).

The program for constructing θ-LGG's is given below. Note that the inverse substitutions found in each step are passed on to the next, so that the literals share variables.

```
% theta_lgg(C1,C2,C) <- C is the θ-LGG of clause C1 and C2
theta_lgg((H1:-B1),(H2:-B2),(H:-B)):-
    anti_unify(H1,H2,H,[],S10,[],S20),           % heads
    theta_lgg_bodies(B1,B2,[],B,S10,S1,S20,S2).  % bodies

% select literal from first body...
theta_lgg_bodies([],B2,B,B,S1,S1,S2,S2).
theta_lgg_bodies([L|B1],B2,B0,B,S10,S1,S20,S2):-
    theta_lgg_literal(L,B2,B0,B00,S10,S11,S20,S21),
    theta_lgg_bodies(B1,B2,B00,B,S11,S1,S21,S2).

% and one from second body
theta_lgg_literal(L1,[],B,B,S1,S1,S2,S2).
theta_lgg_literal(L1,[L2|B2],B0,B,S10,S1,S20,S2):-
    same_predicate(L1,L2),
    anti_unify(L1,L2,L,S10,S11,S20,S21),
    theta_lgg_literal(L1,B2,[L|B0],B,S11,S1,S21,S2).
```

The relation between θ-subsumption and logical consequence

If Clause1 θ-subsumes Clause2, then also Clause1 ⊨ Clause2. The reverse, however, is not always true. Consider the following two clauses:

```
list([V|W]):-list(W)
list([X,Y|Z]):-list(Z)
```

Given list([]), the first clause covers lists of arbitrary length, while the second covers only lists of even length. All lists covered by the second clause are also covered by the first, which is therefore more general. However, there is no substitution that can be applied to the first clause to yield the second (such a substitution should map W both to [Y|Z] and to Z, which is impossible).

It may seem that ⊨ provides a better notion of generality than θ-subsumption. However, such a semantic definition of generality introduces two problems. One is that it does not suggest a simple procedure to generalise clauses, as θ-subsumption does. The second problem is that LGG's under logical consequence are not always unique. Consider the two clauses

```
list([A,B|C]):-list(C)
list([P,Q,R|S]):-list(S)
```

Under logical consequence, these clauses have two LGG's: one is list([X|Y]):-list(Y), and the other is list([X,Y|Z]):-list(V). Under θ-subsumption, only the latter is an LGG. Note that the first LGG looks in fact more plausible!

```
theta_lgg_literal(L1,[L2|B2],B0,B,S10,S1,S20,S2):-
    not same_predicate(L1,L2),
    theta_lgg_literal(L1,B2,B0,B,S10,S1,S20,S2).

%%% same_predicate/2: see Appendix A.2
```

To check the above example, we pose the following query:

```
?-theta_lgg((element(c,[b,c]):-[element(c,[c])]),
            (element(d,[b,c,d]):-
                        [element(d,[c,d]),element(d,[d])]),
            C)
  C = element(X,[b,c|Y]):-[element(X,[X]),element(X,[c|Y])]
```

Exercise 9.3. Determine the θ-LGG of the following two clauses:
```
reverse([2,1],[3],[1,2,3]):-reverse([1],[2,3],[1,2,3])
reverse([a],[],[a]):-reverse([],[a],[a])
```

In the following section we develop a program which generalises the examples by constructing θ-LGG's. This corresponds to a *specific-to-general* search of the space of possible predicate definitions; it is also called *bottom-up* induction. Alternatively, one could start with the most general definition, which is specialised as long as it covers some negative example. A program for *top-down* induction is given in section 9.3.

9.2 Bottom-up induction

The induction program we will develop in this section constructs θ-LGG's of two examples, relative to a partial model M which consists of all positive examples plus ground facts for the background predicates, of which the definitions are given beforehand. Such θ-LGG's are called *relative least general generalisations* or RLGG's. Typically, RLGG's are quite big clauses, that contain many redundant or otherwise useless literals, but also one or two useful literals. For instance, suppose M consists of the following positive examples for the predicate append/3:

```
append([1,2],[3,4],[1,2,3,4])       append([a],[],[a])
append([],[],[])                    append([2],[3,4],[2,3,4])
```

The RLGG of two examples E_1 and E_2 relative to a model M is defined as the θ-LGG of the clauses $E_1:-Conj(M)$ and $E_2:-Conj(M)$, where $Conj(M)$ denotes the conjunction of the ground facts in M. So, the RLGG of the first two examples above is the θ-LGG of the following two clauses:

```
append([1,2],[3,4],[1,2,3,4]):-
     append([1,2],[3,4],[1,2,3,4]),append([a],[],[a]),
     append([],[],[]),append([2],[3,4],[2,3,4])

append([a],[],[a]):-
     append([1,2],[3,4],[1,2,3,4]),append([a],[],[a]),
     append([],[],[]),append([2],[3,4],[2,3,4])
```

The body of the resulting clause consists of 16 literals, constructed by pairwise anti-unification of facts in M:

```
append([A|B],C,[A|D]):-
     append([1,2],[3,4],[1,2,3,4]),append([A|B],C,[A|D]),
     append(W,C,X),append([S|B],[3,4],[S,T,U|V]),
     append([R|G],K,[R|L]),append([a],[],[a]),
     append(Q,[],Q),append([P],K,[P|K]),append(N,K,O),
     append(M,[],M),append([],[],[]),append(G,K,L),
     append([F|G],[3,4],[F,H,I|J]),append([E],C,[E|C]),
     append(B,C,D),append([2],[3,4],[2,3,4])
```

Clearly, this clause contains many redundant literals. First of all, removing the ground facts from M does not change the logical meaning of the clause, since they are known to be true. Furthermore, note that most literals introduce new variables, that do not appear in the head of the clause[20]. For simplicity, we will assume that this does not occur in the intended

---

[20]If X is a variable occurring in Body but not in Head, the formula ∀X: Head←Body is logically equivalent with Head←∃X:Body. Such variables are called *existential variables*.

program, i.e. *all variables in the body of a hypothesis clause also occur in the head.* Such clauses are also called *constrained*. Under this assumption, the clause can be considerably reduced:

```
append([A|B],C,[A|D]):-
    append([A|B],C,[A|D]),append(B,C,D),
```

Note that the first body literal turns the clause into a *tautology*: a clause that is true by definition. We will exclude this literal as well by assuming that hypothesis clauses are **strictly** constrained, i.e. the set of body variables is a **proper** subset of the set of head variables (see Exercise 9.4 for a discussion of the kind of program excluded by this restriction). Under this assumption, we arrive at the recursive clause for append/3:

```
append([A|B],C,[A|D]):-
    append(B,C,D)
```

It is interesting to trace the literal append(B,C,D) back to its origin: it is the anti-unification of the facts append([],[],[]) and append([2],[3,4],[2,3,4]). These are exactly the ground bodies of the last clause, if we unify its head with the two original examples!

The program for computing the RLGG of two examples is given below. It is a slight modification of the program for computing θ-LGG's, given in the previous section. After the head of the clause is constructed, the variables in the head are passed on to the predicate rlgg_bodies/9, which will only construct literals of which all the variables occur in the head.

```
% rlgg(E1,E2,M,C) <- C is RLGG of E1 and E2 relative to M
rlgg(E1,E2,M,(H:-B)):-
    anti_unify(E1,E2,H,[],S10,[],S20),
    varsin(H,V),  % determine variables in head of clause
    rlgg_bodies(M,M,[],B,S10,S1,S20,S2,V).

% varsin(T,V) <- V is list of variables occuring in term T
%               (standard predicate in many Prologs)

rlgg_bodies([],B2,B,B,S1,S1,S2,S2,V).
rlgg_bodies([L|B1],B2,B0,B,S10,S1,S20,S2,V):-
    rlgg_literal(L,B2,B0,B00,S10,S11,S20,S21,V),
    rlgg_bodies(B1,B2,B00,B,S11,S1,S21,S2,V).

rlgg_literal(L1,[],B,B,S1,S1,S2,S2,V).
rlgg_literal(L1,[L2|B2],B0,B,S10,S1,S20,S2,V):-
    same_predicate(L1,L2),
    anti_unify(L1,L2,L,S10,S11,S20,S21),
    varsin(L,Vars),
    var_proper_subset(Vars,V),    % no new variables
    !,rlgg_literal(L1,B2,[L|B0],B,S11,S1,S21,S2,V).
rlgg_literal(L1,[L2|B2],B0,B,S10,S1,S20,S2,V):-
    rlgg_literal(L1,B2,B0,B,S10,S1,S20,S2,V).

%%% var_... uses == rather than unification (Appendix A.2)
```

For simplicity, the body of the RLGG thus constructed is a **list** of literals rather than a conjunction.

The main algorithm of the RLGG-program is relatively simple: construct the RLGG of two positive examples, and remove all positive examples that are extensionally covered by this clause. Such an algorithm, which induces each clause separately, is also called a *covering algorithm*. Positive and negative examples, identified by a sign, are first separated by means of the predicate pos_neg/3, and the positive examples are combined with a (possibly empty) background model for the background predicates, to yield the model to be used for construction of RLGG's.

```prolog
induce_rlgg(Exs,Clauses):-
    pos_neg(Exs,Poss,Negs),    % split pos. & neg. examples
    bg_model(BG),              % ground background model
    append(Poss,BG,Model),     % Model includes pos.exs.
    induce_rlgg(Poss,Negs,Model,Clauses).

induce_rlgg(Poss,Negs,Model,Clauses):-
    covering(Poss,Negs,Model,[],Clauses).

% split positive and negative examples
pos_neg([],[],[]).
pos_neg([+E|Exs],[E|Poss],Negs):-
    pos_neg(Exs,Poss,Negs).
pos_neg([-E|Exs],Poss,[E|Negs]):-
    pos_neg(Exs,Poss,Negs).

% covering algorithm
covering(Poss,Negs,Model,H0,H):-
    construct_hypothesis(Poss,Negs,Model,Hyp),!,
    remove_pos(Poss,Model,Hyp,NewPoss),
    covering(NewPoss,Negs,Model,[Hyp|H0],H).
covering(P,N,M,H0,H):-
    append(H0,P,H). % add uncovered examples to hypothesis

% remove covered positive examples
remove_pos([],M,H,[]).
remove_pos([P|Ps],Model,Hyp,NewP):-
    covers_ex(Hyp,P,Model),!,
    write('Covered example: '),write(P),nl,
    remove_pos(Ps,Model,Hyp,NewP).
remove_pos([P|Ps],Model,Hyp,[P|NewP]):-
    remove_pos(Ps,Model,Hyp,NewP).
```

The two predicates called by the covering algorithm are construct_hypothesis/4 to construct a new clause, and covers_ex/3 to check extensional coverage.

```prolog
% extensional coverage, relative to a ground model
covers_ex((Head:-Body),Example,Model):-
    try((Head=Example,
        forall(element(L,Body),element(L,Model)))).
```

```
% construct a clause by means of RLGG
construct_hypothesis([E1,E2|Es],Negs,Model,Clause):-
    write('RLGG of '),write(E1),
    write(' and '),write(E2),write(' is'),
    rlgg(E1,E2,Model,Cl),
    reduce(Cl,Negs,Model,Clause),!,    % no backtracking
    nl,tab(5),write(Clause),nl.
construct_hypothesis([E1,E2|Es],Negs,Model,Clause):-
    write(' too general'),nl,
    construct_hypothesis([E2|Es],Negs,Model,Clause).
```

`try(Goal)` succeeds if and only if `Goal` succeeds, but without instantiating variables in `Goal` (see Appendix A.2).

The remaining predicate is `reduce/4`. This predicate first removes all the ground facts in the background model from the body of the clause. In a second step, the clause is further generalised by removing as many literals as possible, as long as the resulting clause does not cover any negative example (this is the only point where negative examples are used). This is needed because an RLGG might still contain redundant literals. For instance, given the following model

```
append([1,2],[3,4],[1,2,3,4])     append([a],[],[a])
append([],[],[])                  append([],[1,2,3],[1,2,3])
append([2],[3,4],[2,3,4])         append([],[3,4],[3,4])
```

the RLGG of the first two facts is

```
append([A|B],C,[A|E]):-
    append(B,C,D),append([],C,C)
```

This clause contains the redundant literal `append([],C,C)`, which is true in the intended interpretation. Therefore, removing it will not change the meaning of the clause in the intended interpretation.

```
% remove redundant literals
reduce((H:-B0),Negs,M,(H:-B)):-
    setof0(L,(element(L,B0),not var_element(L,M)),B1),
    reduce_negs(H,B1,[],B,Negs,M).

% reduce_negs(H,B1,B0,B,N,M) <- B is a subsequence of B1
%                              such that H:-B does not
%                              cover elements of N
reduce_negs(H,[L|B0],In,B,Negs,M):-
    append(In,B0,Body),
    not covers_neg((H:-Body),Negs,M,N),!, % remove L
    reduce_negs(H,B0,In,B,Negs,M).
reduce_negs(H,[L|B0],In,B,Negs,M):-       % keep L
    reduce_negs(H,B0,[L|In],B,Negs,M).
reduce_negs(H,[],Body,Body,Negs,M):-      % fail if clause
    not covers_neg((H:-Body),Negs,M,N).   % covers neg.ex.
```

```
covers_neg(Clause,Negs,Model,N):-
    element(N,Negs),
    covers_ex(Clause,N,Model).
```

`%%% var_element/2: see Appendix A.2`

We illustrate the program by applying it to two induction problems, one without and one with additional background predicates. The first example is the familiar `append/3` predicate.

```
bg_model([]).

?-induce_rlgg([  +append([1,2],[3,4],[1,2,3,4]),
                 +append([a],[],[a]),
                 +append([],[],[]),
                 +append([],[1,2,3],[1,2,3]),
                 +append([2],[3,4],[2,3,4]),
                 +append([],[3,4],[3,4]),
                 -append([a],[b],[b]),
                 -append([c],[b],[c,a]),
                 -append([1,2],[],[1,3])    ],Clauses).

RLGG of append([1,2],[3,4],[1,2,3,4]) and
append([a],[],[a]) is
        append([X|Xs],Ys,[X|Zs]):-[append(Xs,Ys,Zs)]
Covered example: append([1,2],[3,4],[1,2,3,4])
Covered example: append([a],[],[a])
Covered example: append([2],[3,4],[2,3,4])
RLGG of append([],[],[]) and append([],[1,2,3],[1,2,3]) is
        append([],Y,Y):-[]
Covered example: append([],[],[])
Covered example: append([],[1,2,3],[1,2,3])
Covered example: append([],[3,4],[3,4])

Clauses = [(append([],Y,Y):-[]),
           (append([X|Xs],Ys,[X|Zs]):-[append(Xs,Ys,Zs)])]
```

Note that, because of the use of extensional coverage, we have to provide complete 'recursive chains' like

```
append([1,2],[3,4],[1,2,3,4])
append([2],[3,4],[2,3,4])
append([],[3,4],[3,4])
```

Note also that the recursive clause is induced before the non-recursive one. This is due to the order in which the examples are presented; of course, it is only possible if we apply extensional coverage rather than intensional coverage.

The second example concerns the use of a non-empty background model. The background predicate `num/2` converts the numbers 1…5 to the numerals one…five and vice versa; the predicate `listnum/2`, which does the same for lists of numbers and numerals, is to be induced.

```
bg_model([  num(1,one),
            num(2,two),
            num(3,three),
            num(4,four),
            num(5,five)  ]).

?-induce_rlgg([  +listnum([],[]),
                 +listnum([2,three,4],[two,3,four]),
                 +listnum([4],[four]),
                 +listnum([three,4],[3,four]),
                 +listnum([two],[2]),
                 -listnum([1,4],[1,four]),
                 -listnum([2,three,4],[two]),
                 -listnum([five],[5,5])      ],Clauses).
```

```
RLGG of listnum([],[]) and
listnum([2,three,4],[two,3,four]) is
    too general
RLGG of listnum([2,three,4],[two,3,four]) and
listnum([4],[four]) is
    listnum([X|Xs],[Y|Ys]):-[num(X,Y),listnum(Xs,Ys)]
Covered example: listnum([2,three,4],[two,3,four])
Covered example: listnum([4],[four])
RLGG of listnum([],[]) and listnum([three,4],[3,four]) is
    too general
RLGG of listnum([three,4],[3,four]) and listnum([two],[2])
is
    listnum([V|Vs],[W|Ws]):-[num(W,V),listnum(Vs,Ws)]
Covered example: listnum([three,4],[3,four])
Covered example: listnum([two],[2])

Clauses =
    [ (listnum([V|Vs],[W|Ws]):-[num(W,V),listnum(Vs,Ws)]),
      (listnum([X|Xs],[Y|Ys]):-[num(X,Y),listnum(Xs,Ys)]),
      listnum([],[]) ]
```

The RLGG of the first two examples is `listnum(X,Y):-[]`, which is too general since it covers the negative examples. Therefore, the first example is temporarily discarded. After construction of the first clause, it is tried again, without success. Finally, since all examples except the first are covered by the two clauses found, the first example is simply added to the hypothesis as a ground fact.

Exercise 9.4. The restriction that the head of a hypothesis clause contains at least one variable that does not occur in the body excludes many useful programs with accumulators, like `reverse/3` (section 3.6). Choose another method to exclude tautological clauses, and demonstrate that your program can learn `reverse/3`.

9.3　Top-down induction

We introduce the second induction method by means of an example. Suppose we want to construct a definition of the predicate `element/2` by means of induction. After receiving the first example `+element(a,[a,b])`, we formulate the simplest hypothesis possible:

```
element(X,Y)
```

This hypothesis states that everything is an element of everything. Suppose our next example is a negative one: `-element(x,[a,b])`. Since this negative example is covered by our current hypothesis, we conclude that it is too general and has to be specialised. Under θ-subsumption, there are two ways to specialise a clause:

(*i*)　apply a substitution to variables in the clause;

(*ii*)　add a literal to the body of the clause.

We can thus specialise our hypothesis in several ways: we can apply substitutions like $\{X \to [\,]\}$, $\{Y \to X\}$ or $\{Y \to [V|W]\}$, or we can add a literal like `element(Y,X)` to the body of the clause. So, the set of specialisations of the above clause includes, among others, the following clauses:

```
element([],Y)
element(X,X)
element(X,[V|W])
element(X,Y):-element(Y,X)
```

Note that each of these clauses is a *minimal* specialisation, in the following sense: each of them is θ-subsumed by the original clause, and there exist no more-general clauses which are also θ-subsumed by the original clause.

Suppose for the moment that we choose the third clause as our next hypothesis:

```
element(X,[V|W])
```

This hypothesis expresses that anything is an element of a non-empty list. Obviously, this clause is again too general, since it still covers the negative example. Possible minimal specialisations include

```
element(X,[V])
element(X,[X|W])
element(X,[V|X])
element(X,[V|W]):-element(X,W)
```

The second of these clauses is true in the intended interpretation, and will therefore never cover any negative example. Since it also covers the only positive example seen up till now, we decide to adopt it as our next hypothesis. Notice that the recursive clause is also among the above specialisations; it will be found if we supply a positive example like `+element(b,[a,b])`.

Thus, we see that the operation of specialisation generates a search space in which the correct clauses defining `element/2` are to be found. Part of this search space, which we will call the *specialisation graph*, is depicted in fig. 9.1. Notice that, in order to generate the specialisation graph, we need to specify the *hypothesis language*: the set of predicates, functors and constants that can occur in the hypothesis. We can further restrict the search

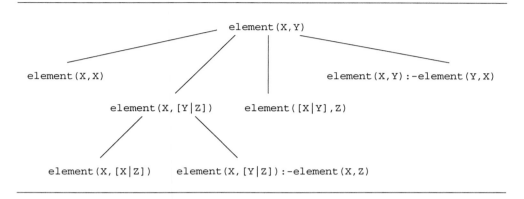

Figure 9.1. Part of the specialisation graph for `element/2`.

space by assigning *types* to the arguments of predicates and functors. For instance, by assigning X and Y in `element(X,Y)` and `[X|Y]` the types 'item' and 'list of items', respectively, it becomes clear that X and Y should not be unified in a specialisation step, and neither should X be substituted by `[]` or `[V|W]`. Such typing would rule out three clauses in fig. 9.1.

Even with such typing restrictions, the branching factor in the specialisation graph is typically quite large, increasing with the number of variables in a clause. Therefore, an agenda-based search procedure will require large amounts of memory. Instead, we will employ an iterative deepening search strategy with backtracking. Each time a clause in the hypothesis is found to be too general, we search the specialisation graph for an alternative, starting from the root and increasing the depth bound until a suitable clause is found. Identifying and removing the too-general clause is a specialisation operation; searching for an alternative and adding it to the hypothesis is a generalisation step.

The program below implements this top-down induction procedure. Its main loop is given by the predicate `process_examples/4`. This predicate processes the examples one by one. Whenever the hypothesis is changed by generalisation or specialisation, the new hypothesis should be checked against all previous examples, which are therefore passed in the list `Done`.

```
induce_spec(Examples,Clauses):-
    process_examples([],[],Examples,Clauses).

% process the examples
process_examples(Clauses,Done,[],Clauses).
process_examples(Cls1,Done,[Ex|Exs],Clauses):-
    process_example(Cls1,Done,Ex,Cls2),
    process_examples(Cls2,[Ex|Done],Exs,Clauses).
```

```
% process one example
process_example(Clauses,Done,+Example,Clauses):-
    covers_d(Clauses,Example).
process_example(Cls,Done,+Example,Clauses):-
    not covers_d(Cls,Example),
    generalise(Cls,Done,Example,Clauses).
process_example(Cls,Done,-Example,Clauses):-
    covers_d(Cls,Example),
    specialise(Cls,Done,Example,Clauses).
process_example(Clauses,Done,-Example,Clauses):-
    not covers_d(Clauses,Example).
```

Intensional coverage of an example by a set of clauses is checked by a simple meta-interpreter. Since the current hypothesis might include circular clauses like `element(X,Y):-element(Y,X)`, the meta-interpreter employs a depth bound to cut off the search for a proof after a fixed number of steps. Additionally, a background theory might be defined by means of the meta-predicate `bg/1`; we will assume that this background theory is non-circular, and does not contain the predicate to be induced.

```
% covers_d(Clauses,Ex) <- Ex can be proved from Clauses and
%                         background theory (max. 10 steps)
covers_d(Clauses,Example):-
    prove_d(10,Clauses,Example).

prove_d(D,Cls,true):-!.
prove_d(D,Cls,(A,B)):-!,
    prove_d(D,Cls,A),
    prove_d(D,Cls,B).
prove_d(D,Cls,A):-
    D>0,D1 is D-1,
    copy_element((A:-B),Cls),       % make copy of clause
    prove_d(D1,Cls,B).
prove_d(D,Cls,A):-
    prove_bg(A).

prove_bg(true):-!.
prove_bg((A,B)):-!,
    prove_bg(A),
    prove_bg(B).
prove_bg(A):-
    bg((A:-B)),
    prove_bg(B).

%%% copy_element/2: see Appendix A.2
```

If the current hypothesis covers a negative example, it follows that it contains at least one clause which is false in the intended interpretation. The predicate `specialise/4` identifies such a false clause by examining the proof of the negative example. Once such a clause is found, it is simply thrown out of the hypothesis. Since this is quite a coarse specialisation step, some of the previous positive examples will now become uncovered, and the predicate process_examples/4 is called again.

```
specialise(Cls,Done,Example,Clauses):-
    false_clause(Cls,Done,Example,C),
    remove_one(C,Cls,Cls1),
    write('.....refuted: '),write(C),nl,
    process_examples(Cls1,[],[-Example|Done],Clauses).

% false_clause(Cs,Exs,E,C) <- C is a false clause
%                              in the proof of E
false_clause(Cls,Exs,true,ok):-!.  % empty proof
false_clause(Cls,Exs,(A,B),X):-!,
    false_clause(Cls,Exs,A,Xa),    % try first conjunct
    ( Xa = ok    -> false_clause(Cls,Exs,B,X)   % 2nd one
    ; otherwise  -> X = Xa
    ).
false_clause(Cls,Exs,E,ok):-       % no false clause for
    element(+E,Exs),!.             % positive examples
false_clause(Cls,Exs,A,ok):-       % no false clause for
    bg((A:-B)),!.                  % background literals
false_clause(Cls,Exs,A,X):-
    copy_element((A:-B),Cls),
    false_clause(Cls,Exs,B,Xb),    % false clause in proof B?
    ( Xb \= ok   -> X = Xb         % yes
    ; otherwise  -> X = (A:-B)     % no; return this clause
    ).
```

As explained above, the predicate generalise/4 searches the specialisation graph for a clause covering an uncovered positive example. Since there might be several uncovered positive examples, the generalised hypothesis is again tested against all previous examples.

```
generalise(Cls,Done,Example,Clauses):-
    search_clause(Done,Example,Cl),
    write('Found clause: '),write(Cl),nl,
    process_examples([Cl|Cls],[],[+Example|Done],Clauses).
```

The current node in the search process is represented by a term a(Clause,Vars), where Vars is the list of variables occurring in Clause, together with their types (see below).

```
% search_clause(Exs,E,C) <- C is a clause covering E and
%                             not covering negative examples
%                             (iterative deepening search)
search_clause(Exs,Example,Clause):-
    literal(Head,Vars),    % root of specialisation graph
    try((Head=Example)),
    search_clause(3,a((Head:-true),Vars),
                  Exs,Example,Clause).
```

```
search_clause(D,Current,Exs,Example,Clause):-
    write(D),write('..'),
    search_clause_d(D,Current,Exs,Example,Clause),!.
search_clause(D,Current,Exs,Example,Clause):-
    D1 is D+1,
    !,search_clause(D1,Current,Exs,Example,Clause).
```

The search ends when a clause is found that covers the uncovered example, while not covering any of the negative examples.

```
search_clause_d(D,a(Clause,Vars),Exs,Example,Clause):-
    covers_ex(Clause,Example,Exs),      % goal
    not((element(-N,Exs),covers_ex(Clause,N,Exs))),!.
search_clause_d(D,Current,Exs,Example,Clause):-
    D>0,D1 is D-1,
    specialise_clause(Current,Spec),    % specialise
    search_clause_d(D1,Spec,Exs,Example,Clause).
```

Here, extensional coverage is tested against the examples and the background theory:

```
covers_ex((Head:-Body),Example,Exs):-
    try((Head=Example,covers_ex(Body,Exs))).

covers_ex(true,Exs):-!.
covers_ex((A,B),Exs):-!,
    covers_ex(A,Exs),
    covers_ex(B,Exs).
covers_ex(A,Exs):-
    element(+A,Exs).
covers_ex(A,Exs):-
    prove_bg(A).
```

The following predicates generate the specialisation graph. The literals that can be added to the body of a clause are given by the predicate `literal/2`. The first argument of `literal/2` is a literal; the second argument specifies the types of variables in the literal. Thus, for the predicate `element/2` the following fact should be added:

```
literal(element(X,Y),[item(X),list(Y)]).
```

Likewise, the possible terms to be used in a substitution are specified with their types by the predicate `term/2`:

```
term(list([]),[]).
term(list([X|Y]),[item(X),list(Y)]).
```

For instance, the clause `element(X,[V|W]):-true` is represented during the search process as

```
a((element(X,[V|W]):-true),[item(X),item(V),list(W)])
```

Consequently, `X` and `V` can be unified with each other but not with `W`, and `W` can be substituted by `[]` or `[Y|Z]`, but `X` and `V` cannot. To restrict the search further, we will again make the assumption that hypothesis clauses are strictly constrained; i.e. the set of variables in a newly added literal is a proper subset of the set of variables in the head of the clause.

```
% specialise_clause(C,S) <- S is minimal specialisation
%                            of C under theta-subsumption
specialise_clause(Current,Spec):-
    add_literal(Current,Spec).
specialise_clause(Current,Spec):-
    apply_subs(Current,Spec).

add_literal(a((H:-true),Vars),a((H:-L),Vars)):-!,
    literal(L,LVars),
    proper_subset(LVars,Vars).    % no new variables in L
add_literal(a((H:-B),Vars),a((H:-L,B),Vars)):-
    literal(L,LVars),
    proper_subset(LVars,Vars).    % no new variables in L

apply_subs(a(Clause,Vars),a(Spec,SVars)):-
    copy_term(a(Clause,Vars),a(Spec,Vs)),    % don't change
    apply_subs1(Vs,SVars).                   % Clause

apply_subs1(Vars,SVars):-
    unify_two(Vars,SVars).    % unify two variables
apply_subs1(Vars,SVars):-
    subs_term(Vars,SVars).    % subs. term for variable

unify_two([X|Vars],Vars):-    % not both X and Y in Vars
    element(Y,Vars),
    X=Y.
unify_two([X|Vars],[X|SVars]):-
    unify_two(Vars,SVars).

subs_term(Vars,SVars):-
    remove_one(X,Vars,Vs),
    term(Term,TVars),
    X=Term,
    append(Vs,TVars,SVars).    % TVars instead of X in Vars
```

We illustrate the program by applying it to the induction problems of the previous section. The first problem is to induce a definition of the predicate append/3. The hypothesis language is specified by the literals and terms to be used, together with the types of their arguments:

```
literal(append(X,Y,Z),[list(X),list(Y),list(Z)]).
term(list([]),[]).
term(list([X|Y]),[item(X),list(Y)]).
```

The following query demonstrates that append/3 can be induced from two positive and four negative examples:

```
?-induce_spec([  +append([],[b,c],[b,c]),
                 -append([],[a,b],[c,d]),
                 -append([a,b],[c,d],[c,d]),
                 -append([a],[b,c],[d,b,c]),
                 -append([a],[b,c],[a,d,e]),
                 +append([a],[b,c],[a,b,c])     ],Clauses)
3..Found clause: append(X,Y,Z):-true
    ...refuted: append([],[a,b],[c,d]):-true
3..Found clause: append(X,Y,Y):-true
    ...refuted: append([a,b],[c,d],[c,d]):-true
3..Found clause: append([],Y,Y):-true
3..4..Found clause: append([X|Xs],Ys,[X|Zs]):-
                                        append(Xs,Ys,Zs)

Clauses = [ (append([X|Xs],Ys,[X|Zs]):-append(Xs,Ys,Zs)),
            (append([],Y,Y):-true) ]
```

The numbers indicate the level of iterative deepening at which the clauses are found. The first two negative examples are needed for the construction of the non-recursive clause, and the remaining two are needed for the construction of the recursive clause.

The second induction problem concerns the predicate listnum/2. The hypothesis language is declared as follows:

```
literal(listnum(X,Y),[list(X),list(Y)]).
literal(num(X,Y),[item(X),item(Y)]).
term(list([]),[]).
term(list([X|Y]),[item(X),list(Y)]).
```

We supply the following background theory:

```
bg((num(1,one):-true)).
bg((num(2,two):-true)).
bg((num(3,three):-true)).
bg((num(4,four):-true)).
bg((num(5,five):-true)).
```

The predicate listnum/2 can be learned from six well-chosen examples:

```
?-induce_spec([  +listnum([],[]),
                 -listnum([one],[one]),
                 -listnum([1,two],[one,two]),
                 +listnum([1],[one]),
                 -listnum([five,two],[5,two]),
                 +listnum([five],[5]) ],Clauses)
3..Found clause: listnum(X,Y):-true
    ...refuted: listnum([one],[one]):-true
3..Found clause: listnum([],[]):-true
3..4..Found clause: listnum([V|Vs],[W|Ws]):-
                                  num(V,W),listnum(Vs,Ws)
```

```
3..4..Found clause: listnum([X|Xs],[Y|Ys]):-
                             num(Y,X),listnum(Xs,Ys)

Clauses =
        [ (listnum([X|Xs],[Y|Ys]):-num(Y,X),listnum(Xs,Ys)),
          (listnum([V|Vs],[W|Ws]):-num(V,W),listnum(Vs,Ws)),
          (listnum([],[]):-true) ]
```

It should again be noted that the examples need to be well-chosen and well-ordered. This is particularly true for the recursive clause. Because of the use of extensional coverage, all positive examples occurring in a proof should be given; moreover, it is good practice to supply negative examples for a particular recursive clause before the positive ones. For this induction program, which induces by specialising overly general clauses, negative examples are particularly crucial.

Exercise 9.5. Replace the iterative deepening search strategy with beam search (see the article by Quinlan, referred to below, for a possible heuristic).

Further reading

The program `induce_rlgg/2` is based on the GOLEM system described in (Muggleton & Feng, 1990). The program `induce_spec/2` is based on the MIS system described in (Shapiro, 1983). (Quinlan, 1990) discusses a hill-climbing heuristic for top-down induction. The notion of generalisation in logic programs is discussed in (Niblett, 1988). (Gottlob, 1987) precisely characterises the difference between θ-subsumption and logical consequence.

The subject of inductively inferring logic programs has been recently named *Inductive Logic Programming*. (Muggleton, 1992) is the first collection of papers on this subject. Recent books are (De Raedt, 1992) and (Lavrač & Džeroski, 1994).

G. GOTTLOB (1987), 'Subsumption and implication', *Information Processing Letters* **24**: 109–111.

N. LAVRAČ & S. DŽEROSKI (1994), *Inductive Logic Programming: Techniques and Applications*, Ellis Horwood.

S.H. MUGGLETON & C. FENG (1990), 'Efficient induction of logic programs'. In *Proc. First Conference on Algorithmic Learning Theory*, Ohmsha, Tokyo. Also in (Muggleton, 1992), pp. 261-280.

S.H. MUGGLETON (ed.) (1992), *Inductive Logic Programming*, Academic Press.

T. NIBLETT (1988), 'A study of generalisation in logic programs'. In *Proc. European Working Sessions on Learning*, D. Sleeman (ed.), pp. 131-138, Pitman.

J.R. QUINLAN (1990), 'Learning logical definitions from relations', *Machine Learning* **5**(3): 239-266.

L. DE RAEDT (1992), *Interactive Theory Revision: an Inductive Logic Programming Approach*, Academic Press.

E.Y. SHAPIRO (1983), *Algorithmic Program Debugging*, MIT Press.

Appendices

Appendix A describes a number of built-in Prolog predicates, and lists a library of utility programs. These predicates are used in various programs throughout the book.

Appendix B gives two programs converting to and from clausal logic. The first program transforms a formula in first-order Predicate Logic to clausal form, as described in section 2.5. The second program completes a given set of general clauses by means of Predicate Completion (section 8.2). The output of this program is a formula in Predicate Logic, which can be transformed back to clausal form by means of the first program.

Appendix C gives detailed answers to selected exercises.

A

A catalogue of useful predicates

Appendix A.1 describes a number of built-in Prolog predicates. Appendix A.2 comprises a small library of utility predicates that are used by programs in this book.

A.1 Built-in predicates

Term manipulation

`Term1 = Term2`	`Term1` and `Term2` are unified.
`Term1 \= Term2`	`Term1` and `Term2` cannot be unified.
`Term1 == Term2`	`Term1` and `Term2` are bound to the same term.
`Term1 \== Term2`	`Term1` and `Term2` are bound to different terms.
`var(V)`	`V` is an unbound variable.
`arg(N,T,A)`	`A` is the N-th argument of term `T`.
`functor(T,F,N)`	`T` is a term with functor `F` and arity `N`.
`Term =.. List`	`List` is a list starting with the functor of `Term`, followed by its arguments.
`varsin(Term,Vs)`	`Vs` is a list of the variables in `Term`.
`numbervars(T,N,M)`	the variables in term `T` are instantiated to terms of the form `'$VAR'`(n), where n is an integer which has a different value for each distinct variable. The variables will be numbered starting from `N`, and `M` is the next unused number.

Database manipulation

`assert(Clause)`	`Clause` is added at the end of the database (can also be a single atom, without a body).
`asserta(Clause)`	`Clause` is added at the *top* of the database.
`clause(H,B)`	`H:-B` is a clause in the database (`H` must be instantiated).
`retract(Clause)`	the first clause unifying with `Clause` is removed from the database.

`retractall(Head)`	all clauses with head unifying with `Head` are removed from the database.
`kill(Predicate)`	all clauses defining `Predicate` are removed from the database.
`save(File)`	save the clauses in the database to `File`.
`consult(File)`	load the clauses in `File` into the database.
`op(P,Type,Name)`	declare an operator `Name` with priority `P` (a number between 0 and 1200, lower priority binds stronger); `Type` is `fx` or `fy` for prefix, `xfx`, `xfy` or `yfx` for infix, and `xf` or `yf` for postfix.

Control

`call(Goal)`	call `Goal` (must be instantiated to a goal).
`not(Goal)`	`Goal` is not provable (must be instantiated to a goal). `not/1` could be defined as

```
        not(Goal):-call(Goal),!,fail.
        not(Goal).
```

`fail, false`	forces failure.
`true, otherwise`	always succeeds. `true/0` could be defined as

```
            true.
```

`repeat`	succeeds indefinitely many times on backtracking. `repeat/0` could be defined as

```
        repeat.
        repeat:-repeat.
```

`findall(X,G,L)`	`L` is a list of `X`'s, one for each solution of `G` (succeeds with the empty list if no solutions are found).
`bagof(X,G,L)`	`L` is a list of `X`'s, one for each solution of `G`, which may be preceded by existential variables (fails if no solutions are found).
`setof(X,G,L)`	as `bagof/3`, but `L` is a sorted list without duplicates.
`forall(G,C)`	for all the solutions of `G`, `C` is true. `forall/2` could be defined as

```
        forall(G,C):-not((G,not(C))).
```

Interaction

`read(Term)`	`Term` is instantiated to the next line typed by the user (must be a Prolog term).
`write(Term)`	write `Term` to the screen.
`tab(N)`	write `N` spaces to the screen.
`nl`	write a newline to the screen.
`get(C)`	`C` is ASCII code of next character typed by the user.
`put(C)`	write character with ASCII code `C` to the screen.
`tell(File)`	redirect output to `File`.
`told`	stop redirecting output.
`see(File)`	redirect input from `File`.
`seen.`	stop redirecting input.

A.2 A library of utility predicates

What follows is a small collection of predicates that are used by various programs throughout the book.

Lists and sets. We start with a couple of simple list predicates.

```
% element(X,Ys) <- X is an element of the list Ys
element(X,[X|Ys]).
element(X,[Y|Ys]):-
    element(X,Ys).

% append(Xs,Ys,Zs) <- list Zs is Xs followed by Ys
append([],Ys,Ys).
append([X|Xs],Ys,[X|Zs]):-
    append(Xs,Ys,Zs).

% remove_one(X,Ys,Zs) <- Zs is list Ys minus
%                        one occurrence of X
remove_one(X,[X|Ys],Ys).
remove_one(X,[Y|Ys],[Y|Zs]):-
    remove_one(X,Ys,Zs).
```

The difference between lists and sets is that the order of elements in a set is not important. Thus, a *subset* is different from a *sublist*. The predicate proper_subset/2 works only if the first argument is a list without duplicates!

```
% subset(Xs,Ys) <- every element of Xs occurs in Ys
subset([],Ys).
subset([X|Xs],Ys):-
    element(X,Ys),
    subset(Xs,Ys).

% proper_subset(Xs,Ys) <- Xs is a subset of Ys, and Ys
%                         has more elements than Xs
proper_subset([],Ys):-
    Ys \= [].
proper_subset([X|Xs],Ys):-
    remove_one(X,Ys,Ys1),
    proper_subset(Xs,Ys1).
```

The following three predicates use syntactic identity rather than unification, which is useful for lists containing variables.

```
var_element(X,[Y|Ys]):-
    X == Y.      % syntactic identity
var_element(X,[Y|Ys]):-
    var_element(X,Ys).
```

```
var_remove_one(X,[Y|Ys],Ys):-
    X == Y.     % syntactic identity
var_remove_one(X,[Y|Ys],[Y|Zs]):-
    var_remove_one(X,Ys,Zs).

var_proper_subset([],Ys):-
    Ys \= [].
var_proper_subset([X|Xs],Ys):-
    var_remove_one(X,Ys,Zs),
    var_proper_subset(Xs,Zs).
```

Conjunctions and disjunctions.   Conjunctions and disjunctions are recursive datastructures, just like lists. However, whereas a single-element list such [1] is a complex term .(1,[]), a single-element conjunction or disjunction is a simple term. Therefore, each of the following predicates needs an extra clause for the single-element case. Note that true is the empty conjunction, while false represents the empty disjunction.

```
disj_element(X,X):-            % single-element disjunction
    not X=false,
    not X=(One;TheOther).
disj_element(X,(X;Ys)).
disj_element(X,(Y;Ys)):-
    disj_element(X,Ys).

conj_append(true,Ys,Ys).
conj_append(X,Ys,(X,Ys)):-     % single-element conjunction
    not X=true,
    not X=(One,TheOther).
conj_append((X,Xs),Ys,(X,Zs)):-
    conj_append(Xs,Ys,Zs).

disj_append(false,Ys,Ys).
disj_append(X,Ys,(X;Ys)):-     % single-element disjunction
    not X=false,
    not X=(One;TheOther).
disj_append((X;Xs),Ys,(X;Zs)):-
    disj_append(Xs,Ys,Zs).

conj_remove_one(X,X,true):-    % single-element conjunction
    not X=true,
    not X=(One,TheOther).
conj_remove_one(X,(X,Ys),Ys).
conj_remove_one(X,(Y,Ys),(Y,Zs)):-
    conj_remove_one(X,Ys,Zs).
```

Preventing variables from getting instantiated.   Whenever Prolog reads a clause from its internal database, fresh copies of the variables in the clause are created. When a meta-interpreter uses an internal list of clauses, this is desirable as well. The predicate

`copy_term/2` uses the internal database to create a fresh copy of any term.
`copy_element/2` uses `copy_term/2` to create a fresh copy of an item in a list.

```
% copy_term(Old,New) <- New is a copy of Old
%                       with new variables
copy_term(Old,New):-
    asserta('$copy'(Old)),
    retract('$copy'(New)),!.
copy_term(Old,New):-     % in case Old and New don't unify
    retract('$copy'(Old)),
    !,fail.

% copy_element(X,L) <- X is an element of L
%                      with new variables
copy_element(X,Ys):-
    element(X1,Ys),
    copy_term(X1,X).
```

`try/1` is a meta-predicate which tests whether a goal succeeds, without returning an answer-substitution. This is achieved by taking advantage of the difference between negation as failure and logical negation.

```
% try(Goal) <- Goal succeeds, but variables
%              don't get instantiated
try(Goal):-
    not not Goal.
```

Various. The remaining predicates speak for themselves.

```
% variant of setof/3 which succeeds with the empty list
% if no solutions can be found
setof0(X,G,L):-
    setof(X,G,L),!.
setof0(X,G,[]).

% same_predicate(L1,L2) <- literals L1 and L2 have
%                          the same predicate and arity
same_predicate(L1,L2):-
    functor(L1,P,N),
    functor(L2,P,N).
```

B
Two programs for logical conversion

The program in appendix B.1 transforms a formula in first-order Predicate Logic to clausal form, as described in section 2.5. The program in appendix B.2 completes a given set of general clauses by means of Predicate Completion (section 8.2). The output of this program is a formula in Predicate Logic, which can be transformed back to clausal form by means of the first program.

B.1 From Predicate Logic to clausal logic

In section 2.5 we discussed a method for transforming a formula in Predicate Logic to an 'almost' equivalent set of clauses (reread this section if you don't recall in what sense the clauses differ from the Predicate Logic formula). Below, a Prolog program implementing this method is given.

The logical symbols used in Predicate Logic formulas are defined as operators:

```
% logical symbols used in Predicate Logic formulas
:-op(900,xfx,'=>').            % implication
:-op(800,xfy,&).              % conjunction
:-op(800,xfy,v).              % disjunction
:-op(400,fy,-).               % negation
```

In addition, a universally quantified formula of the form $\forall X : F$ is represented by the term `forall(X,F)`. For instance, the formula

$$\forall S:\ \texttt{student\_of(S,peter)} \rightarrow \texttt{likes(peter,S)}$$

is represented by

```
forall(S,student_of(peter)=>likes(peter,S)).
```

Likewise, an existentially quantified formula of the form $\exists X : F$ is represented by the term `exists(X,F)`.

The tranformation from Predicate Logic to clausal logic requires six steps:

(*i*)   replace implications by disjunction and negation;
(*ii*) push negations inside, so that each of them immediately precedes a literal;
(*iii*) move quantifiers to the front (the result is said to be in *prenex normal form*);
(*iv*) replace existentially quantified variables by Skolem functors;
(*v*)   rewrite into *conjunctive normal form*, i.e. a conjunction of disjunctions of literals;
(*vi*) rewrite each conjunct to a clause.

The main predicate `transform/2` carries out these six steps:

```
transform(Formula,Clauses):-
     rewrite_implications(Formula,F1),
     negations_inside(F1,F2),
     prenex_normal_form(F2,F3),
     skolemise(F3,F4),
     conjunctive_normal_form(F4,F5),
     clausal_form(F5,Clauses).
```

Predicates for each of these steps are defined below.
     The first two predicates contain one clause for each possible form a formula could have.

```
% rewrite_implications(F1,F2) <- F2 is a PL formula
%                                without implications,
%                                log. equivalent with F1
rewrite_implications(A,A):-        % base case
     literal(A).
rewrite_implications(A => B, -C v D):- % implication
     rewrite_implications(A,C),
     rewrite_implications(B,D).
rewrite_implications(A & B, C & D):-  % no change;
     rewrite_implications(A,C),      % try rest of
     rewrite_implications(B,D).      % formula
rewrite_implications(A v B, C v D):-
     rewrite_implications(A,C),
     rewrite_implications(B,D).
rewrite_implications(-A,-C):-
     rewrite_implications(A,C).
rewrite_implications(forall(X,B), forall(X,D)):-
     rewrite_implications(B,D).
rewrite_implications(exists(X,B), exists(X,D)):-
     rewrite_implications(B,D).
```

```
% negations_inside(F1,F2) <- F2 is a PL formula with
%                             negs. only preceding literals
%                             log. equivalent with F1
negations_inside(A,A):-                   % base case
     literal(A).
negations_inside(-(A & B), C v D):-     % De Morgan (1)
     negations_inside(-A,C),
     negations_inside(-B,D).
negations_inside(-(A v B), C &  D):-    % De Morgan (2)
     negations_inside(-A,C),
     negations_inside(-B,D).
negations_inside(-(-A),B):-               % double negation
     negations_inside(A,B).
negations_inside(-exists(X,A),forall(X,B)):-  % quantifiers
     negations_inside(-A,B).
negations_inside(-forall(X,A),exists(X,B)):-
     negations_inside(-A,B).
negations_inside(A & B, C & D):-        % no change;
     negations_inside(A,C),               % try rest of
     negations_inside(B,D).               % formula
negations_inside(A v B, C v  D):-
     negations_inside(A,C),
     negations_inside(B,D).
negations_inside(exists(X,A),exists(X,B)):-
     negations_inside(A,B).
negations_inside(forall(X,A),forall(X,B)):-
     negations_inside(A,B).
```

In step (*iii*), the quantifiers found at different positions in the formula are moved to the front, preserving their order. This is achieved by means of an auxiliary predicate pnf/4, which separates the quantifiers from the rest of the formula (referred to below as the Body). An additional argument V acts as a pointer to the place of the body in the quantifier structure. For instance, the query

```
?-pnf(forall(X,p(X,X)) & forall(Y,exists(Z,p(Y,Z))),Q,V,B)
```

has the following answers:

```
Q = forall(X,forall(Y,exists(Z,V)))
B = p(X,X)&p(Y,Z)
```

Unifying V with B gives the required formula in prenex normal form:

```
% prenex_normal_form(F1,F2) <- F2 is a PL formula
%                               with all quant.s in front,
%                               log. equivalent with F1
prenex_normal_form(F,PNF):-
     pnf(F,PNF,B,B).
```

```
pnf(A,V,V,A):-                          % base case
     literal(A).
pnf(forall(X,F),forall(X,Quants),V,Body):-
     pnf(F,Quants,V,Body).
pnf(exists(X,F),exists(X,Quants),V,Body):-
     pnf(F,Quants,V,Body).
pnf(A & B,Quants,V,BodyA & BodyB):-
     pnf(A,Quants,QB,BodyA),
     pnf(B,QB,V,BodyB).
pnf(A v B,Quants,V,BodyA v BodyB):-
     pnf(A,Quants,QB,BodyA),
     pnf(B,QB,V,BodyB).
```

Step (*iv*) is called *Skolemisation*. It involves introducing a Skolem functor for each existentially quantified variable. The Skolem functors are named sk1, sk2, etc. The arguments of the Skolem functors are given by the universally quantified variables found before the existentially quantified one. Since all remaining variables are universally quantified, the universal quantifiers can be dropped. (Strictly speaking, the formula is now neither in Predicate Logic form, nor in clausal form.)

```
% skolemise(F1,F2) <- F2 is obtained from F1 by replacing
%                     all existentially quantified
%                     variables by Skolem terms
skolemise(F1,F2):-
     skolemise(F1,[],1,F2).

skolemise(forall(X,F1),VarList,N,F2):-!,    % remove univ.
     skolemise(F1,[X|VarList],N,F2).        % quantifier
skolemise(exists(X,F1),VarList,N,F2):-!,
     skolem_term(X,VarList,N),              % unify with
     N1 is N+1,                             % Skolem term
     skolemise(F1,VarList,N1,F2).
skolemise(F,V,N,F).                 % copy rest of formula

skolem_term(X,VarList,N):-
     C is N+48,                       % number -> character
     name(Functor,[115,107,C]),       % Skolem functor skN
     X =.. [Functor|VarList].
```

We now have a formula containing only conjunction, disjunction and positive and negative literals. Such a formula can uniquely be rewritten to a conjunction of disjunctions of literals, by distributing disjunction over conjunction. The result is said to be in *conjunctive normal form* (CNF):

```
conjunctive_normal_form(A,A):-                  % base case
     disjunction_of_literals(A),!.
conjunctive_normal_form((A & B) v C, D & E ):-!,
     conjunctive_normal_form(A v C,D),          % distribution
     conjunctive_normal_form(B v C,E).
```

```
conjunctive_normal_form(A v (B & C), D & E ):- !,
    conjunctive_normal_form(A v B,D),          % distribution
    conjunctive_normal_form(A v C,E).
conjunctive_normal_form(A & B,C & D):-         % conjuction
    conjunctive_normal_form(A,C),
    conjunctive_normal_form(B,D).
conjunctive_normal_form(A v B,E):-             % other cases
    conjunctive_normal_form(A,C),
    conjunctive_normal_form(B,D),
    conjunctive_normal_form(C v D,E).
```

Finally, the CNF-formula is rewritten to a list of clauses. For simplicity, body and head of each clause are represented by lists:

```
clausal_form(A, [Clause]):-
    disjunction_of_literals(A),
    make_clause(A,Clause).
clausal_form(A & B,Clauses):-
    clausal_form(A,ClausesA),
    clausal_form(B,ClausesB),
    append(ClausesA,ClausesB,Clauses).

make_clause(P,([P]:-[])):-
    logical_atom(P).
make_clause(-N,([]:-[N])):-
    logical_atom(N).
make_clause(A v B,(HeadAB:-BodyAB)):-
    make_clause(A,(HeadA:-BodyA)),
    make_clause(B,(HeadB:-BodyB)),
    append(HeadA,HeadB,HeadAB),
    append(BodyA,BodyB,BodyAB).
```

The program is completed by a number of simple utility predicates:

```
disjunction_of_literals(A):-
    literal(A).
disjunction_of_literals(C v D):-
    disjunction_of_literals(C),
    disjunction_of_literals(D).

literal(A):-
    logical_atom(A).
literal(-A):-
    logical_atom(A).

logical_atom(A):-
    functor(A,P,N),
    not logical_symbol(P).
```

```
logical_symbol(=>).
logical_symbol(<=>).
logical_symbol(-).
logical_symbol(&).
logical_symbol(v).
logical_symbol(exists).
logical_symbol(forall).
```

B.2 Predicate Completion

In section 8.2, we presented Predicate Completion as a technique for explicitly handling negative information. A logic program is viewed as a set of predicate definitions, where the only-if parts are implicitly assumed. Below, a program is given which constructs additional clauses representing the only-if parts.

A program is represented as a list of clauses, where head and body of each clause are lists of atoms, as in the program in the previous section. The output of the Predicate Completion program is a formula in first-order Predicate Logic, which can be transformed to clausal logic by means of the aforementioned program, if desired. Definitions for different predicates are handled separately, so the first step is to partition the program into separate predicate definitions. After completing each of these definitions we add appropriate formulas for each of the undefined predicates.

```
% complete(P,F) <- P is a list of predicate definitions,
%                  and F is a Predicate Logic formula
%                  representing the only-if parts of P
complete(Program,Comp):-
    separate_definitions(Program,Definitions),
    complete_definitions(Definitions,CompDefs,Heads),
    handle_undefined(Program,Heads,CompDefs,Comp).

separate_definitions([],[]).
separate_definitions([([H]:-B)|Cls],[[([H]:-B)|D]|Ds]):-
    get_definition(Cls,H,D,Rest),
    separate_definitions(Rest,Ds).

get_definition([],Head,[],[]).
get_definition([([H]:-B)|Cls],Head,[([H]:-B)|Def],Rest):-
    same_predicate(H,Head),
    get_definition(Cls,Head,Def,Rest).
get_definition([([H]:-B)|Cls],Head,Def,[([H]:-B)|Rest]):-
    not same_predicate(H,Head),
    get_definition(Cls,Head,Def,Rest).
```

Undefined predicates are those which occur in bodies of clauses without occurring in any head. The list `Heads` of defined predicates is obtained while completing each predicate definition. Care must be taken to avoid considering `not/1` as an undefined predicate, and also to check the negated literal itself. After constructing the list of undefined literals

occuring in clause bodies, each of them is transformed into a formula of the form
$\forall X1...\forall Xn:\ \neg p(X1,...,Xn)$:

```
handle_undefined(Program,Heads,CompDefs,Comp):-
     findall(L,
                ( member((H:-B),Program), % pick a clause body
                 ( (member(L,B),not L=not(X))   % unneg. lit.
                 ; member(not L,B) ),      % or a negated one
                 not member(L,Heads) ),   % which is undefined
             Undefs),
        undef_formulas(Undefs,CompDefs,Comp).

undef_formulas([],Comp,Comp).
undef_formulas([L|Ls],Comp0,Comp):-
     quantify(L,F),
     undef_formulas(Ls,F & Comp0,Comp).

quantify(L,F):-
     L =.. [P|As],
     variablise(As,Vs,F,-NewL),      % NB. negation symbol!
     NewL =.. [P|Vs].      % turn arguments into variables

% add quantifiers
variablise([],[],L,L).
variablise([A|As],[V|Vs],forall(V,F),L):-
     variablise(As,Vs,F,L).
```

The main task in Predicate Completion is the completion of each separate predicate
definition. The main steps are

(*i*)   adding explicit unifications to the body of clauses;
(*ii*)   adding existential quantifiers for those variables occurring in the body of a
        clause but not in its head;
(*iii*) combining the clauses into one formula, and adding universal quantifiers for
        the head variables.

The predicate unifications_and_quantifiers/2 takes care of the first two steps,
and the third step is carried out by the predicate complete_formula/3. These predicates
are relatively self-explanatory:

```
% complete_definitions(D,C,H) <- C is the complement of
%                                definitions D, and H is
%                                list of variablised heads
complete_definitions([Def],Comp,[Head]):-!,
     complete_definition(Def,Comp,Head).
complete_definitions([Def|Defs],Comp & Comps,[H|Hs]):-
     complete_definition(Def,Comp,H),
     complete_definitions(Defs,Comps,Hs).
```

```
complete_definition(Definition,Comp,Head):-
    unifications_and_quantifiers(Definition,F),
    complete_formula(F,Comp,Head).

unifications_and_quantifiers([],[]).
unifications_and_quantifiers([Clause|Clauses],[C|Cs]):-
    unifs_and_quants(Clause,C),
    unifications_and_quantifiers(Clauses,Cs).

unifs_and_quants(([Head]:-Body),([NewHead]:-NewBody)):-
    Head=..[Pred|Args],
    explicit_unifications(Args,NewArgs,Body,TmpBody),
    existential_quantifiers(TmpBody,NewArgs,NewBody),
    NewHead=..[Pred|NewArgs].

% explicit_unifications(A,NA,B,NB) <- NA is list A with
%                          non-var. terms replaced by new
%                          var.s; NB is body B extended
%                          with explicit unifications
explicit_unifications([],[],Body,Body).
explicit_unifications([T|As],[V|NewAs],B,[V=T|NewB]):-
    nonvar(T),                % add explicit unification
    explicit_unifications(As,NewAs,B,NewB).
explicit_unifications([Var|As],[Var|NewAs],Body,NewBody):-
    var(Var),                 % no expl. unific. needed
    explicit_unifications(Args,NewArgs,Body,NewBody).

% existential_quantifiers(B,V,NB) <- NB is conj. of lit.s
%                          in B, extended by ex. quant.s
%                          for var.s in B but not in V
existential_quantifiers(Body,HeadVars,NewBody):-
    varsin(Body,BodyVars),          % built-in predicate
    body_form(Body,Conj),           % list -> conjunction
    body_quants(BodyVars,HeadVars,Conj,NewBody).

body_form([not Lit],-Lit):-!.
body_form([Lit],Lit):-!.
body_form([not Lit|List],-Lit & Conj):-!,
    body_form(List,Conj).
body_form([Lit|List],Lit & Conj):-
    body_form(List,Conj).

% body_quants(BV,HV,C,QC) <- QC is conj. C extended with
%                          existential quant.s for all
%                          variables in BV but not in HV
body_quants([],HeadVars,Conj,Conj).
body_quants([BVar|BVars],HeadVars,Conj,exists(BVar,F)):-
    not var_element(BVar,HeadVars),
    body_quants(BVars,HeadVars,Conj,F).
```

```
body_quants([BVar|BVars],HeadVars,Conj,F):-
    var_element(BVar,HeadVars),
    body_quants(BVars,HeadVars,Conj,F).

% complete_formula(C,F,H) <- F is disjunction of bodies
%                            of clauses in C, and univ.
%                            quantified head H
complete_formula(C,Formula,Head):-
    combine_clauses(C,Head,Body),
    varsin(Head,HeadVars),
    head_quants(HeadVars,Head => Body,Formula).

combine_clauses([([Head]:-Body)],Head,Body):- !.
combine_clauses([([Head]:-Body)|R],Head,Body v RBody):-
    combine_clauses(R,Head,RBody).

head_quants([],Formula,Formula).
head_quants([HVar|HVars],Formula,forall(HVar,F)):-
    head_quants(HVars,Formula,F).
```

The following query illustrates the operation of the program, and shows also how it can be combined with the program for conversion to clausal form presented in the previous section.

```
?-P=[([bird(tweety)]:-[]),
     ([flies(X)]:-[bird(X),not abnormal(X)])],
  complete(P,F),
  transform(F,C).

F=forall(Y,-abnormal(Y)) &
  forall(Z,bird(Z) => Z=tweety) &
  forall(X,flies(X) => bird(X) & -abnormal(X))

C=[([]:-[abnormal(Y)]),
   ([Z=tweety]:-[bird(Z)]),
   ([bird(X)]:-[flies(X)]),
   ([]:-[flies(X),abnormal(X)])]
```

C

Answers to selected exercises

Below, answers to selected exercises can be found. Not all answers have been included, due to two reasons. Some of the questions only lead to a new insight when the answer is actually constructed, and the student is encouraged to do so. Furthermore, some other questions embody small programming projects, and don't have straightforward answers.

The remaining questions have been constructed to highlight a particular point in the discussion (which, incidentally, is the reason that they are printed throughout the text, and not at the end of each chapter). They are most advantageous when addressed as soon as they are encountered. The answers provided here can then be used to check and assess one's own solution. Most of the answers contain additional explanatory remarks.

Alternatively, this appendix can be read separately, after the previous chapters have been studied. To this end, some of the questions have been reformulated so as to minimise references to the original text.

C.1 A brief introduction to clausal logic

Exercise 1.2. Construct the proof trees for the query
```
?-nearby(W,charing_cross).
```

There are six answers to this query:

{W→green_park}
{W→piccadilly_circus}
{W→leicester_square}
{W→bond_street}
{W→oxford_circus}
{W→tottenham_court_road}

The proof trees for the first three answers are analogous to fig. 1.2. The proof tree for the fourth answer is given below (the two remaining proof trees are similar):

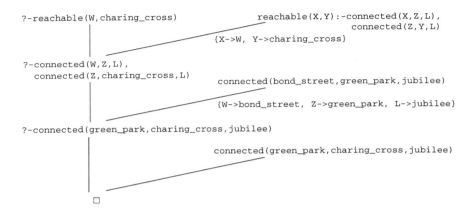

Exercise 1.4. A list is either the empty list `[]`, or a non-empty list `[First|Rest]` where `Rest` is a list. Define a relation `list(L)`, which checks whether `L` is a list. Adapt it such that it succeeds only for lists of (*i*) even length and (*ii*) odd length.

The first specification can immediately be translated to Prolog:

```
list([]).
list([First|Rest]):-list(Rest).
```

A list of even length is either the empty list, or a non-empty list with two more elements than the next shorter list of even length:

```
evenlist([]).
evenlist([First,Second|Rest]):-evenlist(Rest).
```

In order to adapt this definition for lists of odd length, only the non-recursive clause needs to be changed:

```
oddlist([One]).
oddlist([First,Second|Rest]):-oddlist(Rest).
```

Notice that `oddlist` can also be defined in terms of `evenlist` (or *vice versa*):

```
oddlist([First|Rest]):-evenlist(Rest).
```

Exercise 1.5. Construct a query asking for a route from Bond Street to Piccadilly Circus with at least two intermediate stations.

```
?-reachable(bond_street,piccadilly_circus,[S1,S2|Rest]).
```

C.2 Clausal logic and resolution: theoretical backgrounds

Exercise 2.1. Translate the following statements into clauses, using the atoms
person, sad and happy:
(*a*)   persons are happy or sad;
(*b*)   no person is both happy and sad;
(*c*)   sad persons are not happy;
(*d*)   non-happy persons are sad.

The statements should be read as '**if** … **then** …' statements. Thus, the first statement
reads '**if** somebody is a person, **then** she is happy or sad':
    (*a*)   `happy;sad:-person`
The second statement reads '**if** somebody is a person, **then** she is not both happy and sad'.
In clausal logic, only positive conclusions can be drawn; negative conclusions are turned
into positive conditions, as follows: '**if** somebody is a person, and she is happy and sad,
then contradiction'. A contradictory conclusion is signalled by the empty head:
    (*b*)   `:-person,happy,sad`
Following the same recipe, the third statement expresses that '**if** somebody is a person who
is sad, and she is happy, **then** contradiction':
    (*c*)   `:-person,sad,happy`
Thus, sentences (*b*) and (*c*) convey the same logical meaning.
    Finally, the fourth sentence reads '**if** somebody is a person who is not happy, **then** she
is sad'. In clausal logic, only positive conditions can be used; therefore, this negative
condition should be turned into a positive conclusion: '**if** somebody is a person, **then** she is
sad or happy'. We thus obtain the same clause as in case (*a*):
    (*d*)   `sad;happy:-person`

Exercise 2.2. Given the program
            `married;bachelor:-man,adult.`
            `man.`
            `:-bachelor.`
determine which of the following clauses are logical consequences of this program:
(*a*)   `married:-adult;`
(*b*)   `married:-bachelor;`
(*c*)   `bachelor:-man;`
(*d*)   `bachelor:-bachelor.`

(*a*) Any model of the first clause, which additionally makes man **true**, is also a model
of the clause `married;bachelor:-adult`. Likewise, any model of this clause which
additionally makes `bachelor` **false** is also a model of the clause `married:-adult`,
which is therefore a logical consequence of the program.
    (*b*) The body of this clause is **false** in any model of the program, and therefore the
clause is **true** in any such model.

(*c*) The body of this clause is **true** in any model of the program, while its head is **false**. The clause is therefore not a logical consequence of the program (on the contrary, it is **false** in every model of the program, not just in some).

(*d*) This clause is a *tautology*: it is **true** in any interpretation, and therefore a logical consequence of any program.

Exercise 2.3. Write down the six Herbrand interpretations that are not models of the program

```
married;bachelor:-man,adult.
has_wife:-man,married.
```

The six interpretations are:

{man, adult}
{man, adult, has_wife}
{man, married}
{man, married, adult}
{man, married, bachelor}
{man, married, adult, bachelor}

The first two interpretations satisfy the body of the first clause but violate its head; the remaining four interpretations satisfy the body of the second clause but violate its head.

Exercise 2.4. Give a derivation of friendly from the following program:
```
happy;friendly:-teacher.
friendly:-teacher,happy.
teacher;wise.
teacher:-wise.
```

This requires derivations of the clauses friendly:-teacher and teacher:

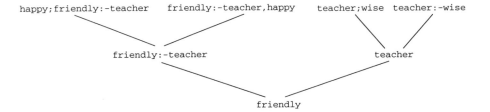

Notice that this derivation can not be recast in the form of a linear tree, where each resolvent is obtained from the previous resolvent and a given clause, as in Chapter 1. This is due to the fact that some clauses are indefinite (have more than one positive literal).

Exercise 2.5. Prove by refutation that `friendly:-has_friends` is a logical consequence of the following clauses:

`happy:-has_friends.`
`friendly:-happy.`

The negation of `friendly:-has_friends` consists of two clauses, `:-friendly` and `has_friends`. Together, these four clauses are inconsistent:

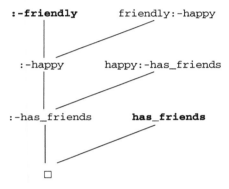

Exercise 2.6. How many models does the following clause have over the Herbrand universe {`peter,maria`}:

`likes(peter,S):-student_of(S,peter)`

The set of ground instances of this clause is

```
{ likes(peter,maria):-student_of(maria,peter),
  likes(peter,peter):-student_of(peter,peter) }
```

and the Herbrand base is

```
{ likes(peter,peter),likes(peter,maria),
  likes(maria,peter),likes(maria,maria),
  student_of(peter,peter),student_of(peter,maria),
  student_of(maria,peter),student_of(maria,maria) }
```

Only the left four ground atoms are relevant for determining whether an interpretation is a model. 9 out of 16 truth-value assignments to these ground atoms result in a model. Because of the 4 irrelevant ground atoms, this yields $9*2^4=144$ models. Notice that this is a rather large number of models for such a modest Herbrand universe, and such a simple clause! This illustrates that *less knowledge leads to more models*.

Exercise 2.7. Write a clause expressing that Peter teaches all the first-year courses, and apply resolution to this clause and the clause

likes(peter,maria):-
follows(maria,C),teaches(peter,C)

This is expressed by the clause

teaches(peter,C):-first_year_course(C)

Resolution with the above clause yields

likes(peter,maria):-follows(maria,C),first_year_course(C)

In words: 'Peter likes Maria **if** Maria follows a first-year course'.

Exercise 2.9. Translate to clausal logic:
(*a*)   every mouse has a tail;
(*b*)   somebody loves everybody;
(*c*)   every two numbers have a maximum.

(*a*) This statement should be read as '**if** X is a mouse, **then** there exists something which is X's tail'. Giving X's tail the abstract name tail(X), we obtain the following clause:

tail_of(tail(X),X):-mouse(X)

(*b*) Here we need to give the person who loves everybody an abstract name. Since this person does not depend on anybody else, it can simply be a constant:

loves(person_who_loves_everybody,X)

Notice the difference with the statement 'everybody loves somebody':

loves(X,person_loved_by(X))

(*c*) This statement should be read as '**if** X and Y are numbers, then there exists a number which is their maximum'. Giving this maximum the abstract name max(X,Y) yields the clause

maximum(X,Y,max(X,Y)):-number(X),number(Y)

Exercise 2.10. Determine the Herbrand universe of the following program:

length([],0).
length([X|Y],s(L)):-length(Y,L).

(Hint: recall that [] is a constant, and that [X|Y] is an alternative notation for the complex term .(X,Y) with binary functor '.'!)

In the intended interpretation, `s` is restricted to numbers and '`.`' is restricted to lists; however, variables are untyped in clausal logic, and the two sets of terms may be mixed. Thus, the Herbrand universe will contain terms denoting numbers, such as

```
0,s(0),s(s(0)),s(s(s(0))),...
```

and terms denoting lists of numbers, such as

```
[],[0],[s(0),0],[s(s(0)),s(0),0],...
```

but also 'strange' terms like

```
[[[0]]] or .(.(.(0,[]),[]),[])
[s(0)|0] or .(s(0),0)
[s([[]|0])]
```

and so on.

Exercise 2.11. If possible, unify the following pairs of terms:
(*a*) `plus(X,Y,s(Y))` and `plus(s(V),W,s(s(V)))`;
(*b*) `length([X|Y],s(0))` and `length([V],V)`;
(*c*) `larger(s(s(X)),X)` and `larger(V,s(V))`.

(*a*) `plus(s(V),s(V),s(s(V)))`.
(*b*) `length([s(0)],s(0))`.
(*c*) Not unifiable.

Exercise 2.13. Write a clause for the statement 'somebody is innocent unless proven guilty', and give its intended model (supposing that `john` is the only individual in the Herbrand universe).

The clause is

```
innocent(X):-not guilty(X)
```

with intended model `{innocent(john)}`.

Exercise 2.14. Translate to clausal logic:
(*a*) ∀X∃Y: `mouse(X)`→`tail_of(Y,X)`;
(*b*) ∀X∃Y: `loves(X,Y)`∧(∀Z: `loves(Y,Z)`);
(*c*) ∀X∀Y∃Z: `number(X)`∧`number(Y)`→`maximum(X,Y,Z)`.

(*a*) This statement translates almost immediately into a clause, replacing the existential quantifier by a Skolem functor `tail`:

```
tail_of(tail(X),X):-mouse(X)
```

(*b*) This formula is already in conjunctive normal form, and each conjunct yields a separate clause. After replacing the existential quantifier by a Skolem functor person_loved_by, we obtain

```
loves(X,person_loved_by(X)).
loves(person_loved_by(X),Z).
```

Notice that the two clauses are 'linked' by the Skolem functor.

(*c*) Here, the Skolem functor has two arguments:

```
maximum(X,Y,max(X,Y)):-number(X),number(Y)
```

See also Exercise 2.9.

C.3 Logic Programming and Prolog

Exercise 3.2. Draw the SLD-tree for the following program:
```
list([]).
list([H|T]):-list(T).
```
and the query ?-list(L).

This is one of the simplest infinite SLD-trees:

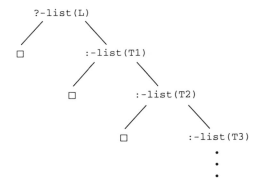

The query succeeds infinitely often, producing the answers:

```
L = [];
L = [X1,X2];
L = [Y1,Y2,Y3];
L = [Z1,Z2,Z3,Z4];
```

and so on. Note that reversing the order of the clauses means that Prolog gives no answer at all.

Exercise 3.3. Draw the SLD-tree for the query `?-likes(A,B)`, given the following program:

```
likes(peter,Y):-friendly(Y).
likes(T,S):-student_of(S,T).
student_of(maria,peter).
student_of(paul,peter).
friendly(maria).
```

Add a cut in order to prune away one of the answers {A→peter, B→maria}, and indicate the result in the SLD-tree. Can this be done without pruning away the third answer?

This program produces three answers:

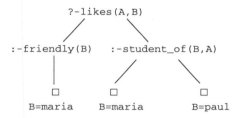

Adding a cut to the first clause (before or after `friendly(Y)`) will prune away two answers (left figure). Adding a cut at the end of the second clause has no effect, while placing it just before the literal `student_of(S,T)` will only prune the answer {A→peter, B→paul} (right figure).

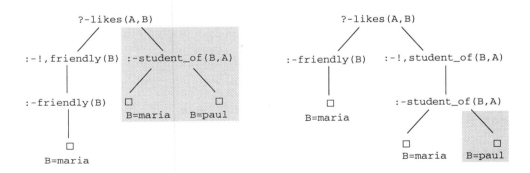

If in addition the last two clauses are swapped, only the second answer {A→peter, B→maria} is pruned.

Exercise 3.5. Given the program
                    bachelor(X):-not(married(X)),man(X).
                    man(fred).
                    man(peter).
                    married(fred).
draw the SLD-trees for the queries ?-bachelor(fred) and ?-bachelor(peter).

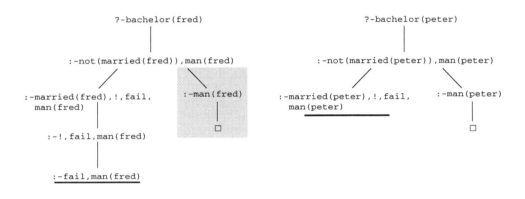

Exercise 3.6. Change the first clause to
                    bachelor(X):-not(married(X)),man(X)
and show that the modified program produces the right answer, by drawing the
SLD-tree for the query ?-bachelor(X).

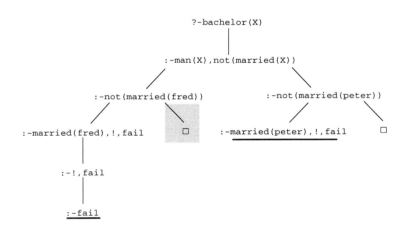

Exercise 3.7. Given the program

```
p:-q,r,s,!,t.
p:-q,r,u.
q.
r.
u.
```

show that the query ?-p succeeds, but that q and r are tried twice.

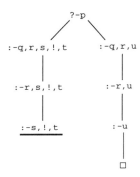

Exercise 3.8. Given the equivalent program with if-then-else

```
p:-q,r,if_s_then_t_else_u.
if_s_then_t_else_u:-s,!,t.
if_s_then_t_else_u:-u.
```

show that q and r are now tried only once.

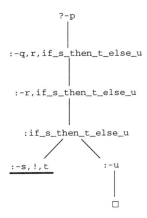

Exercise 3.9. Write a predicate `zero(A,B,C,X)` which, given the coefficients *a*, *b* and *c*, calculates both values of *x* for which $ax^2+bx+c=0$.

```
zero(A,B,C,X):-
    X is (-B + sqrt(B*B - 4*A*C)) / 2*A.
zero(A,B,C,X):-
    X is (-B - sqrt(B*B - 4*A*C)) / 2*A.
```

Exercise 3.10. Given the program
```
             length([],0).
             length([H|T],N):-length(T,M),N is M+1.
```
draw the proof tree for the query `?-length([a,b,c],N)`.

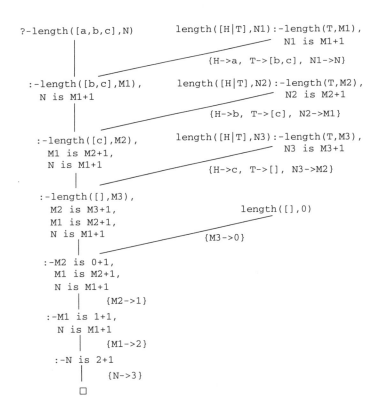

Notice that the maximum number of literals in the resolvent is proportional to the depth of the recursion, which is typical for non-tail recursive predicates. When proofs are long, such programs will be quite inefficient.

Exercise 3.11. Given the program
```
length_acc(L,N):-length_acc(L,0,N).
length_acc([],N,N).
length_acc([H|T],N0,N):-N1 is N0+1,length_acc(T,N1,N).
```
draw the proof tree for the query ?-length_acc([a,b,c],N).

In this program, the is literals are solved immediately after they are added to the resolvent:

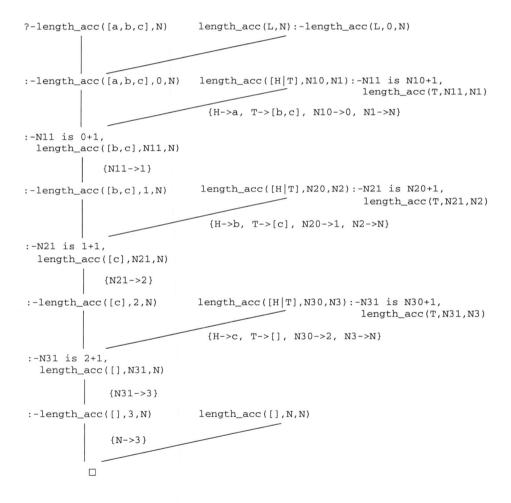

Here, the length of the resolvent is independent of the level of recursion, which makes tail-recursive loops very similar to iterative loops with regard to memory requirements.

Exercise 3.13. In the `naive_reverse` predicate, represent the reversed list by a difference list, use `append_dl` instead of append, and show that this results in the predicate `reverse_dl` by unfolding the definition of `append_dl`.

The reversed lists are represented by difference lists as follows:
- (partly) specified lists are extended with a variable representing the minus list, e.g. `[]` becomes `R-R`, and `[H]` becomes `[H|Minus]-Minus`;
- a variable representing a list is replaced by two variables representing the plus and minus lists, e.g. `R` becomes `RPlus-RMinus`.

```
reverse([],R-R).
reverse([H|T],RPlus-RMinus):-
    reverse(T,R1Plus-R1Minus),
    append_dl(R1Plus-R1Minus,[H|Minus]-Minus,RPlus-RMinus).
```

Unfolding the call to `append_dl/3` means that `R1Plus` should be unified with `RPlus`, `R1Minus` with `[H|Minus]`, and `Minus` with `RMinus`, which yields

```
reverse([],R-R).
reverse([H|T],RPlus-RMinus):-
    reverse(T,RPlus-[H|RMinus]).
```

Renaming the variables results in the same definition as `reverse_dl/2`.

This illustrates that the translation from simple lists to difference lists can (to a large extent) be automated.

Exercise 3.14. Rewrite the program for `rel`, using `=..`

```
rel(R,[],[]).
rel(R,[X|Xs],[Y|Ys]):-
    Goal =.. [R,X,Y],
    call(Goal),
    rel(R,Xs,Ys).
```

Note that, in contrast with the original program, this program conforms to the syntax of clausal logic: there are no variables in functor or literal positions.

Exercise 3.15. Write a program which sorts and removes duplicates from a list, using `setof`.

The basic idea is to use `element/2` to generate the elements of the list on backtracking, and to collect and sort them by means of `setof/2`.

```
sort(List,SortedList):-
    setof(X,element(X,List),SortedList).
```

```
element(X,[X|Ys]).
element(X,[Y|Ys]):-
    element(X,Ys).
```

Exercise 3.18. Implement a predicate `permutation/2`, such that
`permutation(L,P)` is true if P contains the same elements as the list L but
(possibly) in a different order, following these steps. (One auxiliary predicate is
needed.)

As usual, we start with the declarative specification:

```
% permutation(L,P) <- P contains the same elements as L
%                     (possibly in a different order)
```

Taking the first argument as the recursion argument and the second as the output argument,
we obtain the following skeleton:

```
permutation([],[]).
permutation([Head|Tail],?Permutation):-
    /* do something with Head */
    permutation(Tail,Permutation).
```

Inserting `Head` somewhere in `Permutation` should yield `?Permutation`:

```
permutation([],[]).
permutation([Head|Tail],WholePermutation):-
    insert_somewhere(Head,Permutation,WholePermutation),
    permutation(Tail,Permutation).
```

The predicate `insert_somewhere/3` can be obtained in the same way as the
predicate `insert/3` (section 3.9) by ignoring the arithmetic conditions:

```
insert_somewhere(X,[],[X]).
insert_somewhere(X,[Head|Tail],[Head|Inserted]):-
    insert_somewhere(X,Tail,Inserted).
insert_somewhere(X,[Head|Tail],[X,Head|Tail]).
```

This program, which is declaratively and procedurally correct, can be slightly improved by
noting that the first and third clauses can be combined into a single base case:

```
insert_somewhere(X,List,[X|List]).
insert_somewhere(X,[Head|Tail],[Head|Inserted]):-
    insert_somewhere(X,Tail,Inserted).
```

Exercise 3.19. Implement an alternative sorting method by using the
`partition/4` predicate.

This predicate implements the famous *quicksort* algorithm, which is one of the most
efficient sorting algorithms:

```
quicksort([],[]).
quicksort([X|Xs],Sorted):-
    partition(Xs,X,Littles,Bigs),
    quicksort(Littles,SortedLittles),
    quicksort(Bigs,SortedBigs),
    append(SortedLittles,[X|SortedBigs],Sorted).
```

The program can still be improved by employing difference lists.

C.4 Representing structured knowledge

The exercises in this chapter should not provide major difficulties.

C.5 Searching graphs

Exercise 5.3. Consider the following program:
```
                brother(peter,paul).
                brother(adrian,paul).
                brother(X,Y):-brother(Y,X).
                brother(X,Y):-brother(X,Z),brother(Z,Y).
```
Compare and explain the behaviour of `prove_bf/1` and Prolog on the query
`?-brother(peter,adrian)`. Can you re-order the clauses, such that Prolog
succeeds?

Prolog will be trapped in an infinite loop, regardless of the order of the clauses. This is
so because a refutation of `?-brother(peter,adrian)` requires both recursive clauses,
but whichever is found first will also be tried before the second one in all the other refutation
steps. In contrast, `prove_bf/1` will be able to construct a refutation.

Exercise 5.5. Give the models of the program
```
                married(X);bachelor(X):-man(X),adult(X).
                has_wife(X):-married(X),man(X).
                man(paul).
                adult(paul).
```

This program has four models (bachelors may have a wife, and married man may be bachelors):

```
{man(paul),adult(paul),bachelor(paul)}
{man(paul),adult(paul),bachelor(paul),has_wife(paul)}
{man(paul),adult(paul),married(paul),has_wife(paul)}
{man(paul),adult(paul),married(paul),bachelor(paul),
has_wife(paul)}
```

The second and fourth models are non-minimal.

Exercise 5.6. Are all minimal models always constructed by `model/1`?

Yes. The set of all Herbrand interpretations can be seen as a search space, in which the models are to be found. This search space is ordered by the subset relation. `model/1` starts from the empty interpretation, and repeatedly adds ground atoms until a model is constructed. Since one atom is added at a time, the procedure will never jump over a model. Since, on backtracking, all possible ways to satisfy a violated clause are considered, `model/1` performs a breadth-first search (which is complete).

C.6 Informed search

Exercise 6.1. Suppose the call `children(Current,Children)` results in an ordered list of children. Write a predicate `merge/3` which directly merges this list with the current agenda.

This predicate is a little bit special because it requires **two** recursion arguments. Therefore, there are two recursive clauses and two base cases. Note that in the second clause the first argument is required to be a non-empty list. This is done to prevent the query `?-merge([],[],L)` from succeeding twice.

```
merge([],Agenda,Agenda).
merge([Child|Children],[],[Child|Children]).  % empty agenda
merge([Child|Children],[Node|Agenda],[Child|NewAgenda]):-
    eval(Child,ChildValue),
    eval(Node,NodeValue),
    ChildValue < NodeValue,   % Child is better than Node
    merge(Children,[Node|Agenda],NewAgenda).
merge([Child|Children],[Node|Agenda],[Node|NewAgenda]):-
    eval(Child,ChildValue),
    eval(Node,NodeValue),
    ChildValue >= NodeValue, % Child not better than Node
    merge([Child|Children],Agenda,NewAgenda).
```

Exercise 6.4. Find a position for which the third heuristic is too pessimistic.

It is too pessimistic for the starting position (minimal cost 15, estimate 18).

C.7 Reasoning with natural language

Exercise 7.1. Redraw the parse tree of fig. 7.1 in the manner of an SLD proof tree, where 'resolvents' are partially parsed sentences such as

```
            [the],[rapid],noun,verb_phrase
```
and 'clauses' are grammar rules.

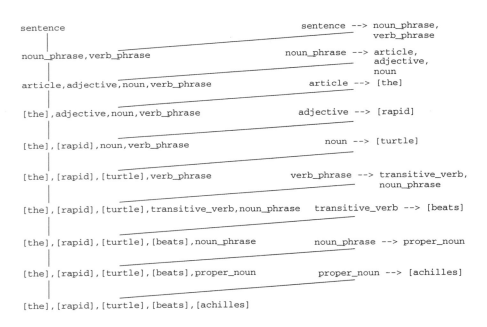

```
sentence                                            sentence --> noun_phrase,
    |                                                            verb_phrase
noun_phrase,verb_phrase                          noun_phrase --> article,
    |                                                            adjective,
                                                                 noun
article,adjective,noun,verb_phrase                   article --> [the]
    |
[the],adjective,noun,verb_phrase                   adjective --> [rapid]
    |
[the],[rapid],noun,verb_phrase                         noun --> [turtle]
    |
[the],[rapid],[turtle],verb_phrase             verb_phrase --> transitive_verb,
    |                                                             noun_phrase
[the],[rapid],[turtle],transitive_verb,noun_phrase  transitive_verb --> [beats]
    |
[the],[rapid],[turtle],[beats],noun_phrase       noun_phrase --> proper_noun
    |
[the],[rapid],[turtle],[beats],proper_noun         proper_noun --> [achilles]
    |
[the],[rapid],[turtle],[beats],[achilles]
```

Exercise 7.2. Draw the search space generated by the grammar in section 7.1 for a top-down parse, if grammar rules are applied to sentences from left to right. Discuss the similarities and differences with SLD-trees.

The search space is partly drawn below; the lower part, which contains all possible verb phrases, re-appears at three other nodes as indicated.

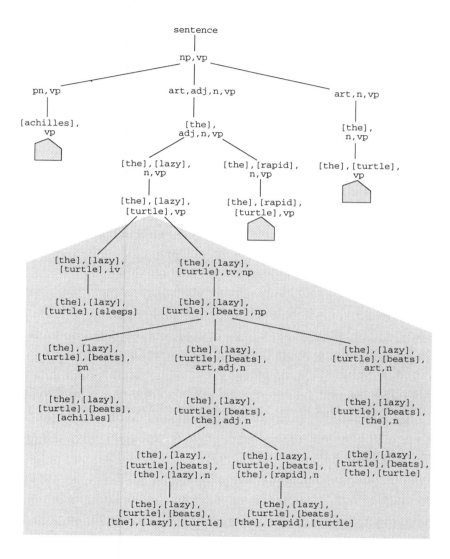

This search space is basically a propositional SLD-tree, with fully parsed sentences corresponding to success branches (failure branches occur only when for some syntactic category no grammar rules are specified).

Exercise 7.4. Extend the following grammar rules with arguments expressing their interpretation:

```
verb_phrase      --> transitive_verb,proper_noun.
transitive_verb  --> [likes].
```

The transitive verb defines a binary mapping `Y=>X=>L`, which is applied to the meaning of the proper noun:

```
verb_phrase(M)  --> transitive_verb(Y=>M),proper_noun(Y).
transitive_verb(Y=>X=>likes(X,Y))  --> [likes].
```

C.8 Reasoning with incomplete information

Exercise 8.1. Give the models of the program
                    bird(tweety).
                    ostrich(tweety).
                    flies(X):-bird(X),not abnormal(X).
                    abnormal(X):-ostrich(X).
(interpreting the general clause as the corresponding indefinite clause). Which one is the intended model (see section 2.4)?

The models are

```
{bird(tweety),ostrich(tweety),abnormal(tweety)}
{bird(tweety),ostrich(tweety),abnormal(tweety),
 flies(tweety)}
```

i.e. Tweety, being an ostrich, is an abnormal bird which may or may not fly. The intended model is the first one, since we have no reason to assume that ostriches fly.

Exercise 8.2. Give the models of the program
                    likes(peter,S):-student_of(S,peter).
                    student_of(paul,peter).

The Herbrand base of this program is

```
{ likes(peter,peter),likes(peter,paul),
  likes(paul,peter),likes(paul,paul),
  student_of(peter,peter),student_of(peter,paul),
  student_of(paul,peter),student_of(paul,paul) }
```

The atoms `student_of(paul,peter)` and `likes(peter,paul)` are **true** in every model. If the atom `student_of(peter,peter)` is **true**, then so is the atom `likes(peter,peter)` (three possibilities). Disregarding the other four atoms, we obtain the following models:

```
{ student_of(paul,peter),likes(peter,paul) }
{ student_of(paul,peter),
  likes(peter,paul),likes(peter,peter) }
```

```
{ student_of(paul,peter),student_of(peter,peter),
  likes(peter,paul),likes(peter,peter) }
```

Taking the four remaining atoms into account, we obtain $3*2^4=48$ models. (See also Exercise 2.6.)

Exercise 8.3. Apply Predicate Completion to the program
```
            wise(X):-not teacher(X).
            teacher(peter):-wise(peter).
```

The completion of this program is

$\forall$X: wise(X)$\leftrightarrow$ ¬teacher(X)
$\forall$X: teacher(X)$\leftrightarrow$ (X=peter $\land$ wise(peter))

The first formula states that somebody is wise if and only if he is not a teacher; the second formula says that Peter is wise if and only if he is a teacher. Together, these two statements are inconsistent.

C.9 Inductive reasoning

Exercise 9.3. Determine the θ-LGG of the following two clauses:
```
     reverse([2,1],[3],[1,2,3]):-reverse([1],[2,3],[1,2,3])
     reverse([a],[],[a]):-reverse([],[a],[a])
```

```
reverse([H|T],A,[RH|RT]):-reverse(T,[H|A],[RH|RT])
```

This is the recursive clause in the version with accumulator of the `reverse/3` predicate (section 3.6), with one small difference: here, the third argument is required to be a non-empty list (which it always is). Notice that this clause is not strictly constrained, and cannot be inferred by the induction programs in sections 9.2 and 9.3 (see als Exercise 9.4).

Index

Page indications in **bold** refer to a definition of the term. `Typewriter` typeface refers to a Prolog predicate.